Freedom in
Rousseau's
Political Philosophy

Freedom in
Rousseau's
Political
Philosophy

Daniel E. Cullen

NORTHERN
ILLINOIS
UNIVERSITY
PRESS
DeKalb
1993

© 1993 by Northern Illinois University Press

Published by the Northern Illinois University Press, DeKalb, Illinois 60115

Manufactured in the United States using acid-free paper ∞

Design by Julia Fauci

Library of Congress Cataloging-in-Publication Data

Cullen, Daniel.

    Freedom in Rousseau's political philosophy / Daniel Cullen.

       p. cm.

    Includes bibliographical references and index.

    ISBN 0-87580-180-3

    1. Rousseau, Jean-Jacques, 1712–1778—Contributions in political science. 2. Liberty. I. Title.

  JC179.R9C85 1993

  323.44—dc20   93-16549

                 CIP

*To my mother
and to the memory of my father*

Contents

Preface

The commentary on Rousseau is replete with efforts to draw from his work a single, self-consistent theory. He has variously been called an asocial individualist, a liberal, a conservative, a majoritarian populist, and a totalitarian. One is tempted to say that any coherent interpretation of Rousseau must be an astigmatism that prevents certain rays of his theory from coming into focus. The unity of his work is indeed a complex one that, in the interpretation I offer here, consists in an effort to ground individual freedom both in constitutional principles of right and in community—to unite the rational assent to principle characteristic of liberalism with the affective community values associated with conservatism and, more recently, communitarianism.

I attempt in this book to delineate and criticize Rousseau's theory of political freedom. The heart of that theory is an explanation of social equivalents for the conditions of the state of nature that supported natural freedom. Rousseau did not share the belief of Hobbes and Locke that self-interest could be enlightened. The social conflicts that self-interest engenders might, in his view, be resolved only by assimilating the individual self to a community self (*moi commun*). Still, in line with Hobbes and Locke, Rousseau conceived freedom negatively, not as self-development through political participation. Freedom for Rousseau meant individual independence of other wills, which in his view was the natural and best condition for humankind. All the prescriptions of his political theory were intended by Rousseau to show how that independence could be established in civil order. Thus moral freedom, possible only in society, was a way to independence, not a value in itself. The expression of the general will similarly had no value for Rousseau as the voice of a mystical "Oversoul." The general will was for him a fence to individual freedom. In Rousseau's theory, freedom also required that the popular role in political decision making be confined to giving and withholding consent to governmental structures, to incumbency of political office, and to policies worked out by representatives. Widespread popular participation in daily politics could only bring factional conflict, culminating in domination by particular wills, and with that the end of individual independence.

Rousseau's political theory has been attractive to those critics (Americans in particular) who lament the withering away of democratic citizenship and who are persuaded that its revitalization requires turning from, rather than toward, the founding principles of liberal-democratic constitutionalism. It is argued that the liberal qualification of democracy systematically weakens it by promoting individualism over citizenship. For those dissatisfied with the result, Rousseau has served as a compelling alternative to liberal democracy's theoretical framers because, while acknowledging (indeed radicalizing) the philosophical case for individualism, he offers a strong version of citizenship in which individualism is tamed by and for political life. In place of liberal democracy, Rousseau offers *democratic freedom*, a conception that is both philosophically and politically superior in acknowledging the primacy of liberty without damning political life with the antagonism of the self to the political order. Rousseau's citizen regains freedom by generalizing, which is to say "politicizing," his will, thereby achieving an unprecedented marriage of the most private dimension of the self to the common life, without the subjugation of either. Rousseau was convinced that at its worst, politics compounded the problems of the precivil condition by "moralizing," that is, exacerbating, the differences among men. But once the precivil condition became irrevocably social, political means were necessary to achieve the "generality" that did not exist by nature. The general will of the democratic citizen defends his civic identity against the eruption of a particularity that has become self- as well as politically destructive, but that may be rendered dormant, if not extinct.

The voluntaristic side of Rousseau's theory both affirms that civil association arises only on the basis of self-imposed obligations and obviates the apparently chronic problem of liberal theories of obligation by emphasizing not the primacy of will per se, but *generalized will*, which is an attribute only of the citizen. In contrast to the liberal theories of obligation, which weaken and limit political life, Rousseau's notion of willing seems to encourage a centripetal force tending toward the convergence of generality and will in democratic freedom. The attractiveness of his democracy thus lies in its apparent achievement of that morality of the common good which seems to exceed liberalism's grasp. Reasoning from liberalism's own presuppositions, Rousseau concluded that the social tie must be knotted by a conservative politics of civic education which, ultimately, would be indistinguishable from the promotion of a substantive morality rooted in national prejudices.

Thus Rousseau eschewed a "thin theory" of the good out of a sense that a well-ordered polity required something stronger. For the common good to be effective, it must appear to citizens as a sacred good, something constitutive of their identity, and not merely as the private good that citizens happen to have in common. Rousseau's regime is conservative and its politics unabashedly normative, aiming, so to speak, at giving to every citizen "the same opinions, the same passions and the same interests." The problematical dualism in such concepts as *moi commun*, general will, and democratic freedom bespeaks the underlying tension between liberal and conservative principles that marks Rousseau's democratic theory and the practical life of peoples who aspire to become *E Pluribus Unum*.

It is my hope that the reading of Rousseau I present here may serve to clarify some of the issues that divide liberals from communitarians, and constitutionalists from participatory democrats in the current debate about freedom, rights, morality, and politics in America. My reading may also show that the terms of that debate need recasting. The historical unfolding of Lockean liberalism and of technological progress has produced in our time a "lonely crowd," widespread anomie, and with it a petulant factionalism that increasingly threatens the workability and governability of our democracy. More than two hundred years before the current communitarian debate, Rousseau predicted this result, and his political theory cogently explains why things are the way they are. In embracing the values now proclaimed by both individualists and communitarians, liberals and conservatives, Rousseau's theory displays in an especially graphic manner the importance of each set of values to the other. It also points up the large difficulties involved in resolving the dangerous tension between them. If I am right in affirming Rousseau's fundamental philosophical agreement about human nature with liberals, and about the nature of society with conservatives, it may be the case that Rousseau has proffered the only possible theoretical resolution of that tension, working from the assumptions of that complex agreement. However, the manifest unacceptability of some of Rousseau's chief prescriptions for this resolution may lead us to ask whether the time has come for us to canvass anew the fundamental questions about human nature and about the nature of democratic freedom that underlie contemporary problems.

Everyone who seeks to reconstruct Rousseau is blessed (and cursed!) with a rich quarry of existing interpretations. In my efforts to chisel the features of Rousseau's theory I have learned much from the works of Allan Bloom, Hilail Gildin, Victor Goldschmidt, Michel Launay, Roger Masters, Arthur Melzer, James Miller, Marc Plattner, Patrick Riley, Judith Shklar, Jean Starobinski, Leo Strauss, Charles Taylor, Robert Wokler, and numerous others. The text that follows will both display this debt and show where I have modified or departed from other views. The reader of course will decide whether I have got Rousseau right.

Acknowledgments

It was in the undergraduate lectures of Charles Taylor that I first heard of Jean-Jacques Rousseau and became aware of the need to engage him in order to treat seriously the issues of democracy. Since that time I have had the good fortune to read Rousseau with several other outstanding teachers who shed more light on this enigmatic thinker. In that regard I am particularly grateful to Donald Maletz, Susan Shell, Ernest Fortin, and David Lowenthal. Robert Faulkner agreed to supervise the dissertation in which this book originated. He waited patiently while I struggled to find my voice, and then sternly insisted that I speak clearly and to the point.

William T. Bluhm read the manuscript and generously made available to me his extensive knowledge of the history of political thought. Larry Arnhart and the reviewers for Northern Illinois University Press both pointed out significant problems and gave helpful advice on resolving them.

My greatest intellectual debt is to Robert Eden, with whom my education truly began. His profound grasp of Rousseau inspired my own attempt to catch this Proteus and hold him through his several transformations. While whatever may be of value in the present book is surely traceable to a thought or suggestion of his, he has always let me live out the consequences of my incorrigibility.

Throughout the period of this writing, my wife, Susanna, showed a forbearance of stoic proportions toward a project that seemed interminable. Her unconditional love is what has made this work, along with everything else in my life, possible. My children—Brianna, Liam, and (at the end) Brendan—gave me a second education in Rousseau. Ever subversive of professional duty, they reminded me of the obligations associated with love.

They taught me, sometimes the hard way, that "exister, pour nous, c'est sentir." Their raucous particularity, which seemed to preclude any expression of a general will, would suddenly give way to a spontaneous union of hearts and show me, at least temporarily, how *tout va tout seul.* It is because of their presence that I have some insight into Rousseau's insistence that "il faut être heureux."

Freedom in
Rousseau's
Political Philosophy

conclude that Rousseau's philosophy is not concerned with freedom at all, that his reasoning is sophistic, and that his political doctrine is sinister.[4] Such, perhaps, are the wages of paradox. Rousseau is the first philosopher to understand man in terms of freedom, or to assert that freedom is indispensable to the human good; by freedom he meant individual independence.[5] According to Rousseau, nothing is more fundamental or better defines man than his independence of his fellow men.[6] Freedom is the specific distinction of man, the "qualité d'homme."[7] Charles Taylor has called this thought "the root of an anthropology that conceives human life as the activity of self-realization, and which locates the tension in the human spirit, not in the opposition of virtue and vice, but in that of self versus other dependence."[8] With this reorientation of human concerns, Rousseau sets the stage for a politics oriented toward liberation, which is the horizon of our own thought and practice.

To his critics, Rousseau has been the architect of an oppressive state who repeated an ancient error in attributing freedom to the polity as a whole rather than to individuals within it.[9] While I take this opinion seriously, I am guided by the assumption that Rousseau offers a new conception of freedom rather than a mistaken appreciation of an old idea, and that his assessment of the requirements of a free regime may be an illuminating account, rather than a scandalous betrayal, of liberty. Perhaps the most puzzling aspect of Rousseau's notoriously elusive political philosophy is the apparent contradiction between his fervent appeals to freedom and a political design that allegedly abolishes it. One might explain away this contradiction as Benjamin Constant did: by appealing to two concepts of freedom (ancient and modern, or social and individual), and by viewing Rousseau as the champion of the weaker or atavistic version; alternatively, one can rest content with two antagonistic Rousseaus: the apostle of natural freedom versus the apologist for social control.[10]

But it is more accurate to say that Rousseau challenges the unstated premise of the liberal understanding of freedom, which locates it in the interstices of a society organized around the self-interested pursuits of commerce.[11] It is precisely Rousseau's dissatisfaction with the liberal project that invites the reinterpretation of freedom. In observing that the satisfaction of one's self-interest could occur at the cost of one's freedom, Rousseau reopens an issue that seemed to have been put to rest by the ascendancy of the paradigm of Lockean liberalism. As John Plamenatz has suggested, "It may be that Rousseau, when he speaks of freedom, has something important to say which is not to be found in Hobbes, Locke or Montesquieu, in the French Encyclopaedists or the Benthamites."[12] This book attempts to recover Rousseauian freedom and limn its significance for his politics and for our own.

The Centrality of Natural Freedom

Rousseau's fundamental insight was "Nature made man happy and good while society corrupts him and makes him miserable."[13] The whole advancement of learning and morality characteristic of civilization has debased mankind. In particular, society is guilty of causing the subjection of one will to another. Rousseau regards the latter as the greatest evil, for the worst condition of man is to be at the discretion of another; and dependence is the source of all the vices.[14] The same thought is echoed in the opening of the *Social Contract*: "Man is born free, and everywhere he is in chains." This aporia epitomizes the human problem.

The idea of "natural freedom" is the obverse of Rousseau's "sad and great system," denoting what man has lost in his fatal progress.[15] It becomes an Archimedean point in Rousseau's critique of modern politics and, I will suggest, informs his own democratic theory.[16] The latter centers on the burning question of whether freedom can be reestablished in a civil order, "taking men as they are" (man's historically acquired nature is a given) and "laws as they can be" (a potential reordering of man's relations with other men). My thesis is that while Rousseau's political goal is freedom within a democratic order, "democratic freedom" is shaped by a standard of value which antedates political association and, arguably, transcends politics altogether. That is to say, Rousseau's democratic vision squints toward natural freedom, which is culled from the most antipolitical context imaginable: the pure state of nature.[17] His political project is the re-creation of a condition of independence within a regime based on popular sovereignty. Complete independence of other wills is to be secured by complete dependence on laws, of which each citizen is the author. Seen in this light, the political order retains a crucial affinity with the natural order, which, for Rousseau, is the only unimpeachable source of value. I suggest that the latter remains normative (structurally, not literally) for Rousseau's political theory. Specifically, I find that the general will is modeled on the condition of natural man, "the savage and uncultured man, who . . . has no need to use his reason, who is governed exclusively by his appetites without the need for any other guide and who, following natural instinct, proceeds by steps that are always right [*toujours droits*]."[18]

As Bertrand de Jouvenel reminds us, freedom is what the West stands for.[19] Yet a politics devoted to freedom is inherently problematic, for freedom exerts a centrifugal force on political order.[20] Our own democracy is confronted by a variety of liberation movements seeking to overthrow the authority of traditional customs.[21] Democratic freedom is consequently as much an issue to be addressed as an ideal to be achieved. What *is* the proper relation of freedom and authority? Because the latter are the alpha and omega of Rousseau's political thought ("[T]he essence of the body politic lies in the harmony of obedience and freedom . . ."), attention to his effort to instantiate democratic freedom, in theory and in practice, opens a window on present concerns.[22]

Synopsis of the Argument

This work focuses on two questions. The first is, What is the essential meaning of Rousseauian freedom? Here one struggles to grasp a protean concept, for Rousseau's writings offer diverse subjects of freedom whose ways of life seem irreconcilable: natural man, the denatured or Spartan citizen, Émile (whose life seems to represent some via media between the savage and the citizen), and the solitary walker. One might add, perhaps, the political philosopher, who appears both as a "citizen of a free state" and as a philosophic founder of such a state, one who is in some sense capable of "choosing his birthplace," and therewith his allegiance, unconstrained by limits of place and time.[23] Rather than systematically consider each of Rousseau's personifications of freedom in its particular context, I examine Rousseau's trichotomy: natural, civil, and moral freedom in search of a hierarchy.

The second question is, How does Rousseau's understanding of freedom inform his conception of politics? I try to fathom his conception of democratic freedom, which has both inspired and appalled generations of readers to the present day. I find that, in politics, Rousseau would restore the independence of other wills that obtained in the state of nature. He portrays the democratic regime as a "condition de la liberté," whose foundation is both legitimate and reliable.[24] In both the natural and the civil contexts, Rousseauian freedom denotes a condition rather than a capacity; that is to say, it has little to do with the metaphysical issue of freedom of the will.[25]

No literal re-creation of the state of nature is possible, but its *structure* is replicable on a new plane. Rousseau reasons as follows. In the state of nature, men were independent because they were solitary and the needs of each were simple enough to be satisfied by his own (minimal) efforts. In the social condition men have needs whose satisfaction requires the assistance of others. Rousseau's political reflections are devoted to conceiving how social and political relations could be arranged in such a way as to import the independence of the solitary, natural condition into the social, civil condition.[26] Independence may still be retrievable if human conventions are artfully designed to maintain it, rather than left haphazardly to destroy it. At the center of Rousseau's design is a social contract that will leave each man as free as he was before the onset of social relations while attending to the enlarged requirements of his preservation.

Whereas previous commentators have found a sharp disjunction between Rousseau's thoughts on natural man and civil man, I discover an enduring correspondence between his natural philosophy and his political philosophy. Rousseau's reflections on man's natural, social, and political milieus are unified by a consistent intention to identify and repair the conditions of freedom. The essence of democratic freedom is the sovereignty of the general will, which is said to be "constant, unalterable, and pure." These attributes are also characteristic of the state of nature.[27] For Rousseau, freedom is always predicated on a certain order. Natural freedom is preserved by cleaving to the path of nature; democratic freedom will involve submission to the supreme direction of the general will.

In chapter 2, I will argue that Rousseau conceives freedom

first and foremost as "natural freedom." Natural freedom is a negative condition of independence characterized by an equilibrium of power and desire. Freedom depends on a carefully structured environment, for which the pure state of nature constitutes the paradigm. By associating freedom with the natural condition, Rousseau ends up with a conception of freedom that is as stripped bare as his notion of natural man. Freedom consists in avoiding the domination, and even the assistance, of others; and natural man is insulated from other wills, be they benevolent or hostile. His freedom is therefore best construed as negative rather than positive.

One meaning of the negativity of freedom is the capacity to resist instinctual determination. Rousseau at first relies on this notion to distinguish man from the animals. Such a cleavage seems required to account for the emergence of a recognizably human being from the natural condition. And yet, Rousseau does not follow this presupposition to the traditional conclusion that man is a spiritual being.

Unexpectedly, the complete argument of the *Second Discourse* does not confirm any spirituality of soul in natural man, nor does it develop the expected distinction between free will and mechanical causation.[28] Man's "openness" appears to be a biological rather than a metaphysical feature. The soul of natural man is shown to be subject to a series of modifications provoked by "new circumstances," which distance him further and further from the tutelage of nature.[29]

However, Rousseau does reveal natural man to be a *spirited* being, who resists dependence on or subjection to others. The contrast of the indomitable savage and the servile bourgeois is the leitmotif of the *Discourse*, and this distinction proves to be far more significant than the metaphysical-moral gulf between noninstinctual and instinctual creatures.[30]

In chapter 3 I examine how Rousseau forges democratic freedom by explaining the relationship of natural, civil, and moral freedom in democratic citizenship. I begin with the problematic genesis of civil society: the developments that make political institutions necessary are the very ones that destroy natural freedom. Since men are compelled to establish a common power over themselves, and since there exists no natural basis for authority, nor even any predisposition toward social life, they will consent only to a form of association that leaves each as free as he was before. However, the pact of association involves the total alienation of each associate (with all his rights and powers) to the whole community. In what sense could this leave the individual as free as he was before? The answer depends on appreciating the distinction between the structure of natural freedom and the particular form it happens to take in the state of nature. In civil association men's hitherto discrete powers are united, and the direction of individual power by natural desire is superseded by the exercise of a general will aiming exclusively at a common good.[31] When citizens are subordinated only to conventions that have common objects, "they do not obey anyone, but solely their own will." The "supreme power," the "public force," is now in equilibrium with a generalized desire.[32] Rousseau will later describe government as the artificial equivalent of the union of soul and body in the individual, as the activity of uniting will and power.[33]

I will explain Rousseau's logic in demanding the total alienation of the individual to the *entire* community, and show how the general will is understood to fulfill the structural requirements of natural freedom in a new form. The general will is the most opaque of Rousseau's concepts, and I will devote considerable attention in this chapter to the difficulties that have befuddled its interpreters. It is necessary not only to grasp what the general will is (and is not) but also to understand the carefully elaborated conditions under which it can (and cannot) function. We shall see that the general will is a will to generalize. Furthermore, since a will to generalize one's desires/interests does not exist naturally in men (who are utterly self-regarding), it must be created. Men must be transformed by the operation of a "political economy" into citizens who are capable of willing the general. Strictly speaking, it is only such a general will (and not the people themselves) that is sovereign.

The only free relations are contractual relations, and civil association is "the most voluntary act in the world."[34] However, defining the legitimate contract is only half the solution to the political problem. The other, as noted above, involves the formation of a certain kind of faithful contractor: the citizen. Rousseau's account of citizenship has long vexed interpreters because it appears to offer two dichotomous models: rational political participation and patriotic enthusiasm.[35] In fact, Rousseau combines the two. Legitimacy requires some act of public willing, but the expression of the general will depends on a prior ordering of the affective dispositions of the people, a precondition that is fulfilled for the people but not by the people. This precondition is necessary, but it has no legitimacy; it is achieved by an intervention of wisdom on the side of democratic will.

Rousseau focuses on the problem of getting men to take contract seriously, a difficulty that is perhaps underestimated in the liberal theory of obligation. The latter neglects what might be called the "affective conditions" of the free regime. Rousseau is keenly aware that while one may speak of the "political machine," men themselves are sensitive beings, a fact that is at once a political problem and an opportunity.[36] A politics rooted in the lure of apparent interest will not succeed. Consequently, Rousseauian citizenship will be a "habit of the heart," which is not to say that citizenship will be either natural or humane.[37] Indeed, the activity of the legislator could be described as a hardening of the heart. Such is the meaning of "denaturing."[38] Rousseau understood as well as anybody that contractual relations are not tender; but in the artificial polity, they are the only legitimate relations among free men.

Chapter 4 considers the affective dimension of citizenship, and analyzes Rousseau's attempt to meld abstract principles of political right with the enthusiasm of communal identification. Rousseau believed that uniting the affections might be one way of solving the problem of generality, of having men perceive the general when they look at political questions, and avoid being "blinded" by their particular interests. Reason is insufficient to bring men to will the general. But in his account of the festival (*fête*), Rousseau depicts another kind of generality, one that comes into being spontaneously rather than as a consequence of rational deliberation: "From all this there resulted such a *general* feeling that I can't really describe but a feeling which, in its *general* joy, one experiences quite *naturally* in the midst of all that which is dearest to us."[39]

I explore what is implied in the *re*-formation of "men as they are," why Rousseau understands it to be necessary, and how it reflects his basic assumptions about the human soul. For this purpose, Rousseau reaches back to ancient political practice, which he understands to be a kind of "psychagogy" or soulcraft. Rejecting received theories of social contract, he approaches the question of the foundations of community from a unique angle. As Bertrand de Jouvenel has noted, the term "contract" is a very bad rendition of the mystical union contemplated by Rousseau. The latter envisions something quite other than the exchange of a certain portion of freedom for a certain portion of security. The Rousseauian social contract marks a transition from the natural to the civil condition, but it involves the "death" of the individual as a distinct unity, followed by his rebirth as member of a "moral and collective body."[40] This "redefinition" of the self as a being whose identity is bound up with its social relations has, interestingly, become influential in contemporary critiques of liberalism. I will remark on Rousseau's possible significance for that critique in my concluding chapter and try to clarify Rousseau's adiaphanous place in contemporary political theory. However, it is appropriate here to broach the subject of Rousseau's stance toward modern political thought, for it explains the genesis of freedom as the central problematic of Rousseau's own reflections and indicates how twentieth-century dissatisfaction with liberalism echoes Rousseau's opposition to his own age.

Rousseau's Rejection of Modern Politics

There exists today a widespread sense that the Enlightenment project has foundered, and that a conception of a citizenship based on the acceptance of impartial and impersonal standards of morality must be jettisoned before the construction of a democratic political culture can begin anew.[41] For many critics the liberal tradition of individual rights has undermined the foundation of democratic political community by conceiving the citizen as an abstract bearer of rights, and by fostering an individualism that exerts a relentless centrifugal force on political institutions.[42] This multifaceted critique of contemporary liberal democratic thought and practice has thus arrived at the very plateau from which Rousseau observed the argument and action of modernity.

Contemporary interest in Rousseau endures out of this deep-seated dissatisfaction with the commercial republic. Rousseau represents the road not taken in "bourgeois-liberal modernity," a condition that for many remains worthy of the judgment Rousseau rendered against his own times. Rousseau accurately appreciated the goal of Enlightenment-liberal thought as a cunning attempt to manage men as they are so that their basic asociality supported social ends; over that project he broke ranks with "the party of humanity." Rousseau's political vision is focused on something nobler than the pursuit of comfortable self-preservation, and his spirited rejection of the "politics of progress" is bound up with a defense of freedom that maintains a current appeal.[43] Autonomy is the watchword in contemporary theoretical discourse, and the singular value of the Rousseauian version is its political character. Rousseau offers autonomy as a form of social self-determination and common self-government.[44]

Thus Rousseau is a lodestar for contemporary critics of "bourgeois freedom." He indicts the entire modern movement in politics and morality on the basis of a full grasp of its logic and intention. While his fulminations against the bourgeois culture of modernity can appear as a confused jeremiad (invoking here the standard of Roman civic virtue, there that of prepolitical savagery), Rousseau's opposition to modern politics is arresting precisely because he attacks from within.

Rousseau adopts the cardinal assumption of modern political philosophy: for the proper understanding of man and his relations, the salient issue is his beginning rather than his end. But Rousseau accuses his predecessors of betraying their own premise, of forgetting the primacy of freedom in their political arrangements by conceiving men as mere subjects of sovereign power.[45] Whereas the philosophic founders of the commercial republic saw in a new system of morals and legislation the promise of greatness and security, Rousseau saw "unfortunate people trembling under an iron yoke, the whole of humanity crushed by a handful of oppressors, a starving multitude overwhelmed by pain and hunger . . . and everywhere the strong armed against the weak with the redoubtable power of the laws."[46] Rousseau rejected the path charted by Hobbes and Locke from the natural to the civil condition out of a deep conviction that civil society, as it has developed historically, is the disease of which it thinks itself the cure.

Hobbes described political justice as a matter of legality wherein right conduct reduces to conformity with the command of the sovereign. The identification of the just with the legal is further traceable to the covenanting act of men who realize that their appetites are best satisfied when they are partially constrained by a common power erected over them by their own consent. The exercise of will in the social contract is also the submission of will to a sovereign power whose commands thenceforth define justice.

From Hobbes, Rousseau learned that a multitude can be conceived as a single person, and that a corporate personality can possess a will. The possession of that corporate will is sovereignty. But whereas Hobbes attributed sovereignty to the representative of the multitude, Rousseau held that it could never be alienated.

Rousseau's notorious principle, that certain citizens might need to be "forced to be free," is really a variation on the theme that justice has no value unless the coercive power of the whole community can be brought to bear on any member who inclines to behave unjustly. Had Rousseau left it at saying that anyone who breaks the social contract would be forced to be *just*, there would be no controversy, since force must often be the instrument of justice. Rousseau was led to a conception of freedom that crucially depended on justice (understood in terms of relations of "right"), and thereby was reconciled with force.

Let us recall that, for Hobbes, the only measure of justice is the edict of the sovereign. But Rousseau's conception of sovereignty is meant to preserve democratic freedom, and he refuses to follow Hobbes in the alienation of sovereignty to a monarch. Of the latter, Hobbes says: "In him consisteth the essence of the commonwealth; which, to define it, is one person, of whose acts a great multitude, by mutual covenants one with another, have made themselves every one the author, to the end he may use the strength and means of them all, as he shall think expedient, for their peace and common defence."[47]

As I will describe in chapter 3, according to Rousseau's democratic concept of sovereignty, the people rule themselves. Hobbes was convinced that such a representative sovereign was required to make the people's social contract reliable as well as legitimate, for only an awesome power would "direct their actions to the common benefit."[48] Rousseau envisions a democratic path to a similar result. The difference is that democratic justice is not to be purchased by the surrender of freedom. Hobbes was so convinced of the power of *amour-propre* (vanity), of the desire for glory, even at the expense of self-interest rightly understood, that he distanced sovereign power from the pull of the distinctly human appetite for power and domination. Rousseau believed that *amour-propre* could be rechanneled toward the common good.[49] Only on the basis of this assumption can Rousseau's concept of sovereignty be rendered coherent, for Rousseau is every bit as aware as Hobbes was of the human tendency to forsake the common benefit for the pleasure of subjugating one another. Hobbes recognized that civil men must cultivate certain virtues if they are to resist the lure of their *amour-propre*, for even the awesome power of the sovereign is in need of a supplement beyond force and fear.[50] Rousseau argues that virtue is itself a passion, and thus the self-renunciation demanded by the civil condition can be felt by the citizen as a force akin to a natural inclination.

Hobbes did not conceal that the passage from the state of nature to the civil state is a transition from the state of freedom to a state of bondage. In the civil condition, freedom is what remains when obedience to the laws has been subtracted from the subject's discretion. The laws are chains by which men agree to be bound. In the interest of peace, men resign their natural independence. Citizenship is precisely the subtraction from freedom that is made by the sovereign power. Law systematically erases freedom, stopping only at the border of those liberties which are of no interest to the sovereign.

Thus, according to Hobbes, it is incoherent to approach political life with an expectation of (let alone enthusiasm for) freedom. Freedom exists only outside the precinct of sovereign authority. "The end of making laws, is no other, but . . . restraint."[51] Hobbes defines freedom in the following way: "A freeman, is he, that in those things, which by his strength and wit he is able to do, is not hindered to do what he has a will to do."[52] The determination of his will is irrelevant to a man's freedom. Will is only the last appetite in deliberating.[53]

Rousseau accuses Hobbes of legitimating what amounts to a surrender of natural freedom in exchange for chains. Heretofore the social contract has guaranteed nothing but servitude in a social order now enclosed by the barbed wire of an irrevocable legality (*un droit irrevocable*).[54] It is because of this swindle that Rousseau reopens the issue of the state of nature. One can undo the chain of reasoning that led Hobbes to a bad formulation of the social contract only by attacking his assumptions about the natural condition. Rousseau insists that the latter is not subject to the terrors portrayed by Hobbes, nor, for that matter, to the "inconveniences" asserted by Locke. Put simply, so long as natural men are isolated and independent, *amour-propre* does not develop. Dissociated men do not detest, fear, gull, and dominate their fellows.[55]

According to Rousseau, previous philosophers have all made the same mistake: "they spoke about savage man and they described civil man."[56] Rousseau argued that the former had no need to exchange freedom for security because men in the state of nature had no antagonistic relations. On the contrary, it is the dependent relations of civil society—the inequalities of rank, power, and property—that create antagonisms in the first place.[57] Rousseau's counterportrait of the state of nature thus removes the negative incentive for the transition to civil society, which is the linchpin of the Hobbesian (and Lockean) social contract argument. This "correction" also allows Rousseau to reach back, as it were, to the natural condition for a standard of freedom.

Critical Appraisals of Rousseau

Some commentators have questioned whether Rousseau's *political philosophy* can genuinely be said to be oriented by the concern for freedom.[58] There appears to be strong evidence for the view that Rousseau regarded political life as the obstacle rather than the vehicle to freedom. At the beginning of the *Social Contract* he states that his intention is to discover how chains can be legitimate. Finding that no one has yet given a satisfactory account of Rousseau's meaning here, W. T. Bluhm suggests that the restoration of freedom on the political and social level was simply not Rousseau's intention. Bluhm detects no correspondence between Rousseau's concept of freedom (which derives from a natural standard) and his political proposals (which apply only to civilized men). He writes, "The values that he found in the patriotic society of the *Social Contract* have nothing to do with freedom in the only sense of that term meaningful to Rousseau."[59] Bluhm argues that Rousseau never seriously intended to design a free regime, and instead focused on nurturing the values of a "patriotic society."

One problem with this interpretation is that the *Social Contract* repeatedly affirms the importance of freedom. Rousseau states that freedom is the *qualité d'homme*, and that to renounce freedom is to renounce the foundation of one's very being. Furthermore, one explicit aim of the social contract is to "leave each man as free as he was before."[60] I will explain below how legitimate chains are not incompatible with freedom if we do indeed grasp "the only sense of that term meaningful to Rousseau," for there are no political values (patriotic or otherwise) that do not derive their importance from a connection with freedom. Although the proximate cause of civil society is self-preservation, freedom is its ultimate justification. Rousseau distinguishes himself from previous contract theorists precisely in questioning the outcome of a political order framed principally by the requirements of peace and security. For Rousseau, freedom is a higher good than life.

Rousseau's political proposals have often been judged to be positively inimical to freedom. Perhaps the most interesting view is that of Benjamin Constant, resolute liberal yet reluctant critic of Rousseau, whose genius he acknowledged. Constant argued that Rousseau's passion for freedom was authentic, but anachronistic. The homogeneous social order may have been functional in ancient times, when public safety was radically insecure, but it is positively dysfunctional in the present. Constant accused Rousseau of resuscitating an ancient form of freedom that is not viable in modern conditions.[61] Repeating the contention of Hobbes, Constant alleged that "ancient liberty" was merely collective liberty, indifferent to the freedom of discrete individuals.

But however accurate that judgment might be regarding the ancient city, it is misapplied to Rousseau, who declared that the worst of all circumstances is to find oneself at the discretion of another individual.[62] Moreover, according to Rousseau, it is the very lack of regulation of the "private sphere" of individual life that destroys freedom in the relations of men. His recurring theme is that, in the "private sphere" of society, citizens do their level best to oppress one another. Rousseau's characteristic self-absorption testifies to his concern for the fate of the individual. Beyond that, the *Social Contract* itself evinces a concern for more or less conventional guarantees of individual freedom.[63]

Rousseau shares with Constant a determination that the conditions of freedom are primary. However, for Rousseau the relevant distinction is not Constant's contrast of modern and ancient conditions but, rather, that of the natural and civil conditions, of which both classical antiquity and modernity are subsets. Rousseau discovers the paradigm of freedom in the natural condition. The good civil society will approximate it by replicating its structure (though not, of course, its substance, which is isolation or solitude). Rousseau does indeed esteem ancient political practice, but not for its own sake and not on the basis of ancient philosophical premises. Rousseau thought that he discovered in ancient citizenship the proof that an artful reconstruction of the conditions of freedom was a possibility for modern men. The Spartan regime, as it appeared in the writings of Plutarch, was for Rousseau a laboratory for the denaturing of men into citizens. That ancient experiment suggested the possibility of freedom in modern circumstances.

Because human freedom is so fragile, it must be fenced in by an elaborate system of "education," a training of the habits and sentiments.[64] This notion of a freedom so hedged about as to be almost impervious to view has both perplexed and enraged Rousseau's critics. But once one grasps that the paradigm of freedom is the condition of natural man cloistered in the state of nature, it is possible to appreciate Rousseau's defensive or preservative intention and to transcend the dichotomies of freedom and order, independence and solidarity, that have bedeviled modern political thought and sustained an increasingly sterile debate between "liberals" and "conservatives." The freedom to be recovered in the well-ordered polity is that "original freedom for which [men] seem to have been born," and which they have forfeited in becoming social.[65]

To the liberal criticism that he failed both to define freedom correctly, as protection from the will of the people, and then to conceive effective barriers against the latter, Rousseau might reply that it misses his point. If defensive barriers are needed, it is to police the relations among persons rather than between the individual and the state. Rousseau's liberal detractors accuse him of ignoring the freedom inherent in the "private sphere," or of undervaluing the freedom that derives from the anonymous relationships of a market system, but Rousseau asserts that the interpersonal ties that human beings construct amount to chains of dependence ab initio.[66] Alleviating this problem requires both more and less of politics: more, because the evils of the human condition stem not from man himself but from man "badly governed"; and less, for the dual reason that the human problem really is a prepolitical one, and the art of legislation remains subject to rare, if not impossible, contingencies.[67]

According to Lester Crocker, however, Rousseau's fertile political imagination conceived only the possibility of modern totalitarianism. Crocker argues that Rousseau's regime is one in which citizens enjoy only an ersatz sovereignty. In fact, citizens are "controlled, by a small elite leadership, in one way or another, in the very depths of their beings."[68] For Crocker, the Legislator (Rousseau's alter ego) is an indoctrinator who conditions the people to a constitutional order, and whose managerial function is later routinized and institutionalized. In Rousseau's republic, government manages citizens and limits them to a plebiscitary ratification of elite proposals. For Crocker, the popular assemblies described in the *Social Contract* are the occasions for a gerrymandered unanimity of opinion. No pluralism, no opposition, loyal or otherwise, is tolerated in Rousseau's disciplinary regime, says Crocker. The general will must be unopposed by particular wills, and the general will is best known by the government. For Crocker, Rousseau's is a tutelary rather than a self-governing regime. Such is the prima facie case against Rousseau as the enemy of freedom.

What Crocker fails to consider is Rousseau's argument as to why such illiberal devices might be required *for the sake of freedom*. Doubtless Rousseau's perspective is peculiar, but Crocker never seems to enter into it, preferring instead to explain away Rousseau's unusual proposals as the expression of a bizarre personality. While Crocker correctly identifies the tutelary nature of Rousseau's regime (and quite rightly finds it foreboding), he fails to adequately consider the rationale for Rousseau's insistence on "political education," and its relationship to "generality." No totalitarian would subscribe to the proposition that "civil association is the most voluntary act in the world" and, as Patrick Riley has convincingly shown, Rousseau was drawn to the idea of "généralité" for reasons that have nothing to do with the logic of twentieth-century totalitarianism. Had Rousseau simply been an authoritarian personality, his political theory would not be marked by the tortured effort to reconcile authority and freedom.[69]

Defenders of Rousseau's democratic bona fides regard the general will to be the instantiation of the popular will that liberal politics systematically frustrates. According to C. B. Macpherson, Rousseau offers democracy without liberalism and affirms "the ultimate worth of the dignity and freedom of the individual."[70] Following Marx, Macpherson sees inequality of property as the cause of the "dehumanization" against which Rousseau reacts, and in his reading of Rousseau's theory, property becomes the principal obstacle to social unity. However, Rousseau identifies a more fundamental obstacle than private property: the passion of *amour-propre* that leads human beings to use each other for their own purposes. This fatal passion does not derive from the fact of private possession, and its oppressiveness antedates the relations of production. Disdaining all parchment guarantees (which cannot address the root cause of human exploitation), the Marxist is untroubled by the absence of a bill of rights in Rousseau's democracy. But like the aforementioned "liberal" critique, the Marxist perspective fails to appreciate the depth of the human problem as Rousseau defined it. It is more fundamental than even Marx imagined, lying, as it does, in the jeopardy of human relations as such.

The sovereignty of the general will requires some limits to the right to private property, for if distinct classes emerge, their particular interests could obstruct the discovery and expression of a general will. But while Rousseau does recognize class interest as a threat to political unity, he understands the social problem to be more basic than the Marxist interpretation would allow. The notion that there must be a socialist completion to Rousseau's political design overlooks the primacy of *amour-propre* in his political pathology.[71]

Rousseau certainly suggests that the disorder of social relations is *connected* to inequality; but it is not reducible to that problem. The latter creates a dialectic of domination and subordination that advances with the progress of civilization. The antidote to this fatal progress is a form of political equality, which will serve the restoration of freedom. Rousseau answers in advance those future liberal critics of "egalitarianism" who see freedom and equality as antagonistic, if not antithetical, principles.[72] He recognizes what all liberals acknowledge: that natural differences in talents become consequential, indeed sharpened, in society.[73] Because dependency accompanies that differentiation, social progress is inimical to freedom. Hence Rousseau is particularly hostile to commercial society, which he understands to be the most dynamic, the most productive of wealth, the most differentiated by rank—in a word, the most "progressive."[74] Yet unlike twentieth-century socialists who occasionally harken to him, Rousseau denied the possibility of equality in material abundance and preached instead equality in poverty, not for the sake of equality but for the sake of freedom. He values equality because it bars dependence. In his preferred regime, no citizen would be rich enough to buy another, and none so poor as to be driven to sell himself. He attacks commercial society not because it is unequal but because it is unfree.

The social web is a trap for the will, and it is commercial society that spins it most elaborately. A society devoted to commerce distorts and corrupts natural desires. Rousseau was surely impressed by the vivid account of this process in Montesquieu's *Spirit of the Laws*. Montesquieu explained (with approval) how the taste for luxury softened *moeurs* (manners/morals) and contributed to a humane society.[75] Rousseau argued that such a society was in fact a condition of depravity, its inhabitants locked in a perpetual struggle for domination. At every turn *amour-propre* ravages the soul by infecting it with the twin spirits of domination and servility. Civilized man "pays court to the great whom he hates and the rich whom he scorns."[76] Living in the opinion of others, it is impossible for him to be free. The servile conformity of civilization extinguishes the taste for independence in the soul. Petty whispers and innuendo are the dagger points of polite social conflict, and there is no exit from the arena.

Rousseau's indictment may emphasize the corruption of commercial-republican *moeurs*, but the root problem is society as such. He vivisects social man or civil man, not merely the bourgeois. The emergence of *amour-propre* is inevitable as soon as man becomes a social and moral, which is to say a "related," being. To appreciate the full extent of Rousseau's radicalism, one must take his analysis of the state of nature seriously. It is only by meditation on the state of nature that one can conceive human beings unblighted. The perfect expression of their nature requires independence, whose pristine form is the solitude of the state of nature. Rousseau negates in advance Marx's thesis that man is a "species-being."[77]

The radicalism of Rousseau's attack on human "sociality" has led some readers to regard him as a moralist who abandoned serious concern with the redemption of the social world. Bertrand de Jouvenel finds Rousseau's authentic interest in the reformation of the individual rather than the polity. Since historical "progress" away from simple societies (which alone could achieve good political form) is irreversible, Rousseau occupied himself with a moral indictment of history. On balance, it is difficult to argue with Jouvenel's characterization of Rousseau as a "pessimistic evolutionist," whose theory elucidates a problem without promising a solution.[78] But the judgment errs in dichotomizing the re-formation of the individual and the polity, for the precise task of Rousseau's political thought is to show how the individual might be restored to freedom *by political means*. As Patrick Riley has noted, Rousseau's emphasis on generality "rules out *particularism*, not individualism"; and after all, Rousseau's reputation as "the father of *modern* democracy" is bound up with his attempt (mentioned above) to do justice to individual freedom and the public good.[79]

This caveat might also be applied to Judith Shklar's rich exegesis of Rousseau's theory. Like Jouvenel, she is struck by Rousseau's pessimism, emphasizes his concern with the reform of the individual, and discounts his visions of political regeneration.[80] Yet it seems to me that her reading tends to portray Rousseau's careful elaboration of the Legislator's activity too much as a theoretical beau geste rather than as an incisive account of a precise and practical political problem. Shklar writes, "He [the Legislator] is, after all, only a brief interruption in the normal course of history which is a tale of otherwise unmitigated popular self-destruction. Indeed, neither he nor his utopia have any other purpose than to illuminate what might be, in glaring contrast to what is, and what will be."[81]

But the interplay of what is and what ought to be does not exhaust the dialectical tension in Rousseau's political theory, which has as much to do with the conflicting imperatives of legitimacy and reliability as with the indictment of the present by a standard beyond time and place. The goal of politics is the sovereignty of the general will, and the impediments to it are known. The issue is how they can be both reliably *and* legitimately overcome. There are resources ("The limits of the possible in moral matters are less narrow than we think.") and limitations ("Each individual can, as a man, have a private will contrary to or differing from the general will he has as a citizen.") affecting this task.[82] For Shklar, "The juxtaposition of what is and what ought to be is not a call for action, but a revelation, a psychological event, not an historical one." Thus, "To understand and condemn are the only fit responses to this spectacle [the historical development of humanity] and Rousseau knew no others."[83] It seems to me that at this point, the "pessimistic" interpretation overreaches and cannot sufficiently explain why Rousseau took pains to address so many facets of political founding and renovation, both in the theoretical *Social Contract* and in the more practical works on the constitutions of Poland and Corsica. If indictment was his exclusive end, surely Rousseau could have left his critique at the level of legitimate principles and would not have descended to the lower ground of political mechanics; and, a fortiori, he could have given his political theory a less paradoxical expression.[84]

But in any case, the question of whether Rousseau was a serious reformer (and let us recall that he knew himself to be *ni prince, ni législateur* [neither prince nor legislator]) must be deferred until his prescription has been properly identified. Shklar makes several fine observations regarding the carefully circumscribed role of the people in Rousseau's democracy. She points out that the radius of the general will is carefully limited.[85]

Rousseau minimizes the substantive political activity of the people, even as he ventures an unprecedented concept of popular sovereignty. The popular assembly has little to do with legislation or "self-determination in a politically active sense."[86] Shklar summarizes Rousseau's plan (in a penetrating characterization) as a "politics of prevention."[87] However, this insight seems to belie her general evaluation of Rousseau's intention. For why would a "utopian moralist" be preoccupied with such constraints? Granted that Rousseau conceives political participation as a mode of civic education rather than legislation, Shklar remarks,

> It is not always perfectly clear what Rousseau meant when he insisted that the liberty and equality of the citizens are the only legitimate ends of civil association. In what forms of behavior do freedom and equality manifest themselves? . . . The political participation that liberty and equality demand is not a matter of self-expression. The citizens are not meant to bring their private interests to bear upon public affairs. On the contrary, political participation is a potent form of civil education. Its importance is not in what the citizen contributes to the polity, but what it does for him. Everything that threatens his *moi commun* is bad. All that supports it is good.[88]

I suggest that Rousseau's meaning emerges clearly if we regard his conception of political freedom as negative. Only a negative freedom is compatible with the demotion of substantive democratic practice. Rousseau's preoccupation with the creation and maintenance of a common civic identity is explainable once we understand it as the condition of the realization of the principles of political right. The latter requires not so much that each citizen propose, deliberate, criticize—in short, engage with his fellow citizens—as a means of recovering his individual freedom, as that he *identify* with them. That is not to say that Rousseau was sanguine about the result. My point is that he considered seriously how such an identification might be achieved in real circumstances, such as those of Corsica and Poland, and that howsoever pessimism colored his theoretical effort, it did not preclude his making a painstaking calculus of real political contingencies.

Jean Starobinski's Rousseau strikes a straightforwardly political pose as the "accuser of society" who opposes the bourgeoisification of society and the concomitant disappearance of virtue after the fashion of a Roman tribune.[89] Starobinski explains Rousseau's intense concern for virtue as the consequence of a desire for "transparency," a mode of communication without dissimulation. I apply Starobinski's insight to my own argument in suggesting that Rousseau's notion of a transparent community is the key to achieving a general will among men as they are, but one that is purchased by abandoning the conventional assumptions of democratic politics. Relations of transparency require a kind of intimacy that is normally (and perhaps simply) foreclosed in political life. In the terms I will later employ, Rousseau's civic vision turns out to be a democratic society whose unity is an affair of the heart and whose politics is a process of "identification" rather than deliberation. One might say that Rousseau anticipated and rejected *avant la lettre* Habermas's ideal speech situation of undistorted communication.[90] In Rousseau's democracy, the crucial activity of citizenship involves the silent peregrination of the will from particularity to generality. The distortions of power and influence are neutralized not by the free give-and-take of democratic discourse but, if anything, by the free play of the heart. Whereas Habermas's ideal speech situation aims "to destroy the effectiveness of the authority of tradition over the present," the latter is, as we shall see, a significant feature of Rousseau's political scheme.[91]

Whatever may be the precise relation of Rousseau's moral and political intentions, it is their union in his summons to democracy that resonates in the contemporary clamor against liberalism.[92] Today Rousseau's illiberalism is a virtue insofar as it challenges the constricted, liberal, "mechanistic" concept of freedom that polarizes coercion and freedom, and therewith freedom and politics. In the current intellectual climate, the traditional socialist opposition to liberalism no longer inspires, for, as Benjamin Barber notes, even the Marxist is duped by the liberal allegation that politics is exclusive, "and freedom the antithesis of politics."[93]

The liberal allergy to strong community is certainly aggravated by Rousseau's democratic theory, which looks like an attempt to give every citizen the same opinions, passions, and interests. According to James Madison, self-love, the fallibility of reason, and natural diversity conspire to thwart attempts to unify a society.[94] Therefore liberal government must bow to human nature and steer clear of strong community if it is to preserve liberty. But while Rousseau, too, recognized reason's weakness, self-love's power, and the diverse capacities of men, he arrived at a different estimate of the requirements of a free society. If for Madison the starting point of political reflection is the acknowledgment that plurality is ineradicable (rooted ultimately, as it is, in the diverse faculties of men), Rousseau's starting point is the assumption of generality as the sine qua non of politics. Rousseau's bold rejection of "pluralistic dissensus" derives from his conviction that the historical development of human beings has been wholly disordered. And since the limits of the possible in moral relations are not constrictive—that is, since varieties of the social tie are permissible—there is no compelling reason to stop short of a rigorous politics of *généralité* that might cure rather than merely palliate the mischiefs of social life.

For those seeking a democratic alternative to the present condition, Rousseau's legislative science is guaranteed to be attractive. It both surpasses the Madisonian framework in realism and outshines it in moral appeal by pointing, as it seems to, toward community through participatory democracy.[95] Rousseauian politics seems to evince a concern for the goods of the soul missing in the liberal politics, which emphasizes constitutional forms rather than character formation.[96] Consequently, Rousseau has filled a void for those antiliberals who have lost faith in Marx but whose goal remains a "politics of authenticity" that would nourish both self-realization and genuine community.[97]

This book will argue that the assumptions and conclusions of Rousseau's theory of political freedom provide no firm support for the enterprise of participatory democracy, and that those who would rely on Rousseau for that purpose are burdened with a theory that hollows out political agency, purchases self-government at the price of passivity, and affirms human beings' "potentialities for creative, moral existence" as objects rather than as subjects of political action.[98] Rousseau was certainly dedicated to "the formation of free men and free communities founded on egalitarian principles," but he was persuaded that the goal depended on removing the contingencies of political life.[99] Democratic freedom would be achieved not by the forceful application of democratic principles but, rather, by their modification at the hand of a philosophic Legislator. The distance between strong democracy and Rousseauian democracy is a measure of the gulf separating "man" and "citizen." It is because human beings have no natural predisposition toward political life, no natural inclination or capacity for willing the general, that the democratic order must be established for them rather than by them. Politics may involve the completion of the moral personality of the individual, but not in an authentic way.

To Tom Hayden's question—Is there "anything innate in man that yearns for attachment to a consuming cause or a transcendent form of being?"—Rousseau's answer is negative.[100] All forms of being beyond the original or natural condition (at least any that would not be wholly corrupt) will be the result of an external artifice. For that reason, the forms of democratic freedom (including, not least, the "true constitution" established in the heart of the citizen) have to be preserved against a certain kind of spontaneous willfulness that *is* innate (or almost so), and that threatens to undo the careful reconciliation of the legitimate principles of political right and the requirements of political stability on which the civic "form of being" depends.

Reflecting on American constitutional forms, Sheldon Wolin has decried the achievement of "democracy without the citizen." The framing of the American republic required the creation of a new kind of citizen, one who would accept an "attenuated relationship with power." According to Wolin, "A citizenry was conceived in terms that allowed the American political animal to evolve into the domesticated creature of media politics." America's constitutional forms threaten to bury the authentic democratic conception of the citizen and an alternative conception of politics, "a politics of experience . . . based on substance rather than image."[101] It turns out that Rousseauian democracy is itself predicated on an attenuated connection between the citizen and power, on a "docile" citizenship, and on unifying images.[102] By

Wolin's standard, Rousseau's regime is also a democracy without the citizen. For if democratic politics is about "not simply discussion and cooperation among friends and neighbours but deliberation about differences, not just differences of opinion and interest, but the different modes of being represented in race, culture, ethnicity, religion, gender, and class," Rousseauian politics may be its antithesis. Rousseauian democracy takes flight from the encounter with difference and from pluralistic dissensus; together they are the nemesis of that *généralité* on which freedom depends.[103]

I argue below that Rousseau framed the problem of achieving such a political goal in terms of the reconciliation of the requirements of "legitimacy" and "reliability."[104] One task of politics is to fulfill the requirement of *droit politique* (political right) by obtaining the consent of the will to the decisions of the civil association: in a word, to achieve a general will. A second task is to secure that goal, to guarantee it, by achieving unity in the body politic. In the absence of political unity, generality is conceivable but remains unreliable; it must be supported by national prejudices that literally predispose the individual to become what he ought to be by arousing enthusiasm for the common good in his heart.[105] It appears that for Rousseau, only the power of love can overcome the intractability of the particular will and incline the individual to prefer his general will. Reason is weak, and unreconstructed individuals have no access to a *volonté générale* (general will) on the basis of their membership in the human species alone.[106] It is only by virtue of membership in a *patrie* (a native land, which is always particular) and an education in its prejudices that a general will can emerge in the citizen. The general will has, ironically, a particular (political) cause.

Whether the "prejudgments" associated with national identity overshadow the individual citizen's judgment and simply preclude the self-determination of his will altogether is a problem of which Rousseau was keenly aware. On the one hand, he recognized that "The most absolute authority is that which penetrates to the inner man and is exerted no less on his will than on his actions." On the other hand, he conceded that the Legislator has "an authority that amounts to nothing," and that "one can never be assured that a private will is in conformity with the general will until it has been submitted to the free vote of the people."[107] This tension between wisdom and will (for it is the wise man who understands what *ought* to be) is the inherent political problem, according to Rousseau, and it is the final reason why his regime must disappoint authentic democrats. For it cannot be denied that, as Rousseau describes it, the work of political education (which is the transformation of the self) occurs not in the continuing process of democratic deliberation but in the founding activity of the Legislator, which is later routinized in the permanent influence of *moeurs*. Rousseauian democratic politics is not an exercise in *self*-transformation because it depends upon a prior transformation of the self that occurs outside the legitimate boundaries of the political.

Several commentators have detected an affinity between Rousseau and Plato; indeed, each conceives a regime whose coming into being depends on a coincidence of philosophy and power. What distinguishes Rousseau's polity is the conjunction of will and wisdom without direct and philosophic rule. As Allan Bloom suggests, Rousseau answers Plato (and, before the fact, Nietzsche) in portraying a democracy that is noble and choiceworthy.[108]

But whatever may be the upshot of Rousseau's vision for the enemies of democracy, it is its ramifications for the friends of democracy that concern me in this book. For while no one did more than Rousseau to revive respect for the worth of democracy, no one seems to have had less confidence in the capacity of citizens to preserve freedom through self-government. His citizens have, so to speak, no gyroscope by means of which they might return antagonistic political relations to a state of equilibrium. Democratic freedom remains fragile and prey, like the independence of natural man, to fatal accidents.

Rousseau's limited appreciation of the possibilities of political life is evident in his analysis of speech, the faculty that endows human beings with a political capacity. Political speech is virtually synonymous with subterfuge, and Rousseau reconceives deliberation as a mutual exercise of silent self-examination. Politics is not an art of association in which individuals assert, modify, and redefine their interests as they explore the paths to private satisfaction and common goals. "The better constituted the State, the more public affairs dominate private ones in the minds of citizens."[109] In this view, the public interest seems to be created ex nihilo and displaces rather than supersedes more partial concerns. Rousseau seems to find in ordinary politics only a relentless tendency toward disassociation, as though no counterweights to the centrifugal forces of pluralism and privatization are available. Political processes carry peril, not promise, and the only institutions that afford a resource as well as a risk are the constitutional devices of the Legislator. "As soon as someone says, *what do I care?* about the affairs of the State, the State should be considered lost," Rousseau submits, as if no appeal to a lapsed citizen were possible.[110] Staking all on the habit of identification with the *moi commun* (common self), Rousseau's democratic regime appears defenseless against the breakdown of routine or the gradual erosion of custom. Should its constitutional roots be damaged, should the prejudice favoring the antiquity of laws wane, what are such a polity's prospects for renewal?[111]

Drawn from the model of natural man cloistered in the pure state of nature, this portrait of the democratic citizen reveals a self that is always menaced, never fortified, by relations with others. Such vulnerability is completely consonant with the first principles of Rousseau's philosophical anthropology, which stresses "a secret opposition between the constitution of man and that of our societies."[112] Yet it rings false as an assessment of democratic life in which citizens do occasionally speak, listen, learn, adjust expectations, modify demands, and retreat from entrenched positions. Rousseau himself underlined the need for "public enlightenment." The general will "must be shown the path it seeks; safeguarded against the seduction of private wills; shown how to assimilate considerations of time and place; taught to weigh the attraction of present, tangible advantages against the danger of remote, hidden ills."[113] One might imagine that democratic politics is itself the path toward this enlightenment, but the letter and the spirit of Rousseau's political philosophy will not support that conclusion.

Rousseau's peculiar conception of democratic "deliberation" aims to isolate each citizen from the influence of others. What ensues is a strangely apolitical process that confines citizens to a reflexive activity; self-examination and self-legislation chart an interior route to the public good. Public affairs are to predominate in the mind of the citizen, but the means is an act of introspection, a private moral choice, through which each of our personal and partial wills becomes general. Thus Rousseau envisages something quite different from an exercise in totalitarian manipulation in which the general will functions as an alien imposition on naive or deluded individuals. Far from being absorbed by a corporate mentality, each citizen gives rise to it by turning *inward*.[114] This isolation from the opinions of others is augmented by a fierce independence from one's own partiality, which now represents the vicious achievement of *amour-propre*.

The logic of Rousseau's retreat from genuine political deliberation derives from his assumption that self-interest is essentially a passion, a disposition that is not merely beyond the reach of reason but reason's superior.[115] Given this premise, his democratic politics resembles not so much the mutual encounter and education of citizens' opinions as a hydraulic channeling of passions (engineered by the Legislator's art), first away from the influence of one's fellow citizens, then against the tendency of one's natural egoism, ending in the confluence that is the general will. Rousseau's conviction that "[t]he limits of the possible in moral matters are less narrow than we think" emboldens this project of directing the passions, but at the cost, finally, of circumscribing democratic politics by a subtle, managerial art.

This result reveals the error in appealing to Rousseau's system as the foundation for a new theory of citizenship. Rousseau's political theory itself (as opposed to the nonpolitical alternative he develops in other writings) is actually antagonistic to the assumptions and aspirations of participatory democracy. Because his political system is modeled on the "equilibrium" found in the prepolitical state of nature, Rousseau's democratic citizen ends up being passive rather than active. Twentieth-century democratic theorists who urge us to recapture what it means to be a citizen, to be a participating member of a moral association rather than a roving contractor in a bazaar of exchange relationships, have occasionally invoked Rousseau's theory to move beyond liberal democracy to genuine community or "strong democracy." But Rousseau shared neither the new democracy's hostility to constitutional forms nor its affirmation of politics as the encounter with difference.

The Natural Paradigm

2

The *Discourse on the Sciences and the Arts* contains the first expression of the *ideé force* of Rousseau's political theory. Social life stifles in men "the sense of that original liberty for which they seem to have been born."[1] With the *Social Contract* Rousseau searches for a form of association that might rekindle that sense by leaving each individual "as free as he was before."[2] These propositions form the starting and ending points of Rousseau's political theory and indicate two crucial assumptions: first, freedom is the fundamental good; second, natural freedom serves as a standard for civil and moral freedom. Rousseau suggests that we can and should discern the nature of freedom *simpliciter* in the state of nature. For if man's historical development has been a process of progressive enchainment, to recover the fundamental value of freedom, one must reach back before the origin of society, which destroyed natural freedom forever.[3] Although such a condition no longer exists (and, indeed, perhaps never existed), it is necessary to have precise knowledge about it "in order to judge our present state correctly."[4]

In this chapter I explore the *Second Discourse*, which is Rousseau's most philosophic writing and his authoritative account of the state of nature, to elucidate the freedom that will be normative for men as they are. Since this interpretation promotes the natural and civil forms of freedom over the moral, one might object that the distinctively human experience of freedom is ignored. For is not natural man somehow prehuman, and is not civil man denatured, or less than human? My suggestion is that Rousseau's attempt to account for man as a "metaphysical and moral" being is incoherent in ways that his definitions of natural and civil man are not. In a subsequent discussion I will turn to the status of moral freedom in Rousseau's thought and argue that the "moralization" of man is subordinate to a political goal and is, therefore, best understood as a moment of, or a stage on the way to, political freedom. The latter, in turn, will be shown to reflect the superiority of natural freedom, passivity, and happiness to virtue.

The *Second Discourse* begins by imagining men as they must have been before society forced the acquisition of new and unnatural characteristics.[5] The first observation made about natural man is that his needs are easily satisfied. Furthermore, he is strong, "advantageously organized," able to endure the rigors of a sometimes harsh Nature.[6] The argument aims to show that in the natural condition, man can preserve himself by means of his own powers. Having done so, Rousseau drops his bombshell: in becoming sociable, man becomes a slave.[7] Social man is weak, fearful, and servile, qualities that Rousseau connects to a "soft and effeminate way of life."

The meaning of natural freedom thus emerges in the first few pages of the *Discourse*. Natural independence is associated with manliness, and with "virtue," if one understands the term "in a physical sense." Subsequently we learn that the "most virtuous" is the one who "least resists the simple impulsions of Nature."[8] Rousseau implies that the most virtuous is also the least servile, or the most free. But an even more astonishing reinterpretation—or, better, revaluation—of virtue is soon ventured. The acquisition of virtue through reason is inferior to the "virtue" of independence. Whereas the former requires minds of the stamp of Socrates, independence guarantees inactive passions, and therewith a kind of spontaneous moderation, in everyone. The sheer fact that men in the natural condition have no relations with one another renders them strangers to the violent quarrels that threaten the preservation of the human race.[9]

Natural freedom is the condition of independence characteristic of the state of nature. Therein man is wholly absorbed by *amour de soi*, an exclusive concern for his own well-being. Such "solipsism" is predicated on isolation from one's fellow men. Natural man cares nothing for the opinions of others, either as master or as servant.[10] This condition of freedom from both an "external" domination by others and an "internal" concern for them, also guarantees man's natural goodness. "Man's goodness is identical to his natural freedom."[11]

The natural condition of man is virtually indistinguishable from that of the animals, the only difference being that the latter have no exit from theirs.[12] By his faculty of perfectibility, man has the possibility of another mode of existence. Although he is ensconced in what seems like a providential condition, natural man is in fact undetermined. However, Rousseau makes it clear that perfectibility is triggered only by accident. The development of all the human faculties is contingent, and man could have remained eternally in his primitive condition.[13] This provocative conclusion is crucial, because only this possibility permits Rousseau to use the natural condition as a critical standard for civilized man.

By "natural" Rousseau does not mean exactly what Hobbes described: the condition antecedent to civil society and the imposition of civil laws. According to Rousseau, the natural condition antedates society altogether. This revision of Hobbes is of capital importance. Rousseau indicates why in note O of the *Discourse*:

> *Amour-propre* and *amour de soi-même*, two passions very different in their nature and their effects, must not be confused. *Amour de soi-même* is a natural sentiment which inclines every animal to watch over its own preservation, and which, directed in man by reason and modified by pity, produces humanity and virtue. *Amour-propre* is only a relative sentiment, artificial and born in society, which inclines each individual to have a greater esteem for himself than for anyone else, inspires in men all the harm they do to one

another, and is the true source of honor.

This being well understood, I say that in our primitive state, in the true state of nature, *amour-propre* does not exist; for each particular man regarding himself as the sole spectator to observe him, as the sole being in the universe to take an interest in him, and as the sole judge of his own merit, it is not possible that a sentiment having its source in comparisons he is not capable of making could spring up in his soul.[14]

Each man is an island unto himself in the natural condition. It is the relation between man and his physical surroundings that accounts for his soul's equilibrium. Natural freedom antedates the dependence of social relations; it is wholly negative, coterminous with solitude.

Self-Sufficiency Through Limited Needs

The *Second Discourse* portrays natural freedom as a homeostatic condition. Natural man feels no spur toward self-development, because he experiences no discontent. Rousseau avers that "The truly free man wants only what he can do and does only what he pleases. That is my fundamental maxim."[15] Natural man is situated in the condition of freedom because his "natural forces" perfectly match his needs.[16] As a consequence, he suffers from neither illusions nor prestige. "His imagination suggests nothing to him; his heart asks nothing of him."[17] Untouched by the ravages of *amour-propre*, natural man is given over exclusively to *amour de soi*; he has no need of others and is, therefore, free of them. When he can no longer do without others (and especially the *opinion* of others), he has already become a slave.

Rousseau regards the animal as "an ingenious machine."[18] Its instinctual endowment ensures its capacity to preserve itself in its environment. Natural man likewise enjoys a self-regulating existence characterized by a relatively effortless satisfaction of needs. Rousseau stresses that while man can stray from the path of instinct, he does so to his detriment.[19] In his animal condition he is independent and content, and independence and contentment operate as mutually reinforcing qualities.

Such is Rousseau's naturalistic explanation of freedom. The

latter is compatible with necessity, in a qualified sense. Rousseau refers at crucial moments in his argument to the impulsion of "true" needs.[20] Natural man is shown to be confined within a sphere of existence whose virtue is its closure, even to his own acts of will. Our true needs are givens; part of our natural constitution, they mark the boundary of our freedom. Rousseau asks, "What can be the chains of dependence among men who possess nothing? . . . The bonds of servitude are formed only from the mutual dependence of men and the reciprocal needs that unite them."[21] So long as their needs remain limited, men have no incentive to unite and progress.[22] Natural man's avoidance of intractable needs guarantees his immunity from the spiritual cruelty of domineering others.[23]

In the *Émile* Rousseau explains that "Every desire supposes privation; misery consists therefore in the disproportion between our desires and our faculties. A sensitive being whose faculties were congruent to his desires would be an absolutely happy being."[24] Rousseau invokes this same congruence of faculties (or power) and desire to define freedom:[25]

> The only one who does his own will is he who, in order to do it, has no need to put another's arms at the end of his own; from which it follows that the first of all goods is not authority but freedom. . . .
>
> Before prejudices and human institutions have corrupted our natural inclinations, the happiness of children, like that of men, consists in the use of their freedom. . . . Whoever does what he wants is happy if he is self-sufficient. This is the case of man living in the state of nature.[26]

The same equilibrium constitutes the sentiment of existence and the "moment of freedom." Rousseau is aware that this moment does not endure, but it remains a standard for the evaluation of human progress. The wise man would seek to draw an impenetrable circle around the original equilibrium.[27]

The Metaphysical Hurdle

Human freedom is an affirmation of nature. To be free is to be as nature intended us.[28] But the astonishing assertion of the

Second Discourse is that nature intended us to be savage.[29] How, then, is natural man to be distinguished from an animal? This question provokes Rousseau's notorious foray into metaphysics, at which point his argument is enmeshed in a conundrum.[30] To locate natural man within the human species, Rousseau must impute to him some attribute that cannot be explained by natural causes:

> Nature commands every animal, and the beast obeys. Man feels the same impulse, but he realizes that he is free to acquiesce or resist; and it is above all in the consciousness of his freedom that the spirituality of his soul is shown. For physics explains in some way the mechanism of the senses and the formation of ideas; but in the power of willing, or rather of choosing, and in the sentiment of that power are found purely spiritual acts about which the laws of mechanics explain nothing.[31]

We are confronted by two conflicting assertions: the nature of man is his freedom, but man's natural state is nonhuman. It would seem that if man is free, he is no longer natural; and if he is natural, he is not yet free. In failing to disjoin nature and freedom, Rousseau's argument seems to founder on conceptual confusion, with the result that metaphysical freedom remains obscure and problematic.

In his preliminary attempt to describe the "metaphysical side" of man, Rousseau suggests that freedom, rather than intelligence, is the specific distinction of man, since even animals have ideas. But precisely how does freedom appear, and what is its content? Rousseau's answer is equivocal. Freedom is first distinguished from instinct, but we learn in the same paragraph that the negation of nature is man's undoing! Are we to regard the man who had "in instinct alone, everything necessary for him to live in the state of nature," as free or as unfree? Can necessity, understood as confinement to primitive needs, if not to instinct, be compatible with freedom? One might understand Rousseau to mean that whereas the animal lives naturally, man lives freely, in the sense of creating his own nature. However, the history of man that Rousseau provides does not support this view. We thus seem to be hard pressed to account for "natural freedom," the goodness of which is the leitmotif of the *Discourse*.

One way to avoid the paradoxical association of freedom and natural necessity is to interpret Rousseau as holding that man is free only potentially. That is, freedom might be understood in the light of perfectibility. This openness to change, which remains dormant prior to the "revolutions" in the state of nature, is eventually aroused and then driven by human intelligence. Freedom would remain primary, provided that the capacity for change is understood to precede the intelligence that triggers it, although ultimately freedom and intelligence operate in tandem. The difficulty with this reading is that natural man could not be understood to be free.

Another interpretative route around the concept of natural freedom suggests itself. Human behavior is not determined by instinct; men can choose alternative means of preservation, whereas animals cannot. But since in the fortunate condition of nature he need not choose, man can remain both free and natural. Here the linkage of freedom and the natural condition is accidental rather than necessary. However, on this reading one cannot account for Rousseau's elevation of the pure state of nature to normative status, nor for his indictment of the historical process for the extinction of freedom.

We are left with the conclusion that it is the natural condition itself which renders man free, in the sense of preserving his independence of others. The freedom Rousseau praises in the *Second Discourse* is thus quite distinct from the capacity for "spiritual acts" that might annul the laws of mechanics. The internal constraints on human behavior and the psyche are less important than the invasion of other wills.[32]

As Robert Wokler has pointed out, Rousseau's notion of "metaphysical freedom" established "no formidable gulf between our higher and lower or collective and private selves but rather marked an initially very faint line between savage man and beast."[33] Rousseau was not the first to assimilate humanity to animality in order to make a critical point about contemporary man. The illustrious Montaigne did precisely this in his *Essays*.[34] Montaigne's intention was to attack the "angelization" of human nature that generated an ethics of asceticism and inhumanity.

But Rousseau appears to have gone Montaigne one better, taking literally a conflation of animal and human that Montaigne made rhetorically. Rousseau also drew on the natural philosophy of his time, deriving his concept of the "sentiment of existence" from Buffon's notion that animals are limited to an idea of their present existence. Rousseau applies the Buffonian idea to natural man, and expands it into a social critique.[35] According to Rousseau's elaboration, social man is unhappy because he derives the sentiment of his existence from the judgments of others. On this ground, social man can be distinguished from natural man, but the *Discourse* has not yet satisfactorily resolved the issue of what separates the human from the animal species.[36] In note J, Rousseau shifts propositions to the possibility that "perfectibility" rather than freedom may be the crucial distinction.[37]

Perfectibility

Concerned that his attack on civilized slavery and misery may become obscured in the fog of arguments over the existence or nonexistence of spiritual substances, Rousseau jettisons free will in favor of *perfectibilité*.[38] Now man appears as the being who is changeable. Perfectibility is openness or indeterminacy. Yet Rousseau reports the effects of perfectibility to be the loss rather than the acquisition of freedom. Thus any account of history as the *unfolding* of freedom founders in incoherence. For on such a reading, freedom is both what explains and what is explained: freedom is purportedly the result of the historical genesis of humanity, and freedom is the spur that forces natural man out of nature. Either way, the "metaphysical perspective" on freedom culminates in the embarrassment that such freedom must be judged a calamity for man. The dramatic action, as it were, of the *Discourse* contrasts the value of natural freedom against the curse of civilized oppression. The text provokes by its insistent claim that the original condition, before the accidental activation of perfectibility and the onset of the historical process, was superior.

What is striking, and seldom remarked, is that after introducing the concepts of metaphysical freedom and perfectibility, Rousseau ignores them in the remainder of the *Discourse*. We are shown instead that, whereas in the pure state of nature man is an open being, possessing the capacity of perfectibility or change, nevertheless his *condition* is one of closure to change. Once man is forced out of the pure state of nature, his career of openness commences, and his fall into unfreedom begins: he becomes "the tyrant of himself and of nature."[39] From this perspective, Nature appears as the guarantor of freedom, in the sense Rousseau finds most relevant. Attributes that set man apart from nature undermine his self-sufficiency; hence perfectibility figures negatively in the account of natural man, which stresses the accidental character of his departure from the state of nature and the unfortunate effects of his own efforts to adapt to new circumstances.[40]

Metaphysical Neutrality

The whole metaphysical argument must be viewed in a strategic perspective. Rousseau shrewdly adopts an attitude of "metaphysical neutrality."[41] Victor Goldschmidt has suggested that Rousseau wished to avoid a contemporary dispute between materialists and dualists (principally Condillac and Buffon), so that his account of the difference between original and "present" man would not be summarily dismissed by this or that faction of the men of science. The retreat from freedom to "perfectibility" as the distinguishing quality of man is occasioned by a rhetorical rather than a philosophical necessity.[42] The crucial thesis of the *Second Discourse* is that the uniquely human quality adds nothing significant to the constitution of "physical man" (*l'homme physique*). Unlike Kant, Rousseau wished to argue that freedom does not necessarily raise man out of nature, even though it appears to raise him above it. Man leaves the state of nature because of the chance operation of external forces, not because of the inexorable unfolding of some internal principle.

Thus any attempt at a metaphysical account of freedom would entrain the consequence of undermining the characteristics attributed to man in the natural condition. Furthermore, a metaphysical account of freedom would compromise Rousseau's insistence that man's capacity to negate the natural does not herald the ascent to an ennobling realm of spirit and self-determination.

Rather, as man removes himself from the state of nature (or, rather, as he is forced out of it by certain "fatal accidents"), his will becomes the hostage of artificial needs and desires. By identifying freedom with the natural condition of independence, Rousseau associates it with the mundane rather than the transcendent. The *Second Discourse* teaches that anything metaphysical, anything "beyond nature," threatens to enslave the self.

Rousseau's argument elides the metaphysical issue because his primary concern is to portray freedom as the original and happiest condition of man, and because the question of the specific distinction of man vis-à-vis the animals raises disputes that deflect attention from the principal issue. As the *Discourse* proceeds, freedom emerges as a circumstantial independence rather than a timeless *qualité d'homme*. The nature of freedom is "natural freedom," the condition characterized by the absence of relations that, in turn, is attributable to the proportionality between each individual's powers and needs. The association of freedom with a metaphysical endowment must be avoided, because to admit any quality that would be incompatible with the constitution of *l'homme physique* would imply that the natural condition is unstable, whereas the entire argument of the *Discourse* hinges on the assertion that the natural condition is a kind of plateau on which mankind could and should have remained.[43] It is only when man leaves the natural condition that his freedom is lost.

By taking up the metaphysical issue, Rousseau was forced to bridge the gulf between men who were born free and contemporary men, who are everywhere in chains. But his argument reveals that it is precisely freedom which distinguishes natural man from contemporary man. The *Discourse* emphasizes the immense distance between man and man rather than between man and animal. The former distance is the profound gulf between the natural and the conventional. Freedom must be associated with the natural, or else the indictment of civil man collapses.

Now Rousseau is surely aware that his emphasis on the distance between "original" and "present" man threatens to push the former so far back that he crosses the barrier between men and animals; but he nonetheless ventures some radical suppositions on this score. The upshot of note J is to associate rather than to dissociate man and animal. There Rousseau points out that while his contemporaries demote the orangutan to a beast, the ancients elevated him to a divinity. But perhaps the orangutan is between beast and god; perhaps he is a man![44]

It is significant that Rousseau assumes an obligation to account for the metaphysical side of man, and then uses the opportunity to debunk the notion of a universal human essence:

> Hence this fine adage of ethics, so often repeated by the philosophical rabble: That men are everywhere the same; that as they have the same passions and the same vices everywhere, it is rather useless to seek to characterize different peoples—which is about as well reasoned as if one were to say it is impossible to distinguish Peter from James, because they both have a nose, a mouth, and eyes.[45]

In Rousseau's "reading" of nature, man is a historical being.[46] His psyche is a construct shaped by social and material influences. It is impossible to regard his spirituality as an essence that remains fixed.[47] Rousseau draws our attention to "the powerful effects of the diversity of climates, air, foods, way of life, habits in general, and above all the astonishing force of the same causes when they act continually upon long sequences of generations."[48] Although "A savage is a man, and a European is a man," the philosopher's attention is drawn to the *external* forces that shape the soul of each. In the case of the European, it is government, the laws, customs, self-interest, and, above all, property that make him a scoundrel. Whereas for the savage man, "It is not possible that he will acquire the habit of doing evil, because to do so would profit him nothing."[49] Rousseau subverts both traditional ethics and the metaphysics on which it is based, by turning attention away from the alleged universal qualities of humanity to the social and physical causes of human depravity.

On the other hand, challenging the traditional barrier between the human and animal species threatens to blunt the critical edge of the concept of natural man, since one could simply deny any relevance of the "natural ideal" for civil man. In addition, some tie between the two must be maintained, or else Rousseau cannot explain how mankind traveled from there to here. Thus Rousseau banks on the "spirituality" of the human soul (first describing it as the capacity of free will) and joins the natural and the civil condition by a purported development of latent capacities. Cartesian dualism is, so to speak, kept in reserve to connect original man and contemporary man. But the intention of the *Discourse* is to *disconnect* them as radically as possible, short of literally denying that they belong to the same species. Accordingly, two points must be emphasized: natural man never evinces any "spirituality" in the pure state of nature; and the aforementioned "capacities" require the trigger of mechanical causation, which is wholly contingent.

Rousseau ignores spiritual causation in hypothesizing about the transition from original to present man. It can be explained in terms of the operation of external forces on man's internal constitution:

> Savage man, by nature committed to instinct alone, or rather compensated for the instinct he perhaps lacks by faculties capable of substituting for it at first, and then of raising him far above nature, will therefore begin with purely animal functions. To perceive and feel will be his first state, which he will have in common with all animals. To will and not will, to desire and fear will be the first and almost the only operations of his soul *until new circumstances cause new developments in it.*[50]

Rousseau distinguishes "willing and not willing" from the functions of perceiving and feeling, which man shares with the animals. It would appear that willing and not willing are manifestations of man's purported capacity "to acquiesce or resist."[51] But Rousseau's point in the passage just quoted is, rather, that man's pristine condition absolves him from the need to do anything but acquiesce. Natural man has no obstacles to overcome. His soul is agitated by nothing, including a will that would confound Nature.[52] Natural man's behavior simulates instinct; he remains within the natural order.[53]

The human predicament is that the social order contradicts the order of nature. Man's historical career is a record of ever-deepening spiritual corruption. But so long as man is enclosed within the pure state of nature, he is confined to perceiving and feeling. His passions are rooted in the instinct of preservation, that is, in *amour de soi*. This "simple operation of the soul" is a direct expression of nature, a feeling anterior to reason; it is explainable without resort to an innate spirituality.[54] Thus Rousseau's earlier remark about man's "consciousness of his freedom" must be labeled an overstatement, for natural man is characteristically unself-conscious. His self-awareness appears to be coeval with his interest in others, at which point he becomes a moral being.[55]

The Moral Side of Natural Man

> It seems at first that men in that state, not having among themselves any kind of moral relationship or known duties, could be neither good nor evil, and had neither vices nor virtues: unless, taking these words in a physical sense, one calls vices in the individual the qualities that can harm his own preservation, and virtues those that can contribute to it; in which case it would be necessary to call the most virtuous the one who least resists the simple impulses of nature.[56]

Because morality presupposes relations with others, it is marred by the general disorder of the social condition. Rousseau challenges the conventional valuation of morality by denying that social men's "subjecting themselves to a universal dependence" results in a condition preferable to "having neither harm to fear nor good to hope from anyone."[57]

Natural freedom is amoral or premoral, but it leaves the heart at peace. Natural man is a being who is neither "dazzled by enlightenment" nor "tormented by passions." His faculties and desires are balanced by a "wise Providence."[58] Rousseau refers twice more to the calm and inactivity of the passions as the explanation for natural man's amoral goodness.[59] Above all, "since they had no kind of commerce among themselves," natural men had no experience of *amour-propre* and no true idea of justice.[60] Rousseau concludes that relations among men are better, happier, freer when they resemble relations to things. The harm that one person might do to another becomes problematic only when it has a moral dimension, that is, when it is perceived as a willful act. It is not the blow but the insult behind it that smarts.[61]

Rousseau carefully distinguishes the physical from the moral element in human relations and sentiments. Using the example of love to make a general point about the effect of society on the passions, he argues that natural men are spared the violence and oppression of the social condition. He unmasks moral relations as a network of opportunities for individuals to yoke each other in an effort to satisfy artificial passions.[62] Throughout the discussion of morality in the first part of the *Discourse*, Rousseau's point is not that men are subjugated by their passions but, rather, that they subjugate each other in order to satisfy their passions. The distinction is crucial and derives from the principle of natural goodness. Far from serving the natural end of the human species, moral relations are inimical to the freedom for which men seem to be born. Morality and reason herald the onset of disorder.

> Whatever the moralists may say about it, human under-standing owes much to the passions, which by common agreement also owe much to it. It is by their activity that our reason is perfected; we seek to know only because we desire to have pleasure, and it is impossible to conceive why one who had neither desires nor fear would go to the trouble of reasoning. The passions in turn derive their origin from our needs, and their progress from our knowl-edge. For one can desire or fear things only through the ideas one can have of them or by the simple impulsion of nature; and savage man, deprived of every kind of enlight-enment, feels only the passions of this last kind. His desires do not exceed his physical needs.[63]

Passions begin as exaggerated forms of primitive needs. Needs stimulate our reason to provide the means for their satisfaction. Reason is the servant rather than the master of the passions. Imagination causes reason to become even more forward look-ing, thereby exaggerating our needs once again.[64] The spawning of new needs and desires stimulates the development of our faculties. And just as our desires are satisfied, imagination produces new discontent. As the servant of the passions, reason has no ordering influence over them; it merely develops in their wake. This dialectic of reason and passion quickly spirals beyond our control; depravity is ineluctable. The natural condition kept man within a proper equilibrium; reason propels him headlong into a vortex.[65] The remedy is apparent: "Let us measure the radius of our sphere and stay in the center like the insect in the middle of his web; we shall always be sufficient unto ourselves."[66]

Rousseau deepens his attack on morality with the claim that natural man has no experience of a moral element in love: "He heeds solely the temperament he received from nature." "Imagination, which causes so much havoc among us, does not speak to savage hearts. Everyone peaceably waits for the impulsion of nature; yields to it without choice with more pleasure than frenzy; and, the need satisfied, all desire is extinguished."[67] The "prediction" that the impulsion of nature will not exceed the limits which preserve the condition of independence becomes an overarching proposition. One might summarize the entire message of the *Second Discourse* as the conviction that man does better to follow the course of nature than to direct himself by rational-moral agency.[68]

The Order of Nature

Natural man breathes only repose and freedom. His happiness stems from his status as a "free being" whose heart is at peace, and whose body is healthy.[69] The state of nature is marked by a uniformity that exempts man from those "brusque and continual changes caused by the passions and inconstancy of united peoples."[70] Rousseau contrasts the "simple, uniform and solitary way of life prescribed to us by nature" with the "immoderate ecstasies of all the passions" that torment the soul of civilized man.[71] The absence of passion explains why natural man has no metaphysical and moral personality; as a being limited entirely to physical needs, his mind does not develop.

What is true of the head is also true of the heart. What does it mean to have a heart at peace? Rousseau explains that it is the passions which agitate the heart, and the most turbulent passion of all is coeval with moral relations.[72] It is only in society that love, like all the other passions, disturbs our existence. Freedom and tranquillity are connected, since independence shields us from the inevitable agitations that accompany encountering other wills. So long as natural man remains independent, neither his head nor his heart will implicate him in the turbulent social passions.

> Let us conclude that wandering in the forests, without industry, without speech, without domicile, without war and without liaisons, with no need of his fellowmen . . . savage man, subject to few passions and self-sufficient, had only the sentiments and intellect suited to that state. . . . There was neither education nor progress; the generations multiplied uselessly; and everyone always starting from the same point, centuries past in all the crudeness of the first ages; the species was already old, and man remained ever a child.[73]

The pure state of nature is indistinguishable from the purely physical condition, wherein "an animal is at the end of a few months what it will be all its life; and its species is at the end of a thousand years what it was the first year of that thousand."[74] Natural freedom inheres in this animal-like existence, which is characterized by the solitude and self-sufficiency of each. Rousseau assimilates natural existence to animal existence and contrasts the result with the "prodigious diversity" of civilized life.[75]

The *Discourse* shifts the traditional focus on an essential, spiritual human nature to a genealogy of the passions, understood as modifications of biological drives: a generic understanding of man gives way to a genetic account. Man's "humanization" results from accidental, mechanical causation. Thus the ontological divide between beast and man is superseded by the distance between natural and civilized man. Rousseau underscores the displacement of metaphysics by history through emphasizing original man's proximity to the animal condition.[76]

The upshot of the reconsideration of natural man's "moral side" is likewise to annul its significance for understanding him. Rousseau explains that in the natural condition, "chains of dependence" are impossible because men are not united by reciprocal needs, and because they possess nothing.[77] This amounts to an admission that men are free precisely because they are not yet moral beings. Rousseau shows the acquisition of moral personality to be as unnatural and harmful to man as the development of his understanding. The reinterpretation of man's natural good as freedom diminishes the status of reason and morality. The latter are tainted by their complicity in the destruction of the pure state of nature.[78]

The Destruction of Natural Freedom

Having established the superiority of the natural to the civil condition, it remains for Rousseau to account for the evolution from one to the other. The crisis of new needs is Rousseau's "apolitical" explanation for the genesis of civil society, one that he will later reprise in the *Social Contract*.[79] In that account, "men as they are" are beings who can no longer preserve themselves. Rousseau prefers this apolitical perspective when describing the *legitimate* institution of civil society, intimating that all men are equally subject to that pressure. But there is another explanation of the genesis of civil society in which the political passion to dominate looms larger than the pressure of needs. This is the explanation Rousseau provides in the *Second Discourse* and masks, at least partially, in the *Social Contract*. Civil society arises not so much from the universal desire for self-preservation as from the specific desire of the rich to preserve their domination.[80]

This "political establishment" of the first societies secured the mastery of the few by making it rightful: "All ran to meet their chains thinking they secured their freedom, for although they had enough reason to feel the advantages of a political establishment, they did not have enough experience to foresee its dangers. Those most capable of anticipating the abuses were precisely those who counted on profiting from them."[81] The origin of civil society "destroyed natural freedom for all time," and necessitated the creation of more such societies as a measure of self-defense. Eventually, laments Rousseau, there was no corner of the universe "where one could free oneself from the yoke."[82] Men were everywhere in chains.

Rousseau remarks that prior to the onset of laws, one could subject his equals only "by attacking their goods or by giving them some of his," a point which forcefully indicates that domination is more important than profit to men as they are.[83] The unstated conclusion is that the laws thereafter permit indefinite opportunities for mastery.

Having portrayed "nascent government," Rousseau exposes its domination as wholly illegitimate by an argument that prefigures the early chapters of the *Social Contract*. It is not reasonable to assume, he says, that "proud and indomitable men" [*fiers et indomptés*] would purchase security at the price of slavery. "In fact, why did they give themselves superiors if not to defend themselves against oppression, and to protect their goods, their freedoms and their lives, which are, so to speak the constituent elements of their being?"[84] Such proud and indomitable men are natural men, the predecessors of men as they are, those who have not been corrupted by the passion for distinction. Their concern is to avoid domination, not to practice it, even at the expense of their own subjugation. Rousseau here identifies freedom not as the distinguishing feature or faculty of man but simply as his natural good. "In the relations between one man and another, the worst that can happen to one is to see himself at the discretion of another."[85]

This knowledge is indispensable to the correct understanding of political right: "It is therefore incontestable, and it is the fundamental maxim of all political right, that peoples have given themselves chiefs to defend their freedom and not to enslave themselves."[86] The true principles of political right are derivable from the goodness of natural freedom. It follows that they cannot be known so long as one reasons from men as they are.

> Savage man and civilized man differ so much in the bottom of their hearts and inclinations that what constitutes the supreme happiness of one would reduce the other to despair. The former breathes only repose and freedom; he wants only to live and remain idle; and even the perfect quietude of the Stoic does not approach his profound indifference for all other objects.[87]

Political right, like the nature of man, seems to require a historical inquiry to discover the proud and indomitable man who is its subject.

Our politicians make the same sophisms about love of freedom that our philosophers have made about the state of nature; by the things they see they make judgements about very different things which they have not seen. And they attribute to men a natural inclination to servitude, without thinking that it is the same for freedom as for innocence and virtue—their value is felt only as long as one enjoys them oneself, and the taste for them is lost as soon as one has lost them.[88]

Recovering the idea of natural freedom is the precondition for ministering to the situation of contemporary men. The *Second Discourse* portrays natural freedom as a kind of spiritedness, a negative disposition to resist the domination of others.[89]

As an untamed steed bristles his mane, paws the earth with his hoof, and breaks away impetuously at the very approach of the bit, whereas a trained horse patiently endures whip and spur, barbarous man does not bend his head for the yoke that civilized man wears without a murmur, and he prefers the most turbulent freedom to tranquil subjection. Therefore it is not by the degradation of enslaved peoples that man's natural disposition for or against servitude must be judged, but by the marvels done by all free peoples to guard themselves from oppression.[90]

Rousseau leaves his portrait of the untamed natural man with the suggestion that freedom is a higher good than life.

This conclusion seems to have an immediate significance for the situation of contemporary men. Rousseau's emphatic denial of any right of slavery by reference to freedom as a gift of nature makes no sense as a metaphysical argument, but powerful sense as a political and moral one. "The jurists who have gravely pronounced that the child of a slave would be born a slave, have decided in other terms that a man would not be born a man."[91] Such a definition of humanity is far more important to Rousseau than the metaphysical issue of whether or to what extent human agency transcends mechanical causation. Between those materialists and dualists who dispute over the latter, Rousseau is prepared to adopt a stance of neutrality; but there can be no neutrality on the political issue of whether man is born free. The philosophers who deny *that* proposition are the agents of despotism.[92] Regardless of natural man's proximity to animal nature, no man is so low as to have natural rulers above him.

Despite the ringing assertion of a natural right of freedom, one might object that the supporting argument leads to a dead end. The natural condition of man is the site of freedom, but only because men have no relations there. The pure state of nature is a condition of solitude, and its freedom is entirely negative. Natural man enjoys a political, moral, economic, and even psychological independence (pity notwithstanding). Such is the meaning of "living within oneself," of experiencing the "sentiment of existence."[93] The case for man's natural goodness requires that the natural condition be located at the extreme of asociality, so that "nature" and "society" become wholly separate spheres. But given that radical separation, can the situation of natural man have *any* significance (negative or positive) for the present?

In the preface to the *Second Discourse* Rousseau insisted that knowledge of natural man was necessary to judge the present correctly.[94] The indictment of contemporary civilization is his fundamental purpose. Rousseau clarifies the saliency of the concept of natural man to this accusatory project in the *Letter to Beaumont*: "This man exists no longer, you say: but he could exist by supposition. Even if the state of nature had not existed, it is necessary to define it: it is the norm on the basis of which we can judge our present civilized condition."[95]

John Charvet protests that Rousseau's extreme disjunction of nature and society causes a fatal incoherence in his thought. Assume natural man to be independent and without *amour-propre*, and social man to be dependent and to have acquired *amour-propre*. Charvet argues, "The problem with which this opposition presents Rousseau is how, if we can neither return to nature in its original form, nor be content with our present corrupt social existence, we can reform man in such a way as to bring about a reconciliation between nature and society."[96] Rousseau's difficulty, according to Charvet, is that natural man's independence and self-sufficiency cannot be imported into the social condition, because the former excludes real social and political relations.[97] But this criticism assumes that we have a standard of adequate social, moral, and political relations to apply to Rousseau's intentions. Charvet's standard is one in which each person is "concerned for the particular identity and value he has for another."[98] But that standard merely begs the question Rousseau raises concerning *amour-propre*. Charvet cannot countenance Rousseau's thoroughgoing critique of *amour-propre*, but neither does he convincingly refute it. It behooves us, then, to attend to how Rousseau thought the natural paradigm might be reconstituted on the level of society in form rather than in substance. For although the natural condition excludes real social and political relations, it does not follow that the latter cannot be reformed in the light of nature.

Granting that Rousseau did understand the natural man to constitute a new norm (in the manner recounted in the letter to Archbishop Beaumont), the question becomes whether that norm is wholly critical, or whether it has some reconstructive significance. Can natural freedom have any bearing on the solution to the social problem?

Natural freedom was a consequence of man's situation or environment. It must thus be regarded as conditional. Natural man can neither be praised nor be blamed for the fact that his powers and desires remained in a happy equilibrium; he simply finds himself in a fortuitous natural order. As subsequent discussion will show, Rousseau conceived a political order in which civil man would be situated in a context that replicates the natural condition. To design and implement that order will require a master artificer, who creates the civil constitution and certain affective dispositions that will reinforce it over time. The goal is to imitate the perfect enclosure of the pure state of nature, and then surpass it by forestalling its destruction. The harmful consequences of man's fall into society might therefore be overcome in a new, artificial context that restores the effects of natural self-sufficiency outside the natural condition per se. According to this logic, civil man can avoid dependence on others by relying exclusively on impersonal or general laws, and each can be subject to the same condition. In this way, the freedom and equality of the natural condition are revived even though civil man no longer breathes the air of the pure state of nature.

Because the natural condition rather than the constitution of natural man is the key to freedom, Rousseau's project avoids the incoherence alleged by Charvet. Nature and society can be connected analytically or structurally, if not substantively. However, Rousseau does flirt with the possibility of the latter kind of link in hypothesizing a privileged stage of history in which man can be said to be both natural and social. Our attention is drawn to the portrait of the "golden age" and the possibility of a freedom that might constitute an acceptable bridge between natural and contemporary man.

The Golden Age of Freedom

The second part of the *Second Discourse* recapitulates man's origin, this time to make the connection with contemporary man rather than break it. In this second version, we encounter possibilities for natural man that did not appear on the horizon of the pure state of nature. The second account of natural man is not about his condition but about his progress beyond the pure state of nature. At one stage of this development, we encounter the possibility of a freedom that is not incompatible with human relations. Rousseau describes the "golden age" as the period of "nascent society," when the development of the human faculties reached the mean between primitive indolence of original man and the petulant activity of *amour-propre*. Rousseau writes:

> The more one thinks about it, the more one finds that this state was the least subject to revolutions, the best for man, and that he must have come out of it only by some fatal accident, which for the common good ought not to have happened. The example of savages, who have almost all been found at this point, seems to confirm that the human race was made to remain in it always; that this state is the veritable prime of the world.[99]

Now Rousseau had earlier described the pure state of nature itself as just such an eternal condition that natural man would never have left, but for an accidental development of his faculties.[100] Consequently, the account of the golden age seems to blunt the radicalism of Rousseau's indictment of society by undermining the privileged condition of the pure state of nature. That critique established the superiority of solitude; but the golden age is undeniably a social condition, albeit of a curiously circumscribed sort. Is there a kind of freedom for men who are beyond the pure state of nature, yet not corrupted, a freedom that might be different from and superior to natural freedom, strictly understood? Is society not, after all, the source of alienation, according to Rousseau?

I believe these queries must be answered in the negative, and that the difficulties raised by the portrait of the golden age can be resolved by reference to the shift in Rousseau's intention in the second part of the *Discourse*. There he is committed to tracing the route from natural man to civilized man, and his philosophical analysis of the distinction between solitary and social man gives way to a polemical distinction between European civilization and savage life.[101] As his argument advances to embrace new issues, Rousseau abandons natural man and the pure state of nature as standards from which to judge the present. His concern now is to account for the transition from one to the other, and deplore it. Society is no longer questionable; rather than explain it away, Rousseau must unfold its genealogy; yet he takes pains to do so in a way that preserves his sweeping indictment of civilization. Rhetorical exigencies require him to make good on his "prediction" (in the exordium to the *Discourse*) that the reader will be moved to seek the age at which the progress of the species should have stopped, and to elaborate the moral of the frontispiece.

But apart from these arguable considerations, the golden age is a privileged moment only because it is a point in the course of the progressive abandonment of the pure state of nature that manages to preserve the latter's essential quality. The nascent society of the golden age is based on "independent intercourse" (*commerce indépendant*).[102]

This paradoxical ideal anticipates the political solution of the *Social Contract*. Society could be compatible with freedom if, and only if, it could be founded on *independent* relations. In reconstructing the historical process, Rousseau is compelled to connect the two conditions that he had separated for analytical purposes: the "first times" and the present. In the former, the self is at the limit of its contraction, given over to the immediacy of *amour de soi* in the sentiment of existence. In the present, the self has reached the limit of its expansion, and becomes dispersed, so to speak, in the eyes of others. While Rousseau treats the golden age as a lost opportunity on this continuum, he does not mean to suggest that history itself discloses a form of freedom essentially different from what is given in the pure state of nature. The standard remains independence. The golden age represents the time when the original contraction of the self is loosened. One might say that at this juncture of nascent sociality, man begins to express himself without asserting himself. The first speech gives voice to feeling rather than to need. It cannot be denied that by identifying this tentative social expression of selfhood as natural, Rousseau stretches the latter concept in a way that blunts its critical edge. But I would emphasize that in this evocation of the golden age, Rousseau *extends* (illicitly) his notion of the natural rather than proffers a new one. His main concern is to underscore the fact that the first expressions of the self have nothing to do with the dissimulations of *amour-propre*; if they did, or could, how could one avoid the conclusion that *amour-propre* is itself natural?

By representing a moment when independence was preserved, despite nascent sociality, the golden age suggests the possibility of freedom for social men. But it does not teach us that freedom is social, that is, nonnatural. We are soon reminded of the fatal logic of social relations. In the disordered circumstances of human progress, "independent intercourse" does not long endure, as the remainder of the *Discourse* documents. It is revealing that in his eulogy of the golden age, Rousseau reverts to the language of eternity. The notion of a state wherein man remains a unified and independent being while related to others is an exception that proves the rule; but it is also a prefiguration. It will take the artifice of civil order to maintain the independent social relations conjured up in the golden age, before men became expansive selves interested in exerting power against one another. The savage existence of the golden age is beyond the state of utter isolation, but it remains a close approximation: "How are we to imagine the kind of pleasure a savage takes in spending his life alone in the middle of the woods?"[103] What is crucial is that it antecedes the spiritual dependence of men on one another. Rousseau indulges in the conceit that the savage could see and reject the present form of life, in which "all our labors are directed toward only two objects: namely, the commodities of life, and consideration among others."[104]

I suggest, then, that the golden age is a rhetorical rather than a philosophical peak in Rousseau's account of the passage from the pure state of nature and freedom to chains, and that it does not represent a new concept of "natural sociality"; the latter would nullify Rousseau's entire critique. Rhetorically, the notion of the golden age refutes both Hobbes and Aristotle by revealing an alternative to asocial sociability and natural sociability. But analytically, Nature and society must represent discrete and closed systems; otherwise Rousseau must concede the argument of "Philopolis" that nature intended man for society.[105] By situating the golden age in the middle of the stages of the state of nature, Rousseau seems to suggest that mankind suffered a double decline: first from the sheer isolation of the pure state of nature, and then from the plateau of transparent social relations. As the *First Discourse* juxtaposed simple *moeurs* to sophisticated hypocrisy, so the golden age stands for a moment before the laws under which "nations" were unified by *moeurs* and "character."[106] It is a chimera, located outside history, that at least might serve to correct the mistaken prejudices of the present.[107]

A Strategy of Redemption

Once the disruption of natural man's equilibrium occurs, reason becomes disoriented and disorienting. Deflected from the path of nature, it is merely the instrument of the passions. Yet Rousseau also intimates that reason might arrest the vicious dialectic. At least in the wise, reason may eventually seize control and direct the passions toward a new order.[108]

At first glance, the solution to human disorder seems to be buried with the state of nature, for "It is in the disproportion of our desires and our faculties in which our unhappiness consists."[109] However, Rousseau does not condemn passion as such; rather, he distinguishes between natural and artificial passions. He remarks that "A man without passion would be a very poor being." The flaw in man's historical development is that it has been unregulated. Natural man is a model because he stands outside the fatal dialectic of reason and passion. Rousseau intends to extirpate neither reason nor passion. Rather, passions must be controlled in a manner that replicates the natural equilibrium. The passions are the principal instruments of our preservation, and society is for passionate men; but the proper ordering of the passions is discovered in the constitution of the natural man.[110] For, as Rousseau asks, "What type of misery can there be for a free being whose heart is at peace and whose body is healthy?"[111]

Natural freedom is the model of the order of desire and power, but that order is not necessarily confined to the state of nature. Its structure is replicable, if we can escape from the dialectic of corruption. Blocking our exit lies *amour-propre*. It extinguishes our taste for the natural and depraves our reason. Natural man's equilibrium was preserved by, among other things, his ignorance.[112] Civil man's rational capacity induces a kind of vertigo. Yet reason now affords some insight into the prerational, natural order. If its structure is knowable, there is hope that it may be reproduced.

> Meditating on the first and simplest operations of the human soul, I believe I see in it two principles anterior to reason . . . it is from the conjunction and combination that our mind is able to make of these two principles, without the necessity of introducing that of sociability, that all the rules of natural right appear to me to flow: rules which reason is later able to re-establish upon other foundations when, by its successive developments, it has succeeded in stifling nature.[113]

Such is the presupposition in Rousseau's suggestion that the laws imitate the natural order so that the polity may enjoy its advantages.[114] Laws might work to restore the condition of freedom.

At this juncture Rousseau begins to conceive a positive value in morality. The passions are excited by the exaggerated attachments to men and to things characteristic of *amour-propre*. That attachment must be broken; men must be "freed" from the grip of unnatural desires. Out of this logic develops the concept of moral freedom as the control of desire. But the goal of moral freedom is a simulation of natural freedom. When man was naturally free, he was removed from the stimulus of *amour-propre* and therefore could not be subjugated by it.

The first "moralization" of man occurred accidentally in the course of human evolution. It was coeval with relations with others, the point at which man could no longer be utterly self-regarding. But while Rousseau first associates the genesis of morality with the eclipse of freedom, he eventually attempts to reconcile the two. Morality is a potential auxiliary of freedom, so long as *des rapports moraux* (moral relations) remain modeled on the natural paradigm of independence.

In a famous utterance, Rousseau defined moral freedom as the obedience to the law that one prescribes to oneself.[115] Previous interpreters have taken it to constitute a new paradigm of the individual good. But the political metaphor is revealing. Rousseau assimilates moral freedom to the political mode of freedom, which is collective legislation. Moral freedom should be construed neither as the highest nor as a new model of existence for social men, for its goodness remains instrumental to political concerns and dedicated to recovering independence in a civil context. Together with the political freedom to which it is subordinated, the aim of moral freedom is the restoration of an original good.

The Kantian Interpretation of Rousseauian Freedom

This reading of Rousseau's intention is challenged by another that views Rousseau as a precursor of Kant and finds in Rousseau's writings an *evolving* standard of freedom which rests finally on the identification of morality and freedom.[116] Given Rousseau's notable references to the will as a "moral cause" and Kant's acknowledgment of Rousseau's influence on his thinking, there is a strong prima facie case for this view.[117] In an influential study, Ernst Cassirer has argued that Rousseau introduces an epochal formulation by identifying the capacity for voluntary action as the distinguishing feature of man, and the faculty of will as the foundation of moral obligation. For Cassirer, Rousseau's greatness is bound up with his anticipation of Kant.[118] I believe this interpretation errs through a misinterpration of a celebrated passage in the *Social Contract* and that Rousseauian freedom remains informed by the natural standard consistently throughout his writings. Rousseau's ideal of freedom derives not from pure practical reason but from the pure state of nature.

We have seen that in the state of nature, the will has no commission. If the natural condition holds the key to defining man and discovering his good, morality qua freely willed duty cannot be part of it. The question is whether Rousseau adopts a radically different perspective in the *Social Contract* and abandons independence in favor of moral autonomy. The second chapter of the *Geneva Manuscript* provides a detailed account of the transition to the civil condition, about which Rousseau feigns ignorance in the final version of the *Social Contract*: "Man's force is so proportioned to his natural needs and his primitive state that the slightest change in this state and increase in his needs make the assistance of his fellow men necessary; and when his desires finally encompass the whole of nature, the cooperation of the whole human race is barely enough to satisfy them."[119]

Rousseau concedes that once this disruption of the original equilibrium of power and desire occurs, the old independence is no longer desirable. He also says, notably, that such "perfect independence" and "unregulated freedom" always had an essential vice: they obstructed the development of "our most excellent faculties."[120] Here, apparently, is solid support for the "Kantian" perspective on Rousseau, for the worth of natural freedom is cast in doubt; the latter appears now as a condition inimical to the development of the faculties we associate with being human.

I suggest that this "departure" from the philosophical argument of the *Second Discourse* is both ironical and compelled by a rhetorical necessity. In the *Social Contract* (and in the apologetic *Lettres écrits de la montagne*) Rousseau is arguing in favor of a certain social order; and it is hardly conducive to his purpose to reprise his critique of sociality as such. But even so, Rousseau does not forsake his foundational principles and abandon, at the eleventh hour, nature for culture. In Kant's vindication of history, the loss of independence, the disordering of power and desire, and the conflict generated by the forcing together of asocial men—all these are stages on the way to humanity. Kant celebrated these evils for precisely that reason, viewing them as crucial episodes in the liberation of humanity from nature; in so doing, he transformed Rousseau's attack on civilization and the Enlightenment into a defense.[121]

Kant removes the ironic tension between natural freedom and humanity that Rousseau took pains to preserve by defining freedom in terms of a break with the natural condition. Cassirer reads this revision back into Rousseau's original argument: "The return to the simplicity and happiness of the state of nature is barred to us, but the path of *freedom* lies open; it can and must be taken."[122] According to Cassirer, for Rousseau freedom meant:

> the overcoming and elimination of all arbitrariness, the submission to a strict and inviolable law which the individual erects over himself. . . . To be sure, with this they give up the independence of the state of nature, the *indépendance naturelle*, but they exchange it for real freedom, which consists in tying all men to the law. And only then will they have become individuals in the higher sense—autonomous personalities. Rousseau did not hesitate for an instant in elevating this ethical conception of personality far above the mere state of nature.[123]

Cassirer concludes that by the time of the *Social Contract*, Rousseau had abandoned the thesis of the *Second Discourse* and ceased holding out for nature against spirit.

The "ethical conception of personality" is synonymous with rational autonomy; freedom here is the determination of our will under the guidance of reason. The free man wills what he ought to will. Hence the model of the free man cannot be natural man, who avoids dependence on others; it must, rather, be the moral man, who becomes master of himself by obeying his reason rather than his passions.[124] Rousseau's natural man seems to have no occasion even to exercise his will; he is premoral and virtually a creature of instinct. His will appears to be but a correlate of his *amour de soi*. In the state of nature, man is free by virtue of the law of nature, which commands him and everything else.[125] On the other hand, the moral man gives laws to himself. Does natural man's velleity disqualify him from real freedom? Does he somehow fall short of the genuine human good?

It seems to me that Rousseau withdraws from the idea that freedom depends on the strength of the will. Natural man is free precisely because his will encounters no obstacle. Or, as Rousseau put it in the *Reveries*:

> As long as I act freely, I am good and do only good. But as soon as I feel the yoke either of necessity or of men, I become rebellious, or rather, recalcitrant; then I am ineffectual. When it is necessary to do what is opposite to my will, I do not do it at all, no matter what; I do not even do what accords with my will, because I am weak. I abstain from acting, for all of my weakness is with regard to action, all of my strength is negative, and all of my sins are of omission, rarely of commission. I have never believed that man's freedom consisted in doing what he wants, but rather in never doing what he does not want to do; and that is the freedom I have always laid claim to, often preserved, and most scandalized my contemporaries about.[126]

The freedom to which Rousseau lays claim is passive, immature, negative, and weak. Reflecting on his own moral career, the Savoyard Vicar declares that "there is an age when the heart is still free."[127] I submit that Rousseau always considered that time the privileged moment of freedom, which remains normative for freedom in different circumstances. It is the same moment as the sentiment of existence.[128] Natural man enjoys "perfect independence" and "freedom without rule."[129] His actions have no moral element, and he is ignorant of the transports of virtue; but these characteristics are lacking only in the perspective of civil men, who must be united by moral ties. Rousseau judges civil man by the standard of natural man, not the reverse. But the practical reformation of the former is subject to political considerations that necessitate a certain veiling of that critical standard in whose light moral and political life remain permanently questionable.

A teaching concerning moral freedom is necessary because the original form of independence is ruled out for social beings. But it is misleading to interpret Rousseau's advocacy of moral freedom as the promotion of a "higher freedom."[130] That Rousseau's standard remains natural freedom is nicely expressed by the choice of Robinson Crusoe as Émile's model and the injunction to "judge every thing as would this isolated man (*juger de tout comme cet homme isolé*)."[131] In this rare condition man knows no other happiness than "the necessities and freedom." Necessity, or dependence on things, is not incompatible with freedom, precisely because it is devoid of morality. From Rousseau's perspective it is the conjunction of freedom and morality, rather than freedom and nature, that is problematic.

The elevation of natural independence as the norm for rational autonomy seems to entail the primacy of objective conditions over the subjective experience of freedom. On the other hand, and according to the Savoyard Vicar's teaching, we simply *feel* that we are free.[132] However, our experience may depend on conditions beyond our control, and avoidance of dependence on other wills requires something beyond the operation of our own will. In this way, freedom is objective or circumstantial. Throughout his education, Émile experiences a sense of freedom, but that inner sense always depends on the manipulation of his circumstances. The Tutor strives to arrange things so that freedom will never fail; Émile's will is guaranteed against frustration because potential obstacles are removed in advance. The goal is to situate Émile in a milieu resembling that of natural man, whose isolation guarantees him against obstacles to his will.

Thus moral freedom or rational autonomy has a certain role in Rousseau's political scheme, but it remains an approximation of the natural paradigm and the status of reason is less exalted. According to Rousseau, reason is both too strong and too weak to surmount the obstacles thrown up by *amour-propre* and social relations. On the one hand, rationality is the servant of particular interest, and thus exacerbates the antagonisms of social men, making them not merely wolves to one another but cunning wolves. On the other hand, enlightened self-interest gives way to the irreducible preference one has for oneself. As Rousseau remarked, "The voice of nature and that of reason would never contradict each other if only man would not impose on himself duties that he is afterwards *forced* to always prefer to his natural inclinations."[133] "All institutions that put man in contradiction with himself are worthless."[134] In other words, Rousseau has no confidence that man can overcome internal contradictions by the force of his own rational will. Whatever contradictions exist are not the work of nature but the consequence of a development in which reason itself is complicit.

Because Rousseau views reason and morality as problematical engines of human "progress," it is unlikely that he would regard them as the lineaments of a new and superior freedom. They are, rather, faits accomplis in human historical progress, disruptive forces that must eventually be harnessed to the project of a restored equilibrium. But it is a restoration that Rousseau contemplates, and here one sees the unbridgeable gulf between his thought and Kant's: freedom as the end of nature versus freedom as the end of reason in history.[135] Rousseau's philosophic boldness derives from his conviction that previous thinkers have misconstrued, and therefore undervalued, the original human condition. The answer to human misery must be implicit therein, not in the trajectory that leads away from it.

The state of nature is the first and paradigmatic site of freedom. At the same time, independence of others is the condition of happiness. Rousseau remarks of natural man, "His soul, agitated by nothing, is given over to the sole sentiment of its present existence without any idea of the future."[136] Only the tranquil soul can be independent, and only the solitary soul will be at rest. Traffic with others triggers the contest for domination. Rousseau's account of this condition anticipates the unforgettable definition of happiness in his final work:

> But if there is a state in which the soul finds a solid enough base to rest itself on entirely and to gather its whole being into, without needing to recall the past or encroach upon the future; in which time is nothing for it; in which the present lasts forever without, however, making its duration noticed and without any trace of time's passage; without any other sentiment of deprivation or enjoyment, pleasure or pain, desire or fear, except that of our existence, and having this sentiment alone fill it completely; as long as this

state lasts, he who finds himself in it can call himself happy, not with an imperfect, poor, and relative happiness such as one finds in the pleasures of life, but with a sufficient, perfect, and full happiness which leaves the soul no emptiness it might feel a need to fill.[137]

Such a condition has a certain privileged status for Rousseau that is reconfirmed throughout his diverse writings. It has been said that "Rousseau's political thought points away from the present in both directions: to man's happy freedom of the past and to the establishment of a regime in the future which can appeal to the will of those under its authority."[138] But what appeals to the will in the regime of the future remains the independent condition of the past. The threat to freedom is not some supposed assault on one's self from within, which would bespeak a natural division in the soul. The uncontrollable desires are stimulated from without, by the trespass of our fellow citizens.

It is the "happy freedom" of the origins that accounts for Rousseau's preoccupation with the natural. As Marc Plattner observes,

> In the true state of nature, man is happy because he is in harmony with himself; he is able to satisfy all his desires through his own efforts, and, therefore, he is always able to follow his own inclinations. Man is happy in the true state of nature because he is wholly self-sufficient and, therefore, totally independent. Man's happiness is identical with his freedom.[139]

What Rousseau marries, Kant's philosophy would put asunder.[140]

Thus the Kantian interpretation of freedom is incompatible with the deepest presuppositions of Rousseau's thought. Cassirer offers us a Rousseau who sees natural goodness as grounded in man's capacity for self-determination. It is not an original quality of feeling but a fundamental orientation and fundamental destiny of man's will. Man is "by nature good"—to the degree in which this nature is not absorbed in sensual instincts but lifts itself, spontaneously and without outside help, to the idea of freedom.

Due to his perfectibility, man does not tarry in his original condition but strives beyond it. Discontent with the range and mode of his natural life, he devises for himself a new form of existence that lifts him, so to speak, from the natural to the spiritual realm. But, clearly, Rousseau's understanding of natural goodness is otherwise. *Bonté* is something at odds with all culture, religion, and philosophy. If it appears to be lowly, it nonetheless has a value that Rousseau persistently defended.

Cassirer illicitly imports a teleology into Rousseau's account of man's development. According to Rousseau, man is not "destined to be free"; he is *born* free. His "progress" confounds that freedom, and all of Rousseau's constructive exertions are devoted to somehow correcting or compensating for its difficulties. Echoing Kant, Cassirer construes perfectibility as the midwife of freedom: "For freedom is not a gift put into man's cradle by benevolent nature. It exists only insofar as he acquires it for himself, and its possession is inseparable from this ever renewed acquisition."[141] But Rousseau does view freedom as a gift, and the story of humanity is the loss of freedom, not its unfolding.[142] Recognizing the givenness of freedom is crucial to an accurate appraisal of Rousseau's project. No teleology guarantees freedom in the context of society; its possibility depends on an uncertain artifice.

To hold that "man was born free" is to assert that "The bonds of servitude are formed only from the mutual dependence of men and the reciprocal needs that unite them. It is impossible to enslave a man without first putting him in the position of being unable to do without another."[143] As we have seen, for Rousseau it is not the determinism of the laws of matter that constitutes the negation of freedom but the yoke, the indignity that can be imposed on man only by other men. The natural condition leaves each individual free of it. Whereas Kant would later contend that Nature itself "humiliates" man, Rousseau portrays Nature (or the natural condition) as the ally of freedom.[144]

The "Return to Nature"

The upshot of Rousseau's analysis of the natural condition is that everything conspires to keep man in that state. His freedom cannot be regarded as the spur that causes him to leave it.[145] Rousseau stresses that natural man is a free being by virtue of his independence.[146] The avoidance of other wills matters more than the exercise of one's own. As Rousseau will declare in *Émile*, "dependence on things" does not destroy freedom; only moral relations can do that. To be free is to live according to nature, not against it.

So it is that natural freedom comes to light as a condition rather than a capacity. One might say that conditions shift, while capacities develop. Rousseau's account of the former involves a history of man without a teleology of the soul. Born free, happy, and good, man loses these gifts in history. His progress results in a disordered soul, an anarchy of passions, and a tyrannizing will. Natural man was guided by a rudimentary concern for his preservation that was effectively redundant, given the *order* of the original condition. But social man can no longer distinguish his true needs from the artificial needs stimulated by *amour-propre*. All the distinctions between natural man and social man derive from the fact that the former is independent and the latter is dependent.

The condition of freedom is the natural condition.[147] Therein one carries oneself "entirely within one."[148] Rousseau declares, "There is, I feel, an age at which the individual man would want to stop."[149] We have addressed these points above in connection with the question, What relevance can Rousseau's natural man have to postnatural human beings? I suggest that to penetrate the logic of Rousseau's political scheme, the question must be revised to, What bearing can this primitive, autarkic condition have for civilization and politics? More precisely, can the conditions of freedom be *legislated*?

Understood as an equilibrium, the state of nature is a *structural* rather than a *temporal* condition. As a condition of balance or harmony, freedom may be replicable at diverse points in time by different means.[150] If to be natural is to resist the artificial and corrupting acquisitions of civilization, then presumably the only way in which civil man could "liberate himself" would be by sloughing off his civility and sophistication, divesting himself of *amour-propre* and the yoke of opinion. While that is an impossible alternative for the democratic citizen, perhaps the road "back to nature" can indicate a road ahead, toward independence in civil association.

In chapter 3 I will argue that Rousseau tries to align the spheres of nature and right in a subtle way. Freedom is the agent of the process that will establish the legitimate society (the society that accords with the principles of political right) on the foundation of individual autonomy. The latter is "the most asocial principle there is," but it is also the most natural.[151] The social condition can be made to mirror the natural condition if the citizen consents to a regime of general laws that will insure him against oppression by any of his fellows. According to Rousseau, the true principles of political right point to a regime in which each citizen obeys only himself, and "returns" to his natural situation of independence. What Pierre Manent calls "the Rousseauist desire to establish the just society on pure right, on the imperative of autonomy," far from deepening the chasm between nature and convention, actually closes it. Freedom becomes the bridge between the two.[152]

Conclusion

The idea of natural freedom emerges as the peak of Rousseau's political thought. From an investigation of man's privileged origin, Rousseau derives a conclusion about his proper end. This conclusion has been resisted by previous interpreters because it appears to promote man's freedom at the cost of his dignity. Some regard Rousseau's "supposed primitivism" as at most a way station in his elucidation of the true moral destiny of humankind that unites reason and freedom; autonomy is understood to be the core of morality.[153]

The standing interpretation of Rousseauian freedom is that man achieves freedom in history. Yet this account neglects both the surface of Rousseau's work and its fundamental principles. Rousseau disconcerts precisely by challenging that teleological view. The critical force of the concept of natural freedom derives from the fact that it locates man's fulfillment at the beginning rather than the end of history. Rousseau's suggestion is iconoclastic, because the influential modern account of freedom as "moral freedom" is premised on the dichotomy of nature and freedom. As we have seen, Rousseau abjures that separation. He found it possible to speak of "moral freedom," and to dissociate nature and morality, while maintaining the connection of freedom with nature. To grasp his meaning, we must correctly rank the natural and the moral lives.

The significance of morality and moral freedom to Rousseau is misunderstood when he is characterized as a theorist of "positive freedom."[154] Rousseau's understanding of freedom, like his understanding of "education," is profoundly negative.[155] Natural freedom prevents man from falling prey to other wills, and from subjecting them to his own. Natural man's circumstances absolve him from effort, thought, and association with his fellows. He has no occasion for moral behavior, for his circumstances obviate the need for deliberation or the exercise of will.[156] He has no "long-term" desires that might require planning. The natural condition is so structured that man follows his impulses unintentionally, without obstacle and without harm.

Reversing the hierarchy of nature and morality misconstrues Rousseau's norm by substituting for natural goodness an ideal of man as a social, moral, and rational being; it also tends to erase Rousseau's radicalism. On such a reading, Rousseau becomes intelligible (and perhaps more palatable) only when he is no longer preaching a revaluation of values. John Plamenatz's revision of Rousseau's argument is worth examining in some detail.

> A man is "true to his nature" when his passions are not insatiable, when they can all be satisfied, and when the attempt to satisfy them brings him not enemies but friends. He is then at peace with himself and his neighbours; he is vigorous, free and happy. His freedom is not independence, for he needs his neighbours as much as they need him; it is mutual dependence cheerfully accepted. Nor is his happiness either the successful pursuit of pleasure or passive contentment with his lot. . . . his happiness is inconceivable except to a social, rational and moral being. . . . Anyone who has tasted or even imagined the happiness possible to civilized man could not wish to live from hand to mouth like a savage, whose happiness consists only in his being

untroubled by desires beyond his power to satisfy.[157]

In clarifying Rousseau's argument, Plamenatz has inverted it completely. In the *Second Discourse*, Rousseau shocks us precisely by preferring the savage's happiness to the fullness of civilized life, which is inimical to happiness. Social relations are similarly condemned because they are incompatible with independence. Plamenatz professes to be nonplussed by Rousseau's reasoning: "Rousseau could have described this condition without calling it *natural goodness*. The name he gave it is misleading. . . . As often as not, when he calls this condition natural, he is speaking of its origins and not of what it is in itself, but what he is then trying to say, I cannot make out."[158]

But Rousseau could not convey "what it is in itself" without speaking of man's origins, for natural goodness, like natural freedom, cannot be understood apart from its conditions. Only in the natural condition does man enjoy an equilibrium of power and desire, a happy self-sufficiency. A man is free to the extent that he can obtain what he desires without the interference or the assistance of others. Freedom persists only so long as man's desires are few and simple. His powers must be considered finite, since independence is incompatible with using others to augment one's capability. It is because man's desires originally correspond to his physical needs that the state of freedom obtains in the natural condition.[159] Since natural man has no desires that he cannot satisfy, he neither needs nor cares about others, and his freedom is perfect. Only later will he experience desires that are impossible to fulfill on his own. While one might object that the effortless satisfaction of desire qua physical need is at best a passive kind of freedom, Rousseau emphasizes the fact that it is unimpeded. That man's desires or needs impinge on him, that his intentions are apparently not part of his stance toward his desires, does not trouble Rousseau. What matters is that *others* do not impinge on us.

Natural freedom qua self-suffiency is negative rather than developmental; it is a condition to be preserved against all "progress." The development of man's faculties is his first step toward others, toward new passions, toward unfreedom. Rousseau sees the moral world as a problematic addition to the physical or natural order. Because the onset of moral relations is contingent and unnatural, morality provides no standard of human excellence. Rousseau's philosophical anthropology excludes moral norms, as is revealed in his predilection, in the *Discourse*, for physical metaphors like "strength of soul" or "health of soul." Rousseau is attentive to the genesis of morality because moral relations threaten to deform the soul. The coming into being of morality is critical precisely because there is no innate "moral faculty" whose unfolding completes the soul.

Rousseau believed that once human relations become unavoidable, the philosopher cannot shirk the responsibility for ordering them as best he can. Whereas the natural condition regulated the psychic equilibrium of natural man, civilized man requires a new "governor" who will restructure his milieu so that his acquired passions enslave neither himself nor others. The challenge to Rousseau is to conceive such a management of the passions in the context of a democratic regime.

The
Achievement
of Democratic Freedom

3

Are free relations possible? Can the avoidance of personal dependence characteristic of solitude somehow be imported into community? Rousseau's political thought is devoted to finding a form of association that avoids the inherent tendency of social relations toward domination and submission; its project is negative in that political relations are regarded as defensive relations designed to protect citizens from mutual domination.

Rousseau indicates that freedom might be susceptible to a political form, that there are circumstances in which freedom, nature, citizenship, and virtue might be compatible.

> There are two sorts of dependence: dependence on things, which is from nature; dependence on men, which is from society. Dependence on things, since it has no morality, is in no way detrimental to freedom and engenders no vices. Dependence on men, since it is without order, engenders all the vices, and by it, master and slave are mutually corrupted. If there is any means of remedying this ill in society, it is to substitute law for man and to arm the general wills

with a real strength superior to the action of every particular will. If the laws of nations could, like those of nature, have an inflexibility that no human force could ever conquer, dependence on men would then become dependence on things again; in the republic all of the advantages of the natural state would be united with those of the civil state, and freedom which keeps man exempt from vices would be joined to morality which raises him to virtue.[1]

Democratic freedom will involve putting the laws above men, a problem that Rousseau likens to squaring the circle.[2] While a free society can be based only on the will of its members, the latter must will what is right if the conditions of freedom are to be maintained. The people must freely will the kind of yoke that alone may guarantee them against dependence on men. But the achievement of the condition of freedom will be the work of wisdom rather than of will. Rousseau describes putting the laws above men as a suprahuman task, by definition beyond the capacity of a self-governing people.

The Last Stage of the State of Nature

From the origin of man and natural freedom, we turn to the origin of political society and civil freedom. Rousseau describes how men have become what they are before turning to the legitimate principles of right. Understanding that process discloses the obstacles to the establishment of a community of right by revealing what the people must be in order to live according to its principles.

The rupture of the natural condition is coeval with the disequilibrium of power and need that renders the individual dependent on others. Rousseau assumes human development to have reached a point where self-preservation compels men to unite; but in becoming dependent, they remain selfish and uncooperative. In a chapter of the *Geneva Manuscript* that was omitted from the *Social Contract*, Rousseau depicts the unsociability of men as radically as possible, thereby underlining what it means to "take men as they are" as the elements of a new association: "Our needs bring us together in proportion as our passions divide us, and the more we become enemies of our fellow men, the less we can do without them. Such are the first bonds of general society."[3] This fortuitous combination of "Hobbesian" individuals, generated by mutual need rather than by right, is wholly disordered.

> This new order of things gives rise to a multitude of relationships lacking order, regulation and stability, which men alter and change continually—a hundred working to destroy them for one working to establish them. And since the relative existence of man in the state of nature in this later stage is dependent on a thousand continually changing relationships, he can never be sure of being the same for two moments in his life.[4]

From an individual who is entirely for himself, who acts on fixed and invariable principles, man becomes a relative and inconstant being, dependent and miserable. The kind of society that mutual need engenders aggravates this condition, and man "finally perishes as a victim of the deceptive union from which he expected happiness."[5]

In Rousseau's analysis of the last stage of the state of nature, a new dimension of natural freedom comes to light. By the "natural order of things" Rousseau now means a condition that is social (dependent) but precivil. In one sense, freedom has simply been lost and men are entangled in the relations of domination occasioned by *amour-propre*. But since the mutual subjection of slaves and masters is devoid of legitimacy, men retain natural freedom in the sense that they have not given up their power and discretion to provide for their needs.[6] Still, natural freedom has ceased to mean independence based on isolation. Men retain their diverse quotients of power, but the latter is no longer in harmony with needs. Consequently, they find themselves in a vicious dilemma. Need exceeds individual power, compelling the assistance of others; but the latter corrupts and degrades by generating relations of "masters and slaves."[7] The final stage of the state of nature resembles the Hobbesian war of all against all.[8]

In the *Social Contract*, Rousseau initially confines the "inconvenience" of the state of nature to the proliferation of obstacles to self-preservation and the inadequacy of individual power to surmount them. The problem is couched in terms of social physics:

> I assume that men have reached the point where obstacles to their self-preservation in the state of nature prevail by their resistance over the forces each individual can use to maintain himself in that state. Then that primitive state can no longer subsist and the human race would perish if it did not change its way of life.
>
> Now since men cannot engender new forces, but merely unite and direct existing ones, they have no other means of self-preservation except to form, by aggregation, a sum of forces that can prevail over the resistance; set them to work by a single motivation; and make them act in concert.[9]

Now one might imagine a solution to the problem of preservation that did not require the union of forces to have a *single* motivation. That was the very point of Adam Smith's famous dictum that the butcher and baker work to someone else's advantage while being wholly uninterested in his well-being. But while Rousseau appreciates the ingenuity of asocial sociability, he condemns it for cementing a system of dependence that is spiritually debilitating. His exposition of the social contract is unique in its concern to exclude personal dependence in the new, civil mode of being.[10]

The Tug-of-War between Nature and Right

In a situation where each individual sees his maximum advantage in others' adhering to the law while he remains free of obligation, there appears to be no hope that the common good might prevail against particular interest.[11] Contradicting the dominant thought of his time, Rousseau suggests that interest is a principle of separation rather than of union.[12] Their disorderly evolution away from the pure state of nature leaves men competing in a zero-sum game. "The reason of each individual dictates to him maxims directly contrary to those that public reason preaches to the body of society, and . . . each man finds his profit in the misfortune of others."[13]

Outside the pure natural condition, the "state of things" or the "new order of things" puts men at cross-purposes.[14] No collection of such beings can be a community, and no mere sum of their interests can constitute a common good. "There are a thousand ways to bring men together; there is only one way to unite them."[15] An aggregation is not a viable political form, because the interest of each remains separate. "It has neither public good nor body politic."[16] Establishing civil association would appear to be an insoluble problem.[17] The qualities of men as they are in the final stage of the state of nature seem inimical to a common good. Rousseau keeps those dangerous propensities before our eyes:

> Indeed, each individual can, as a man, have a private will contrary to or differing from the general will he has as a citizen. His private interest can speak to him quite differently from the common interest. His absolute and naturally independent existence can bring him to view what he owes the common cause as a free contribution, the loss of which will harm others less than its payment burdens him. And considering the moral person of the State as an imaginary being because it is not a man, he might wish to enjoy the rights of the citizen without fulfilling the duties of a subject, an injustice whose spread would cause the ruin of the body politic.[18]

In his critique of Diderot's understanding of natural right, Rousseau offers a stark portrayal of the problem of social cooperation. Diderot had argued that the existence of natural right was evident to any reflective person, although its precise determination might be elusive. Because the "general will" was "a pure act of understanding which reasons in the silence of the passions," the rules of natural right were accessible to any rational being. One who "refused to reason" would be guilty of "renouncing his human status" and would have to be regarded as a "denatured being."[19]

Rousseau replied that man's moral disposition is not, as Diderot supposed, a concomitant of his humanity. The consequence of man's natural asociality is that morality has no ground outside of society. Futhermore, while morality indeed implies that man consults his reason before heeding his inclinations, reason only directs him to seek his own good. Rousseau accepts Diderot's "violent reasoner" as the representative rational individual, and concludes that deliberation among such merely mirrors a recalcitrant egoism. Precisely so long as they listen only to their reason, men will fail to progress beyond considerations of private interest, to a common good.

> Even if the general will is determined by a pure act of the understanding which reasons in the silence of the passions about what man can demand of his kind . . . where is the man who can thus separate himself from himself? And if the concern for his own preservation is the first precept of nature, how can he be forced to look at the species in general, to impose on himself some duties whose connection with his own constitution he does not see in the least?[20]

Whereas Diderot spoke of natural right as the expression of a "general will" or, more precisely, a universal understanding that signified the needs and goods of all men everywhere, Rousseau spoke of "political right," which could only be the expression of the will of a particular political community.[21] Diderot believed that the general will could be discovered in the laws of "all nations." Rousseau insisted that a general will could only be attributed to this or that nation, for it is a will that one has in common with one's fellow *citizens* rather than one's fellow men.[22] Morality is a political construct.

The way out of the final stage of the state of nature thus required a "new association" that would express the general will of a particular people, respect the *qualité d'homme* (defined as freedom rather than reason), and "denature" man into a citizen. Rousseau opposed Diderot's cosmopolitanism not out of a truculent misanthropy but on the basis of a superior political sense. The principles of political right must be rooted in a particular political context if they are to avoid the defect of natural law that is, in the final analysis, promulgated to no one: "It is only from the social order established among us that we derive ideas about the one we imagine. We conceive of the general society on the basis of our particular societies; the establishment of small republics makes us think about the large one, and we do not really begin to become men until after we have been citizens."[23] Rousseau anticipates Edmund Burke, who declared, in a celebrated phrase, that our first attachment is to "our little platoon."[24]

The *Social Contract* conceives a rapprochement between individual and general interest.

> The engagements that bind us to the social body are obligatory only because they are mutual, and their nature is such that in fulfilling them one cannot work for someone else without also working for oneself. Why is the general will always right and why do all constantly want the happiness of each, if not because there is no one who does not apply this word each to himself, and does not think of himself as he votes for all? Which proves that the equality of right, and the concept of justice it produces, are derived from each man's preference for himself and consequently from the nature of man.[25]

The play on the words "each" and "all" indicates that the social contract "cancels yet preserves" *amour de soi* in effecting the transition from individualism to social unity. But there is an important difference between the coincidence of individual and general interest and an identification of the two. At the beginning of the *Social Contract*, Rousseau insists that duty and interest not be divided. Since the great maxim of morality is "to avoid situations which put our duties in opposition to our interests," the terms of the contract must be acceptable to "men as they are," men with no prior disposition to duty.[26] The free will of precivil man is the exclusive source of right and the sole ground of civic obligation.[27] Each will consent to bind himself to authority only if it is manifestly in his interest, that is, if it conduces to his self-preservation and freedom.

Now "the total alienation of each associate, with all his rights, to the whole community" is not initially associated with an act of morality or virtue. As Rousseau first describes it, adherence to the contract appears to require nothing more of anyone than that he prefer himself.[28] On the basis of Rousseau's preliminary account, solidarity with the *moi commun* rests upon the coincidence rather than the identification of public and private interests. However, as long as the citizen secretly regards his own good, while ostensibly considering the good of the whole, he has not adopted a "civic disposition" and not achieved a general will. The fact that the political good is contingent upon a civic orientation is a grave defect that repeats the very flaw Rousseau criticized in the "bourgeois" social contracts, which left men with one foot in and one foot out of civil association.[29]

Rousseau initially suggests that the social contract has the internal resources to withstand a secret appeal to each individual's calculation: "It is so false that the social contract involves any true renunciation on the part of private individuals that their situation, by the effect of this contract, is actually preferable to what it was beforehand."[30] Each contractor (who has not surrendered his independent reason) will presumably recognize that the social pact is an advantageous bargain. This scenario is subsequently revealed to be facile.

To accomplish its purpose, the social contract must "lift" its adherents to a new plane that transcends the calculation of interest. It aims to integrate the individual into a community, to change the perspective of "each" to that of "us." Rousseau hints at the magnitude of this change in describing the social order in terms of "sacred right," but, as we shall see, its full significance emerges only gradually and in response to an inherent dilemma of the social contract.[31]

The political community is a new order of right in which individuals no longer relate to each other qua individuals. Each part must "act for an end that is general and relative to the whole."[32] As Rousseau puts it: "Instantly, in place of the private person of each contracting party, this act of association produces a moral and collective body, composed of as many members as there are voices in the assembly, which receives from this same act its unity, its common *self*, its life and its will."[33]

The social contract gives birth to a "moral being," with qualities separate and distinct from the natural beings who constitute it.[34] As the operative principles of the *moi commun* are elaborated, it becomes clear that a new *identity* is in the making: "The general will, to be truly such, should be general in its object as well as in its essence; . . . it should come from all and apply to all; and . . . it loses its natural rectitude when it is directed toward any individual, determinate object. Because then, judging by what is foreign to us, we have no true principle of equity to guide us."[35] Citizens are now so far removed from their antecedent individualism that partiality toward individual interests is deemed alien to their (collective) judgment: it has become "foreign to us."[36] Such is the goal of the juridical community that would repair the defects in the natural order of things.

The Logic of Civil Association

Since they are compelled to establish a common power over themselves, and since there exists no natural basis for authority, nor even any predisposition toward social life, men will consent only to a form of association that leaves each as free as he was before. However, the pact of association involves the total alienation of each associate (with all his rights and powers) to the whole community. In what sense could this leave the individual free?

The peculiarity of Rousseau's contractual formula stems from the requirement that it reconcile individual and common good while avoiding *personal relations*:

> This formula shows that the act of association includes a reciprocal engagement between the public and private individuals, and that each individual, contracting with himself so to speak, finds that he is doubly engaged, namely toward private individuals as a member of the sovereign and toward the sovereign as a member of the State.[37]

The contract is not an ensemble of mutual obligations one with another, but a form of contract with oneself. When "each unites with all," mutual relations are superseded by an exclusive relation of each part to the whole.[38] Political relations are such that "each" encounters "all," but never "another," and so the individual preserves his independence in the very act of association.[39] Each contractor considers himself in the relation of sovereign to individuals, or as subject to sovereign, but never as one individual toward another. For his own emphatic reason, Rousseau insists on the liberal-democratic principle of a government of laws and not of men. The fundamental purpose of civil association is to escape the evil of personal dependence, to restore the condition of natural freedom.

We may now appreciate the sense in which the social contract might fulfill the mandate to reconcile what right permits with what interest prescribes.[40] On the level of *right* (as opposed to "the natural order of things"), the gulf between private and general interest can be bridged: "The Sovereign, formed solely by the private individuals composing it, does not and cannot have any interest contrary to theirs."[41] The tie that binds individual and public is so tight that the citizen may regard the *moi commun* as his own self writ large. Since sovereignty is deemed to be fully compatible with the concern for self-preservation, and since it guarantees freedom from individual rulers, it can be said to restore the principal features of the natural condition.

But whereas the precivil mode of being was individualized, civil life must be socialized so that the common force has a single source and a single end. Only in this way can each individual, though uniting with all, obey only himself and remain as free as he was before.[42] As Rousseau put it in the *Second Discourse*, "It is the fundamental maxim of all political right, that peoples have given themselves chiefs to defend their freedom and not to enslave themselves."[43] If the purpose of civil association were merely utilitarian, the union of individual powers would not need to be absolute. One might, for instance, acquire in ad hoc fashion whatever assistance one needed under some market arrangement.[44] However, in Rousseau's scheme, civil man must ascend to the plane of right if the tendency of *amour-propre* toward competition and domination (in a struggle for personal recognition) is to be forestalled. Existence on this level requires that a new disposition arise, one capable of adding force to "public reason." *Amour-propre* itself will have to be modified so that it attaches rather than detaches "men as they are."[45]

The General Will

The logic of Rousseau's demand for the total alienation of the individual to the *entire* community emerges once the general will is understood to fulfill the structural requirements of natural freedom in a new form. Rousseau describes the general will sometimes as a will to generalize on the part of the individual who, as a natural being, may have a particular or private will, and sometimes as the predicate of a collectivity with a "moral personality."[46] The general will is presented as both the subject and the object of political activity. In the first instance, the general will is an attribute of the individual as a newly constituted moral subject.[47] In the second instance, the general will is the outcome of a process of voting subject to certain strictures.[48]

Rousseau portrays the social problem arising out of the destruction or corruption of the natural. The *Second Discourse* employs the myth of the statue of Glaucus to suggest that the original human soul has been so altered by society's effects ("a thousand continually renewed causes") that man no longer acts by "fixed and invariable principles."[49] But in submitting to "the supreme direction of the general will," men may once again act according to a fixed and invariable principle, and recapture their original "constancy" as *citizens*. As Rousseau explains, the general will is "toujours droite"; if one follows it, rather than the variable principle of particular interest, one will always act rightly.[50] When all submit to the direction of the general will, society will be governed exclusively on the basis of the common good.[51]

Rousseau juxtaposes the particular and general wills, emphasizing the latter's superior constancy: "The order of human things is subject to so many revolutions, and ways of thinking as well as ways of being changed so easily, that it would be foolhardy to affirm that one particular will, will want tomorrow what one wants today; and if the general will is less subject to this inconstancy, nothing can protect the private will from it."[52] Because the citizen's good is bound up with the good of the *moi commun*, the general will becomes his pole star. It is "always right and always tends toward the public utility," which is to say, "the most general will is always the most just."[53] The general will may be regarded as a collectivized form of *amour de soi*.[54] Like the latter, the general will is "always constant, unalterable, and pure."[55]

Through the social contract, the citizen exchanges one "fixed and invariable principle" for another.[56] Thus "the remarkable change" produced by the transition from the final stage of the state of nature to the civil state nevertheless preserves an important feature of the *original* natural condition.[57] Before the contract, the individual is exclusively self-regarding and merely follows his desires; after the contract, he is "forced to act upon other principles and to consult his reason before heeding his inclinations."[58]

The reference to force must be put in context. Rousseau means that the individual qua contractor chooses to submit to a new necessity, to act according to a new principle. Whereas natural man was immediately dependent on nature (and thereby independent of men), civil man must bring his immediate desires into agreement with the artificial necessity of laws to regain that independence. Since his particular interests and desires have unnaturally proliferated, and now subject him to the will of others, only adherence to law enables him to avoid such private constraints. As we have seen, in Rousseau's mind necessity is not inimical to human freedom so long as it excludes all traces of personal oppression. Accordingly, Rousseau envisions an equal subordination, on the plane of right, to the general will that restores individuals to the same footing they enjoyed in the natural condition. In the words of Eric Weil, "The general will is, in this sense, nature recovered, the human cosmos in whose bosom the individual is free."[59]

The order of right reflects the natural condition of freedom and equality. Each individual wills that order in willing the general, in submerging his particular interests and desires, in acting as "an indivisible part of the whole."[60] The general will is "toujours droite" because it is the expression of a community that exists *by right*. It can be declared only by citizens who regard themselves as members of a collective body, never by individuals who define their good "idiosyncratically." According to the logic of principles of right, the sovereign "by the sole fact of being, is always what it ought to be."[61]

Patrick Riley has argued that a general will is a philosophical and psychological contradiction in terms: "Will is a conception understandable, if at all, only in terms of individual actions."[62] Rousseau does suggest that will can be predicated of collective entities: the general will is "the will of the people as a body."[63]

At the same time, the general will can be expressed only if "each citizen gives only his own opinion."[64] Rousseau himself certainly did not perceive a contradiction in the simultaneous attribution of the general will to the individual and to the collective, for he regarded it as a positive virtue: "Why is the general will always right and why do all constantly want the happiness of each, if not because there is no one who does not apply this word each to himself, and does not think of himself as he votes for all?"[65]

One purpose of the social contract is to blur the distinction between individual and collective altogether.[66] Hence, when Rousseau states that the general will must be general in its essence or source, he plays on the latter's ambiguity: "It should come from all to apply to all."[67] He might as well have said, "It should come from each and apply to all." If we resort to the "expansiveness" of moral freedom at this juncture, we can, I think, account for the ambiguities surrounding the "authorization" of the general will.

Riley's chief objection to Rousseau's formulation is that it requires the object of the will to be general ("will must take the form of general laws"), whereas "will tends to the particular."[68] However, Rousseau does not say that will *simpliciter* tends toward the particular but, rather, that "The particular will tends by its nature to preferences, and the general will tends by its nature to equality."[69] Or again, "Indeed each individual can, as a man, have a private will contrary to or differing from the general will he has as a citizen."[70] The former will emanates from the individual's "absolute and naturally independent existence"; but the transformation that civil man undergoes invests him with a "moral existence," and the latter is the source of his general will, manifested in his capacity for moral freedom.[71] Rousseau later distinguishes no fewer than three "essentially different" wills in the person of the magistrate.

> First the individual's own will, which tends only toward his private advantage. Second, the common will of the magistrates, which relates uniquely to the advantage of the prince; which may be called the corporate will, and is general in relation to the government and private in relation to the State, of which the government is a part. The will of

the people or the sovereign will, which is general both in relation to the State considered as the whole and in relation to the government considered as part of the whole.

In perfect legislation, the private or individual will should be null; the corporate will of the government very subordinate; and consequently the general or sovereign will always dominant and the unique rule of all the others.[72]

As Rousseau observed in the *Political Economy*, all private individuals who constitute the political association may also be members of other, partial associations: "A given man can be a pious priest, or a brave soldier, or a zealous lawyer, and a bad citizen."[73] Conversely, the good citizen suppresses his possible particular wills when they might conflict with his general will. He cleaves to the civic identity, which is impersonal and general: "Several men together . . . [must] consider themselves to be a single body, so that they have only a single will, which relates to their common preservation and the general welfare."[74]

On the whole, the *Social Contract* is indeed more concerned with the object of the general will than with its source, because Rousseau is after a defense mechanism rather than a positive mode of "agency." In the apt formulation of Judith Shklar, Rousseau conceives "a politics of prevention." The object of the will must be general—the general will must never apply to individuals—to accomplish the condition of negative freedom.[75] To summarize: Each individual, by generalizing his will, prescribes the law to himself and obeys only himself in an act of moral freedom. As a citizen and member of the sovereign, he is free in adhering to the general will because the latter can be said to be his own. His individual will qua citizen blends into the single will of the whole.

Sovereignty of the People

The *Social Contract* bears the subtitle *Principles of Political Right*. The goal is a community of right, rather than an association that is permanently challenged by the assertion of prepolitical rights. Herein lies the important difference between the Rousseauian and Hobbesian contracts. From Rousseau's perspective,

Hobbesian civil society accomplishes nothing. It is both informed and limited by the right of the individual to self-preservation; but that right has no place inside the state so long as the sovereign maintains internal peace. In Hobbes's scheme, the people alienate their sovereignty for the sake of peace and prosperity; but the political consequence is merely the "neutralization of the war of all against all" rather than the institution of right.[76] Right is only residual, an ultimate limit to a public order resting on force; there is no *relation of right* between the people and the sovereign.

Rousseau reconceives the form and purpose of sovereignty by attributing it to the people themselves and by barring its transfer to an agent. Hobbes acknowledged that the union of the people's wills was the legitimate basis of the civil order, but he thought that it could be "sure" only if the united popular will was alienated to a monarch. For Rousseau, sovereignty cannot be alienated from a collective to an individual, because while the former is only a moral being, the latter must remain a natural being. Sovereignty "consists in the general will, and the will cannot be represented."[77] The significance of Rousseau's refusal to countenance such a transfer is that sovereignty no longer authorizes the domination of a monarch, but serves instead as the foundation of popular freedom. The revised purpose of sovereignty is to call into being a new (social) existence *in right* by confining human relations to relations *of right*. With Rousseau, the function of sovereignty shifts from being the principle of differentiation within the body politic to the principle that defends against differentiation: "The sovereign knows only the nation as a body and makes no distinctions between any of those who compose it. What really is an act of sovereignty then? It is not a convention between a superior and an inferior, but a convention between the whole body and each of its members."[78] The political condition of freedom joins the force of sovereignty to the freedom of the people, so that "they obey and no one commands, that they serve and have no master, and are all the freer, in fact, because under what appears as subjugation, no one loses any of his freedom except what would harm the freedom of another."[79] In relations of right, equality guarantees that sovereignty remains a principle of freedom rather than domination; political freedom will be egalitarian or democratic.

Rousseau's turn to *popular* sovereignty also underscores his abiding concern for negative freedom, for the avoidance of subjection to alien rule. In attributing sovereignty to the people collectively, Rousseau revises the traditional conception of sovereignty as a relation of ruler and ruled; as a consequence, he rigorously distinguishes sovereignty and government.[80] The sovereign must never govern, because government involves administration or the cognizance of particulars, with the attendant threat of personal domination. To the criticism that the individual is powerless before an absolute sovereign, Rousseau replies that the one thing sovereign authority cannot do is oppress individuals: "The general will . . . changes its nature when it has a particular object; and as a general will, it cannot pass judgement on either a man or a fact."[81] Indeed, the sovereign may not even punish one who has broken the social treaty.[82] The absolute authority of the sovereign is designed as a guarantee against dependence on others. In Rousseau's view, it is individual authority or "private government" that truly menaces individuals, whereas the force of the state preserves the freedom of its members.[83] Relations of right must be "enforced" because they establish only an artificial order that remains vulnerable to violation.

The absolutism of Rousseauian sovereignty is a corollary to the absolutizing of convention, which removes men from the last stage of the state of nature into new relations of right. No individual can be secure from the depredations of private power so long as some men remain in the state of nature while others are subject to the civil condition, or so long as all are only partly "civilized." It is the general and complete immersion in the civil order that prevents men from becoming wolves to one another.[84] Identification with the sovereign authority, and adherence to its legitimate commands, is the only way for men who have become social and desire to avoid mutual oppression to recoup their independence. The sovereign people create the law that obliges them, and they are related to one another only through that medium. Law is the regulative principle of human relations on the plane of right.[85]

The purpose of Rousseau's democratic constitution is to avoid oppression, but for that reason it cannot dispense with force. The social contract would be an ineffectual guarantee against *private* oppression (the ruthless politics of difference) if it did not include sanctions. Citizens are admonished only to keep their word, to abide by the terms of their own contract. That is the straightforward reasoning behind the notorious injunction that whoever refuses to obey the general will must be forced to be free. Rousseau means that such a person would be "compelled" to obey *his* will, qua citizen. Since it is his will, the recalcitrant individual continues to obey only himself; but he now regards himself *as citizen* and no longer as private man in his relations with others. These are, again, right or moral relations. By Rousseau's lights, the force-freedom paradox arises only because the civil condition may need to be reattuned to the original condition of independent relations; public force aims only to defend everyone against the failure of anyone to be moral, and so merely elaborates what membership in the community of right entails.[86] To force someone to be free is to pitchfork him into the condition of freedom on the civil plane. Rousseau believes that because this manifestly serves the individual's good, it is therefore not against his will. Let us turn next to the precise relation of morality and freedom in the context of defensive politics.

The Political Significance of Moral Freedom

If both natural and civil freedom appear to be negative, one might still expect moral freedom to involve a positive project, and to point to a mode of being that transcends the desire for independence. Yet moral freedom is auxiliary to civil freedom; it, too, serves the goal of independence. Moral freedom is defined as obedience to self-prescribed law.[87] The latter can refer only to general laws, which is to say, to expressions of a general will. In Rousseau's conception, a moral will is a general will, in contradistinction to the particular will of a "natural" and independent being. When he remarks early in the *Social Contract* that "to take away man's freedom of will is to take away all morality from his actions," Rousseau does not mean that anything a man might freely will must be considered moral.[88] His point is negative and fundamentally political: there can be nothing legitimate about an act that represents a concession to sheer force, and no one can alienate his freedom to a master.

According to Rousseau, the height of immorality is to subject oneself to another. Only free conventions have moral weight.[89] When Rousseau finally considers how one's actions do acquire moral status, he reveals that morality is indeed conferred by the operation of will, but it is a will aimed exclusively at general objects. The "moralization" of man signifies his admission into a community of right that entails adherence to the general will on the part of each individual.[90]

Moral freedom does emphasize one aspect of the general will: its source, as opposed to its object. Moral freedom involves the stance of the individual toward his particular civil obligation. Here the question for the citizen is not so much, How can acts of the sovereign collective be confined to general rather than particular objects? but, rather, Will *I* prefer the general will I have as a citizen and moral being to the particular will I continue to have as a "natural person"? Moral freedom involves "mastery of self" in the sense of preferring the *moi commun* to the *moi particulier*; the moral conquest is the victory of one's *moi commun* in achieving the vantage point from which one can the prefer the general to the personal. It is an elaboration of Rousseau's understanding of political existence on the plane of right.

Seen in this light, moral freedom is a precondition of civil freedom. The latter requires that the individual choose to regard himself as part of the whole, or regard himself under a new aspect. Through the practice of moral freedom, the citizen reaffirms his original integration in the civil unity. Rousseau analyzes this dimension of contractual obligation in the following passage from *Political Economy*:

> If . . . men are trained early enough never to consider their persons except as related to the body of the State, and not to perceive their existence, so to speak, except as part of the State's, they will eventually come to identify themselves with this larger whole; to feel themselves to be members of the homeland; to love it with that delicate sentiment that any isolated man feels only for himself.[91]

Moral freedom aims at the achievement of an inner disposition modeled on that of *l'homme isolé*, who was independent outside the state. But the citizen can establish his independence only *within* the state on the basis of a polemical confrontation with his own *volonté particulier*. *L'homme isolé*, innocent and pure without effort because he lacks the corruption of social life, is the model for the citizen who must struggle to purge himself of the corruption that natural existence (in the last stage of the state of nature) threatens to import into civil existence. The "dualism" that menaced original man or *l'homme isolé* was that he would fall into social existence and become other-regarding; the dualism that menaces the citizen is that he will fall out of civic existence into a corrupt form of self-regardingness.

Civil freedom rests on the unique relation of the individual to the whole community and the consent of each to the supreme direction of the general will; but that relation, and that consent, assume a prior transformation in the relation of the individual to himself. If we unfold the concept of the general will, we discover that each individual must first prescribe it to himself. The general will emerges out of opposition to one's private and particular will.

Because the citizen never really sheds his natural and independent existence, and because "the private will tends by its nature toward preferences," moral freedom is a permanent political requirement. Preferences must be routinely examined and brought into conformity with equality, which is to say, the particular will must be generalized.[92] Rousseau indicates that this cannot be accomplished once and for all.[93] It is to the habit of self-scrutiny that Rousseau refers when he states that civil man is forced "to consult his reason before heeding his inclinations."[94]

Given Rousseau's fundamental assumptions about the goodness of the natural inclinations, as a stance toward oneself, the disciplinary act of moral freedom makes sense only as a means toward civil unity and civil freedom. The latter make possible the escape from the last stage of the state of nature, in which natural inclinations have become corrupt and disordered. Man must become "master of himself" because the victory against his particularity is a prolegomenon to rightful relations with others. The only moral will that concerns Rousseau is a general will; morality is inherently political. It provides no detachable ethics of individual conduct.[95]

I argued earlier that the Kantian perspective errs in construing the new imperative of moral freedom as a "higher will" that is somehow beyond the individual's good, or even at odds with his happiness. The "moralization" that the citizen undergoes, and that requires the suppression of particularity in his will, is understood by Rousseau to be in his interest as a member of a new association. To correctly appreciate the significance of Rousseauian moral freedom, instead of imagining a "higher self," we should picture a "larger self," the self "in association": a *moi commun*.

It is because Rousseau regards freedom in terms of a condition to be achieved that he subsumes moral freedom under political considerations. But then those very considerations come to overwhelm the activity of moral freedom itself. Because it is "a permanent political requirement," Rousseau seeks to *guarantee* the outcome of moral freedom, to do away with its contingency. As we shall see, this move becomes the recurrent tendency in Rousseau's political thinking.

"In order for the general will to be well expressed, it is . . . important that there be no partial society in the State, and that each citizen give only his own opinion."[96] As an instance of self-legislation, moral freedom required that law conform to a person's will or, more precisely, that each freely prefer the general to an exclusive preference of his own. Moral freedom appeared as a "moment" of political freedom in which the individual gives the law to himself "before" expressing it as part of the sovereign. Political freedom per se requires that the law express the will of everyone who belongs to the community. In expounding on that criterion, Rousseau introduces a new attribute of the good citizen: the "constant will."

Rousseau explicitly denies that the "natural individual" has a constant preference for the general will over his particular will. "Though it is not impossible for a private will to agree with the general will on a given point, it is impossible, at least, for this agreement to be lasting and unchanging"; hence the need for recurrent exhibitions of moral freedom.[97] Anticipating that at least some members of the community may find themselves at odds with the authoritative expression of the general will, Rousseau suggests that they remain free even while being forced to obey laws to which they have not consented. We are told that such members really have consented through their "constant will": "The citizen consents to all the laws, even to those passed against his will, and even to those that punish him when he dares to violate one of them. The constant will of all the members of the State is the general will, which makes them citizens and free."[98] This thought echoes the suggestion that an individual might be "forced to be free." On what grounds can Rousseau adduce a constant will to conform to the general will when he had denied such constancy in particular individuals?

Rousseau defends his conclusion by introducing a distinction between choice and discovery.

> When a law is proposed in the assembly of the people, what they are being asked is not precisely whether they approve or reject the proposal, but whether it does or does not conform to the general will which is their own. Each one expresses his opinion on this by voting, and the declaration of the general will is drawn from the counting of the votes. Therefore when the opinion contrary to mine prevails, that proves nothing except that I was mistaken, and what I thought to be the general will was not. If my private will had prevailed, I would have done something other than what I wanted. It is then that I would not have been free.[99]

The implicit reasoning is that in the circumstances in which my particular will prevails, *I will not be in a condition of freedom* because I will have left the plane of right for the plane of "natural existence." In other words, the activity of moral freedom, which was to keep the individual from "relapsing" into the wrong existence, is now assumed. My mistaken choice is not a *moral* failure but merely an error that can be overlooked because my good has been accomplished by the majority decision. Once again the substitution of what is good for a person for what that person wills, signifies that Rousseau's goal is the reestablishment of a condition; the *agency* that brings it about becomes a subordinate matter.

The notion of a constant will derives from the distinction between a private will and a general will. As a member of the sovereign body, the citizen is asked only to express a general will. In the terms of our earlier account, the citizen is presumed to have made the moral determination to choose the general over the particular (one might say that he has made a "general determination"). The argument also trades on another previous point: "The general will alone can guide the forces of the State according to the end for which it was instituted, which is the common good."[100] Qua citizen, no individual wants his private will to dominate, because his interest is freedom, which can be secured only if the general will prevails exclusively.

> What really is an act of sovereignty then? It is not a convention between a superior and an inferior, but a convention between the body and each of its members. A convention is legitimate because it has the social contract as a basis; equitable, because it is common to all; useful, because it can have no other object than the general good; and solid, because it has the public force behind it. As long as subjects are subordinated only to such conventions, they do not obey anyone, but solely their own will.[101]

The latter phrase refers to the people's own general will. Such a will is constant in that, qua citizen, no one can want anything other than the general good, for that is his insurance against harm.[102] Rousseau can therefore maintain that "What generalizes the will is not so much the number of votes as the common interest that unites them."[103]

The common interest of each citizen is to avoid oppression, so there is really no objective disproportion between the individual good and the common good. Rousseau reasons from the perspective of the democratic citizen rather than of the free rider who seeks an advantage in every relation. The former's desire not to be oppressed gives him an interest in justice. The people desire only to be left alone.[104] Rousseau suggests that democratic man seeks equality because it guarantees freedom, whereas the powerful and the rich want exemptions from general rules because, for them, the pleasure of domination exceeds the desire for freedom.

But what of the occasion when some individuals mistake what the common interest requires? Rousseau anticipated that eventuality in the following passage from the *Geneva Manuscript*:

> But even if the bond of which I speak were as well established as possible, all the difficulties would not disappear. The works of men—always less perfect than those of nature—never go so directly toward their end. In politics as in mechanics one cannot avoid acting more weakly or more slowly, and losing force over time. The general will is rarely the will of all, and the public force is always less than the sum of the private forces, so that in the mechanism of the State there is an equivalent of friction in machines.[105]

The general will is not always the will of all because "the people's deliberations" are sometimes flawed.[106] Rousseau explains that while one always wants one's good, one does not always see it. The people's good is nonoppression, and the general will always serves it. But since the people are made of flesh and blood, they are prone to substitute their private wills for the general will, or to fail to properly generalize their private wills. Even if the latter converge, the "will of all" remains the mere sum of private wills and forfeits its "rightfulness."

Rousseau suggests that to desire to follow one's private will in the civil order is to forsake one's own interest and, so to speak, to confuse one mode of being with another. He repeatedly reminds us that the state is only a "moral being," and that its members remain private persons, "whose life and freedom are naturally independent of it."[107] But citizens must act *as if* they were "moral beings" with a general rather than a private will. The latter must now be viewed as a counterfeit relic of "natural independence," which has become "uncertain" and "precarious." Rousseau emphasizes the advantage in substituting the new "manner of existence" for the old by characterizing it as the exchange of independence for freedom. By the time civil relations have become necessary, man's "natural independence" no longer means his literal isolation, but merely his personal "right" and capacity to fend off others. That kind of independence no longer guarantees nonoppression, and thus no longer serves the individual's good.[108]

The great danger now is that relations of right will be ruptured by men who want to do as they please on the civil plane.

It seems to be Rousseau's thought that it is not enough to punish violations, to force recalcitrants to be moral. It is necessary that no real violations be found, that political recalcitrance and the moral failure it reflects be explained away as *errors*.

What can account for this strange insistence? A possible explanation emerges when we recall that all "works of men" (as opposed to the works of nature) are peculiarly vulnerable. Because they are merely conventions, the relations of right are fragile. Presumably, repeated ruptures by some will eventually erode the hard-won disposition of others to live justly. The civil condition would be shattered, and individuals would revert to the old form of relations, dominating where they can, submitting where they must. Apart from reasoning such as this, it is difficult to account for Rousseau's desire for unity (for an implicit unanimity) rather than a norm of generality that would punish or correct violations. The appeal to a "constant will" seems designed to preserve the fiction that there are no authentic violations, that all citizens have "good will" or pure intentions, even when they fail to choose the general. Rousseau appears to transmute the *actual* expression of a free will into the *assumption* of a constant will because the latter guarantees a condition of independence, whereas the former necessarily leaves it contingent.

In a passage from *Letters Written from the Mountain*, Rousseau sharply distinguished "independence" from "freedom," asserting that "these things are so different as to be mutually exclusive." This statement seems to undermine the thesis that Rousseau's "ideal" is the condition of independence. However, seen in the context of the transition from the *last* stage of the state of nature to the civil condition, the difficulty is resolved. For it is only when mankind has progressed to the point where civil association becomes necessary that freedom and independence (understood as following one's private will) are at odds. Rousseau elaborates as follows:

> When each person does as he pleases, he often does what displeases others, and that cannot be called a free condition. Freedom consists less in doing one's will than in not being subjected to the will of another; it consists further in not

subjecting the will of another to our own. Whoever is a master cannot be free, and to rule is to obey. Your magistrates know that better than anyone, they who, like Otho, omit nothing servile in order to command. I would only regard as truly free a will which no one had the right to resist; in the common freedom no one has the right to do what the freedom of another forbids. Thus freedom without justice is a veritable contradiction; because however one looks at it, everything prevents the execution of a disordered will.

Therefore, there is no freedom without Laws, nor where anyone is above the Laws: even in the state of nature, man is free only because of the natural Law which commands everyone. A free people obeys, but it does not serve; it has leaders, but not masters; it obeys Laws, but it obeys only Laws and *it is by the force of Laws that it does not obey men.* . . . In a word, freedom is always tied to the fate of Laws, it reigns or it perishes with them; I know of nothing more certain.[109]

These remarks show that political freedom does not represent an entirely new value for Rousseau. It is not really distinguishable from independence, so long as one bears in mind the latter's fundamental meaning of insulation from the will of others. In the context of legitimate civil society, it is accurate to say that freedom from oppression is made more secure, because formerly it had been a mere fact of existence, which became nullified in the last stage of the state of nature. Through the social contract, that fact is converted into a right that cannot be canceled under any circumstances.

The essential identity of independence and freedom is clearly indicated in the following passage from Book 2 of the *Social Contract*: "Each citizen is in a position of perfect independence from all the others and of excessive dependence upon the City. This is always achieved by the same means, because only the force of the State creates the freedom of its members."[110]

Civil freedom is a new *form* of independence. It consists not in the power to do what one pleases but in the condition of independence from the particular wills of others. As we saw above, this is how the democratic citizen defines his good. And it is in this light that Rousseau concludes that "The constant will of all the members of the State is the general will, which makes them citizens and free."[111]

The Superior Individual

If the general will is a constant will, could it not be declared by an individual of superior constancy? Would not the declaration of the most virtuous citizen be the greatest safeguard of the integrity of the general will? Since there will always be friction in the political machine, since some citizens will inevitably either lose sight of their constant will or fail in their constancy, why rely on voting to discover the general will in each legislative situation? Granted that the general will alone should guide the forces of the state according to the ends of preservation and mutual independence, is it not a separate question as to who should declare it?[112]

Rousseau defends the inalienability of sovereignty by claiming that while a private will may sometimes agree with the general will, it is impossible for that agreement to be lasting.[113] The reason is that the two are different sorts of will which pertain to different "modes of being": the former to a "natural and independent existence," the latter to a civil and communal existence. In the very place where Rousseau concedes a crucial role in the polity for "superior intelligence," he explains why such a person is disqualified from ruling. The Legislator's task is to convert man's natural and independent existence into a moral existence.[114] But this artificer of the moral personality remains outside the moral horizon he creates; that is, *he* remains a natural, albeit superior, being. Rousseau understands sovereignty to be an attribute of moral beings exclusively, and he denies that moral personality can be predicated of an individual: "It is apparent . . . that the sovereign is by its nature only a moral person, that it has only an *abstract and collective* existence, and that the idea attributed to this word cannot be likened to that of a simple individual."[115]

Even assuming that the Legislator is the equivalent of Plato's philosopher-king, he cannot have any role *within* the polity.

Rousseau insists that one who has authority over men should not have authority over laws; and, conversely, one who has authority over laws should not have authority over men. "Otherwise his laws, ministers of his passions, would often only perpetuate his injustices, and he could never avoid having private views alter the sanctity of his work."[116] Since he stands apart from the collective moral personality, even the superior individual remains someone whose good is not united with that of others. Although Rousseau imagined a "superior intelligence, who saw all of men's passions yet experienced none of them," he recognized that such a being's happiness was independent of the people's.[117] Such godlike indifference could never be a regular part of the polity; greatness of soul is incompatible with democratic equality.[118]

The people must have leaders who will, inevitably, exhibit the passions of men. The best of such leaders will be tied to the people by affection; but they should all be subordinate to the laws as well. Rousseau makes this point in distinguishing natural or paternal authority from magistracy:

> Although the functions of the father of a family and of the prince should be directed toward the same goal, the paths they take are so different, their duties and rights are so dissimilar, that one cannot confuse them without forming the most erroneous ideas about the principles of a society, and without making mistakes that are fatal to the human race. Indeed, while heeding nature's voice is the best advice a father can heed to fulfill his duties, for the magistrate it is a false guide, working continuously to separate him from his people. . . . To do what is right, the former need only consult his heart; the latter becomes a traitor the moment he heeds his. Even his own reason should be suspect to him and he should follow only the public reason, which is the law.[119]

A correct understanding of the "principles of a society" excludes any authoritative individual expression of "the public reason" or, more precisely, the public will.[120] When it comes to securing the people against oppression, there is greater safety in numbers than in the virtuous self-restraint of a few. Hence Rousseau's skepticism about the superior man: "Even if one were to suppose that this man had existed and worn a crown, does reason allow the rule for governments to be established on a marvel?"[121]

Considerations of prudence aside, as a matter of right, Rousseau flatly denies that sovereignty is transferable: "The people itself cannot, even if it wanted to, divest itself of this incommunicable right, because according to the fundamental compact, only the general will obligates private individuals, and one can never be assured that a private will is in conformity with the general will until it has been submitted to a free vote of the people."[122]

If the ascription of sovereignty to an individual, even a superior one, is illegitimate, how can Rousseau defend the undeniable dependence of the sovereign people on the activity of the Legislator?[123] How can authority and will be reconciled? Rousseau's answer involves distinguishing dependence on the Legislator's wisdom from dependence on his will. While the latter would be destructive of democratic freedom, the former is not incompatible with it. The role of wisdom is to re-create the order within which freedom will be maintained. All of Rousseau's superior "artificers" (the Legislator, the tutor, Wolmar) are "ordinateurs."[124] The wisdom of the latter consists in knowing how to remain faithful to the standard of nature, even in unnatural circumstances; they strive to make their artificial constructions perfect after the model of nature.[125] Although the Legislator "denatures" citizens to fit them for "moral relations," he can be said to "renature" the civic milieu by restoring the order conducive to freedom.

The Problem of Social Unity

Rousseau's concern with wisdom or a superior intelligence reflects the conclusion he reached in his argument with Diderot about the essential incapacity of the individual to adopt a common or general perspective. That deficiency, we recall, was rooted in the relative power of reason and feeling. In another passage from the first version of the *Social Contract*, Rousseau elaborated on it:

> Since the social union has a determinate object, its fulfill-
> ment must be sought as soon as the union is formed. In
> order for each person to want to do what he ought to do

according to the engagement of the social contract, each must know what it is that he ought to want. What he ought to want is the common good; what he ought to avoid is the public ill. But since the state has only an ideal and conventional existence, its members have no natural, common sensitivity by means of which they are promptly alerted to receive a pleasant impression from what is useful to it and a painful impression as soon as it is harmed.[126]

Citizenship has a foundation in reason by virtue of the legitimate principles of political right; but the reason of "men as they are" only reinforces the feeling of particularity. This problem left the social contract subject to contingency, which in turn led to Rousseau's elaboration of a new form of (civil) existence that might escape it. Relations of right are a solution for men as they are, but they must undergo a "remarkable change" in order to make the transition from a disordered social existence (in the last stage of the state of nature) to the new order of right.

The political condition to be achieved is clear: "As long as several men together consider themselves to be a single body, they have only a single will, which relates to their common preservation and the general welfare."[127] However, this corporate sensibility is a prodigious requirement that turns out to involve the "denaturation" of man by means of "public education." In the words of *Émile*, "Good social institutions are those that best know how to denature man, to take his absolute existence from him in order to give him a relative one and transport the 'I' into the common unity, with the result that each individual believes himself no longer one but a part of the unity and no longer feels except within the whole."[128]

The deep antagonism between the individual and society is the starting point of Rousseau's philosophy. As we have seen, he condemns not merely the injustice of this or that historical society but the social situation itself.[129] Nevertheless, for human beings in their present predicament, "everything is radically connected to politics."[130] It is because men's circumstances now require the perfection of the political order that Rousseau declares, "Everything that destroys social unity is worthless. All the institutions which put man in contradiction with himself are worthless."[131]

The latter point suggests that in the present condition, social unity and individual unity are linked. If Rousseau's principal concern is individual integrity, the latter now requires a seamless "integration" of the individual into the social whole.[132] Social unity must be perfected so that the individual experiences others only as part of the undifferentiated whole to which he also belongs. As in the state of nature, where the individual's life is consumed in the activity of *amour de soi*, there is no "I-thou" relation in the perfected social state. The ego is fully integrated into a "moi commun," so that the "moi" imperceptibly becomes "nous." In a *perfect* metamorphosis, the utter self-regardingness of *amour de soi* would be collectivized without any rupture in the individual's consciousness of unity and independence. Civil man could avoid contradiction with himself so long as his ego was represented to him exclusively as a *moi commun*. The oblivion of otherness, which was characteristic of the natural order, is the extraordinary goal of Rousseau's political order. But the other to be avoided now includes a dimension of the self; in the civil condition, one's own particularity represents a threat no less than the particular wills of others. In Rousseau's considered judgment, the function of moral freedom is taken up by civic education, and the Legislator becomes the true artificer of the moral personality.[133]

While principles of right dictate that social contract be the indispensable foundation of political existence, contract does not by itself achieve the *perfection* of political order. We have seen that Rousseau's plan appears to hold out for nothing less. In conformity with the principles of political right, the perfection of generality must be *willed*, but Rousseau indicates that citizens will not freely choose the political remedy they desperately need. Notice that Rousseau does not say that "So long as men continue to submerge their particular wills and will only the general, they will have but a single will." That would imply that their community is, in the words of Renan, "a plebiscite every day," or that the community is indeed the ongoing project of a common will. Rousseau holds the opposite: men must regard themselves as a unified body *if* they are to have that will. The coming into being of community is not the effect of the unified will but its precondition. This fact is explicitly granted in the *Social Contract*:

> For a nascent people to feel *[sentir]* the great maxims of justice and the fundamental rules of statecraft, the effect would have to

become the cause, the social spirit which must be the product of the founding would have to preside over the founding itself, and men would have to be prior to the laws that which they ought to become by means of them.[134]

It might be suggested that the foregoing dilemma is confined to the problem of a nascent people, that is, to the circumstances of founding alone. It might then follow that after certain minimum conditions were established, the people would develop the capacity to legislate the common good on the basis of their own deliberations. But for Rousseau, the problem of founding reflects the essential problem of politics as such. For justice and interest to be reconciled, the diversity or plurality of men (in which none sees beyond self-interest) must give way to a unity that apprehends a common good. But *individuals* reject the common good even while seeing it, because understanding fails to move the will. The perfect political order can be conceived in theory, but its actualization depends on the denaturing art of the Legislator because man's "natural constitution" resists the disengagement of the self from its own particularity.

To be both legitimate and reliable, democracy must rest on contract and community. Rousseau's plan synthesizes a politics of obligation and a politics of solidarity, and strives to satisfy their respective imperatives. The requirement of solidarity arises from the inability of the rational will to lead each individual to choose on the basis of right (to will the general rather than particular interest), even though such a choice is both just and advantageous. On the level of right, the sovereign is always what it ought to be and the general will is always right; but men as they are must first ascend to that level. Rousseau is forced to confront the psychological obstacles to the community of right, and to consider how men as they are might be made to identify with the *moi commun*. In response to this problem he elaborates the politics of virtue.

The Politics of Virtue

As to the relation of virtue and civic education, the first thing to be said is that, for Rousseau, the polity does not exist for the promotion of virtue; rather, virtue exists for the sake of the polity. Virtue consists in putting the good of the whole before one's particular good; it aims at the same goal as the generalizing of one's will. Virtue involves a suppression of one's natural existence in favor of a different identity.[135] Rousseau took over from Montesquieu an understanding of civic virtue as a passion for self-renunciation.[136]

We recall that, initially, the social contract was to avoid any real renunciation.[137] To participate in the general will, the citizen was only to consult his reason.[138] But as the *Social Contract* unfolds, we learn that citizenship must have a foundation in the passions, and that the formation of citizens is a task not for principles of right but for political art. The intervention of the Legislator is required to denature men, to transform them from individuals who prefer themselves into members of a body who cannot conceive of themselves apart from it, to create "a larger whole from which [the] individual receives, in a sense, his life and his being."[139] This requirement is "concealed" in the original statement of the terms of the contract; it comes to light if we unfold the notion of "moral freedom," which Rousseau does not choose to do in the *Social Contract*. One reason for that hesitation may be that civic virtue is overtly problematical in a way that moral freedom was not. Virtue cannot be accounted for by the principles of political right, because citizens do not make themselves virtuous through an exercise of choice. Civic virtue is the work of the Legislator, and thus cannot be grounded in the civil constitution.[140] The denaturing of men into citizens who choose the common good involves educating or "conditioning" the will rather than expressing it. This requirement indicates the gulf between the legitimate and the reliable constitution of the state. To use more familiar language, the constitutional framework must be supported by a "political culture."[141]

Rousseau conceives civic education as a process that takes over the function and purpose of moral freedom in the operations of "political economy." "If it is good to know how to use men as they are, it is better still to make them what one needs them to be. The most absolute authority is that which penetrates to the inner man and is exerted no less on his will than on his actions. It is certain that people are in the long run what the government makes them."[142] The function of government extends beyond the execution of the sovereign will to encompass the formation of citizens inclined to will the common good. As we shall see, the activity of the Legislator is merely the first instance of a continuing "governmental" function devoted to strengthening the social tie.

Civic education is a disciplinary management of the passions, but one that emphatically does not involve the subordination of the passions to reason. The passions themselves are to be manipulated or redirected, by reconstituting their objects. As Émile's tutor declares: "One has a hold on the passions only by means of the passions. It is by their empire that their tyranny must be combatted; and it is always from nature itself that the proper instruments to regulate nature must be drawn."[143] Passion can be made to counteract passion. "Love of country can be more ardent than love of a mistress."[144] Once modified, *amour-propre* can become the foundation of civic virtue; its force can be harnessed for the common good.[145] A skillful manipulation of this passion can inspire enthusiasm for the laws.[146]

Rousseau was not the first to contemplate the management of the passions; Descartes had already indicated the path toward transforming virtue into a science of the passions.[147] But Rousseau advocates the kind of *dirigisme* that Michel Foucault would later associate with the "disciplinary society." Rousseau's regime resembles a *dirigiste* or plebiscitary democracy, with the twist that the citizen submits willingly, indeed *lovingly*, to discipline. The themes of *Poland*, *The First Discourse*, and Rousseau's meditations on civic virtue in general point to the disciplinary society as the sine qua non of democratic freedom:[148]

> Do you want the general will to be fulfilled? Make sure that all private wills are related to it; and since virtue is only this conformity of the private will to the general, to say the same thing briefly, make virtue reign.
>
> If political theorists were less blinded by their ambition, they would see how impossible it is for any establishment whatever to function in the spirit of its institution if it is not directed in accordance with the law of duty.[149]

Civic virtue is not part of the legitimate constitution, but it is nevertheless in tune with its spirit. Without virtue, citizens will fail to regard themselves as a single body, and they will consequently lose the freedom guaranteed by the sovereignty of the general will.

The operation of civic education and the rule of virtue make what ought to be the *effect* of civil life become its *cause*. But must not free men be their own cause? This is the question mark left after moral freedom is absorbed by civic education. If the "moralization" of men is the effect of political economy or "governance" rather than of their own reason, does not civic virtue eclipse the freedom of the citizen altogether by superseding the function of the will?[150]

Rousseau's answer appears to be that civic education serves the free regime by protecting the sovereign will from the danger of its own contingency. In one sense the very purpose of civic education is to overcome the obstacle that sovereignty presents to the perfection of the disciplinary regime or, more generally, to reconcile will and order. Sovereignty by its nature inescapably weakens the force of the law. The yoke of the laws is a fiction, since the sovereign citizenry remains paramount to all laws, including the social contract; will is inherently threatening to order, and a disorderly or particular willfulness permanently threatens to rupture the relations of right that guarantee freedom. It is because Rousseau understands freedom as a condition of order rather than an agency that wills (always contingently) order into being that he emphasizes the stability of sovereignty over its activity. Rousseau's political economy imagines how to perfect *the illusion* of being bound by law, and finds the answer in attaching citizens to their country by their passions.[151] The goal is to bind the heart of the citizen with its own enthusiasm for the law, to exploit the spontaneity of the affections by directing *them* toward what ought to be the object of the will: the maintenance of civil order; the effect (allegiance) becomes the cause.

This conception is clearly at odds with the model of a citizenship understood as the exercise of rational will.[152] "Political economy" and "political right" constitute separate spheres. The latter concerns the legitimate foundations of political institutions, while the former concerns their artful design and operation. The tension between freedom and authority inheres in this distinction. The principles of political right make freedom the cause and the effect of political obligation. The contract is "the most voluntary act in the world," and leaves each contractor "as free as he was before." The ineluctable meaning of sovereignty is that men remain above the law. However, when Rousseau reflects on the requirements of political *order*, he finds that the best social order puts the law above men.[153] Civic virtue aims to resolve this dilemma by changing the perspective of men such that when they look up, they see the law they must obey as an inflexible necessity. Although his sovereignty is incontrovertible, the virtuous citizen regards the law as his master.

For Rousseau, obedience to law *enables* freedom: "the force of the State creates the freedom of its members." It is only the sovereignty of the general will that guarantees the citizen against all personal dependence. By causing the citizen to generalize his will, "by giving each citizen to the *patrie*," civic virtue becomes the fence to freedom.[154]

Whereas rational or deliberative citizenship is legitimate, passionate citizenship is "sure." Without denying that citizens, by right, are masters of their laws, Rousseau argues that the practice of citizenship must nonetheless involve a passionate affirmation of the laws that seems incompatible with genuine choice. At stake, then, in this scheme is the conception of citizenship as a rational choice versus the product of spontaneous identification. Rousseau's hesitation about the capacity of reason to produce the remarkable change in man, his conviction about the primacy of the sentiments, his equivocation about the rank order of laws and *moeurs* as the regulative principles of civil relations—all these ambivalences can be traced to the difficulty of reconciling legitimacy and reliability, of perfecting political order. Genuine choice calls for the exercise of deliberation, but Rousseau regards the latter more as an opportunity to *undo* the general will than to express it.

Rousseau's perfected constitution thus entails a community of right and a parallel "community of the heart" which promotes political freedom by ensuring that the general will is not menaced by eruptions of partiality. In the democratic regime, strict fidelity to constitutional forms is one barrier to the "unforming" of the general will; but that formalism must be supplemented by a disposition of communal sentiment which transcends respect for formal procedures. The planes of right and fact must be joined in such a way that men as they are act *as if* they considered justice alone.

Rousseau elaborates on this requirement in his discussion of the Legislator and the character of the people. The relative existence of the citizen in the community of right, which is a relation only to a whole, is reiterated for the patriotic citizen through membership in a community of the heart. Political freedom is refracted in these two theoretically distinct but experientially united communities. Each fulfills a requirement of freedom (will and order), but on separate planes. This dualism accounts for the complexity of Rousseau's political formulas.[155]

The Two Poles of Democratic Freedom

In light of the dual imperatives informing the design of the free regime, two separate questions arise: What would the terms of a free association be? And what kind of government would be required to make men respect those conditions? We have seen how Rousseau struggles to conceive a reestablishment of freedom in a political condition, and we have tried to unravel his logic in articulating the operative assumptions of the sovereignty of the general will. The *Social Contract* strains even more, however, when it addresses the second question, for it concerns the issue of political economy or governance, which cannot be approached with the same directness and confidence as matters of political right.[156] One might say that the complete argument of the *Social Contract* evinces both a liberal concern for protecting individuals from oppression (albeit predicated on Rousseau's redefinition of the threat) and a conservative regard for the character of the people, but not out of an ambivalence concerning the relative merits of individualism and collectivism. Both concerns arise out of the present crisis of human affairs; their divergence bespeaks the underlying dilemma of human relations as such: men are not naturally suited for social relations.

Rousseau first grapples with the problem by casting the question of social relations in the precise terms of contract: What sort of contract will be legitimate and reliable from the standpoint of free men? This orientation signals what James Miller has called an "epochal transvaluation" of democracy. As Miller describes it, that transvaluation is rooted in a conviction that "all human beings possess, in their own free will, the capacity and the desire for goodness essential to govern themselves."[157] But Rousseau also problematizes that very assumption. Although the autonomy and integrity of the principles of political right (to say nothing of human beings themselves) would seem to be fatally compromised if their actualization required something beyond consent, Rousseau is persuaded of that requirement. He reveals that the social contract faces a communitarian imperative, which it cannot fulfill through the agency of contract alone. Legitimate principles of political right depend on a practice of virtue, which itself is without legitimate foundation.[158] Men require a certain education, a discipline of their opinions, passions, and interests, in order to be capable of respecting their contractual obligations. This requirement that the free regime be "governable" is not concealed in the *Social Contract*, but its full significance emerges belatedly. In the *Political Economy*, Rousseau acknowledged the need forthrightly:

> The homeland cannot subsist without freedom, nor freedom without virtue, nor virtue without citizens. You will have all these if you train citizens; without doing so, you will only have wicked slaves, beginning with the leaders of the State. Now training citizens is not accomplished in a day, and to have them as men they must be taught as children. Someone may tell me that anyone who has to govern men should not seek, outside of their nature, a perfection of which they are not capable; that he should not want to destroy their passions, and that the execution of such a project would not be any more desirable than it is possible. I will agree the more strongly with all this because

a man who had no passions would certainly be a very bad citizen. But it must also be agreed that although men cannot be taught to love nothing, it is not impossible to teach them to love one thing rather than another, and what is truly beautiful rather than what is deformed. If, for example, they are trained early enough never to consider their persons except as related to the body of the State, and not to perceive their own existence, so to speak, except as part of the State's, they will eventually come to identify themselves in some way with this larger whole.[159]

In this seminal passage, Rousseau describes a synergy among political stability, freedom, and virtue. Citizenship is the key to freedom and stability of right. Recognition of the true principles of political right requires that political life be constituted on a foundation of reason and law rather than of force and violence, and the *Social Contract* offers a juridical doctrine which accomplishes precisely that. At the same time, reason and law must be supplemented by a force in the soul for which the principles of right do not account.

Citizens must be virtuous enough to prefer the common good to their particular good. In Rousseau's terminology, the virtuous citizen will be a good subject.[160] The suppression of private interest manifests itself in obedience to law, which becomes the emblem of the citizen's identification with the *moi commun*. Rousseau maintains that the citizen is simultaneously sovereign and subject.[161] But since sovereignty consists in the maintenance of the general will, dutiful obedience becomes the "effectual truth" of citizenship. The task of the citizen is not to participate in the steering of the general will from issue to issue but to identify with it. For this reason, the relation between the collective citizenry qua sovereign and the same collective qua subject is, in Starobinski's words, "almost narcissistic."[162]

Contract and community involve two separate and contradictory operations. Citizens must be denatured to accept the dictates of *droit politique*, and "renatured" to become members of a *patrie*. Although an austere stance toward oneself is required for the moral choice of the general against the particular, Rousseau's patriot will also be a citizen by inclination and passionate choice. Democratic freedom thus oscillates between the logics of legitimacy and reliability, vibrating here with forms of a legitimate constitution and there with the spontaneity of a community of feeling.[163] This variation might be unobjectionable were spontaneous feeling only a reinforcement of legitimate democratic procedures; but the former threatens to supplant the latter altogether by supplying the consensual unity that democratic procedures aim at but cannot guarantee.

The argument of the *Social Contract* consequently shifts from juridical to "sociological" considerations.[164] Whereas contract and community are initially portrayed as coeval, their simultaneity is later acknowledged to be fictitious. On the juridical level, members unite in an association of free and equal partners. But that association, to be a true community, must be rooted in a unity of feeling. The sovereignty of the general will is the first principle of political right, but the latter abstracts from what the people must be in order to express a unified will. Only contract can confer sovereignty, because civil association must be voluntary; however, only the Legislator's art can give rise to solidarity, without which sovereignty is unreliable.[165] Contract itself does not give rise to community.

The Promise of Political Art

Already in his early writings, Rousseau had indicated the usefulness of "political and moral researches." "The mind revolts," he wrote in the preface to the *Discourse on Inequality*, at "the violence and oppression of society."[166] Yet there was evidence that "All these vices belong not so much to man as to man badly governed."[167] "It is certain that peoples are in the long run what the Government makes them be." Indeed, Rousseau's plan for a comprehensive political teaching began from this conviction:

> I came to see that everything was connected radically to politics, and that however one took it, any people would only be what the nature of its government would make of it, thus this great question of the best possible government

seemed to me to reduce itself to this. What is the nature of Government capable of forming a People, the most virtuous, the most enlightened, the wisest, and ultimately, the best, taking this word in its widest sense.[168]

These considerations suggested to Rousseau that men might be bound together in an association without succumbing to domination and servility. The *Social Contract* is an exploration of that possibility. It inquires whether men as they are can be united and subjected to authority, and yet remain free. But how is submission to authority compatible with freedom? Rousseau asked and answered this question in the first version of the *Social Contract*: "By what inconceivable art could the means have been found to subjugate men in order to make them free; . . . to bind their will by their own consent? . . . How can it be that all obey while none commands, that they serve and have no master? . . . These marvels are the work of the laws."[169]

Rousseau's proposed reconciliation of freedom and authority was already implied in his famous statement of the fundamental political problem: "Each one, uniting with all, nevertheless obeys only himself and remains as free as before."[170]

The act of identification with the whole is the means of reconciling the requirements of authority and freedom.[171] While Rousseau maintains the distinction between "participants" in authority and "subjects" of authority, he means to erase the distinction between one or some privileged members of the political association and others; the sovereign is no longer understood as someone apart from the people, and obedience no longer appears as submission to an alien will.[172] But this abolition of the traditional sovereign-subject separation is predicated on the unification of "each" to "all," which is fraught with difficulties.

The idiom of governability pervades Rousseau's discussion of what the people must be in order to bear the civil constitution of freedom. He refers to "subjection to laws," "discipline," "molding," overcoming the "centrifugal force" of each people, "the true yoke of the laws."[173] The physical nature of the task is exemplified in a military analogy: "For the time when the State is organized, like that when a battalion is formed, is the instant when the body is least capable of resisting and easiest to destroy."[174] The genesis of democracy is the creation of an identity, which may entail the destruction of the old. But, his forthright avowal of force notwithstanding, Rousseau's exemplary founding advances against minimal resistance. The people will be docile, passive, and accepting.[175] The force of the Legislator must be sufficient to create a new identity, but not so great as to break the free spirit of the people. Presumably, if the latter experience their subjection to law as a *painful* yoke, they may become either rebellious or slavish as a consequence. Rousseau suggests that the discipline of law is eased by the preexisting habits of communal identity, although this chronology would seem to lie outside real political time.[176] Together, law and communal character make a people free and governable.

Government

The foregoing considerations amply testify to Rousseau's clear-eyed appraisal of the political problem. A social contract is necessary to restore human beings to a condition of freedom, but men as they are, are disinclined to take contract seriously. Government, in the most comprehensive sense, is devoted to instilling that disposition. Is the cause of freedom betrayed by an overriding concern for the governability of democracy, for the inculcation of conservative habits? Rousseau challenges the dichotomy by conceiving (and implicitly justifying) civic virtue as the fence to freedom. The government or management of the people is dedicated to preserving a civic identity that is indispensable to the general will (that is its sole rationale); and it is only the mutual subordination to the supreme direction of the general will that guarantees each individual against all personal dependence.

However, this apology for authority does not yet render it safe. Beyond the founding activity of the Legislator, the need for ordinary government imports a dangerous inequality into real political time. While acknowledging its exigency, Rousseau wants to limit the inequality of the government and the governed, and, to some extent, disguise it. He is adamant that the institution of government in no way implies a pact of submission.[177] Government necessarily entails inequality, and Rousseau maintains that it can be legitimated only by consent. Government is only a device that the sovereign requires as a mediator of its relations with subjects, who are the same individuals considered under a different aspect.[178] Rousseau's model aims to avoid the subordination to government that characterized previous sovereign-subject relations. The evils of traditional politics stemmed from the confusion of government and sovereignty, a false connection that Rousseau severs. As a consequence, government fulfills a single function, regardless of its form.

On the basis of Rousseau's reinterpretation, the form of government is no longer a regime question, and governmental power is somewhat disguised by the impersonality of the rule of law. No one emphasized more than Rousseau the distinction between a government of laws and a government of men. The law embodies no other will than our own, and it guarantees us against personal dependence. But there remains the necessity for particular applications of general rules, which entail the exercise of power by a separate and distinct political body. Although the *Social Contract* evinces a superficial hostility to government, Rousseau does not flinch at what the governability of democracy may require. If things can be so arranged that *tout va tout seul* (everything goes of itself), if the people govern themselves through *moeurs* and right opinion, the weight of the laws will be light and the need for government diminished. On the other hand, Rousseau acknowledges that circumstances might require a period of dictatorship to repair the essential defects of a government of laws.[179]

The question of government is a matter of "social physics," and Rousseau precisely calculates the appropriate quotient of "strength" required for good government. Some readers may see in this exercise only an arcane enthusiasm for mathematics; but Rousseau's recondite discussion points up a fundamental issue.[180] The state is artificial, and consequently permanent vigilance must be exercised over the forces acting upon this "moral body." It turns out that numerous departures from direct democracy are required to preserve the free regime: the Legislator, fundamental law, formalism, tribunes, elective aristocratic government, a re-designed Roman Senate, censorship, civil religion—all of these devices (or their equivalents) may be necessary to the stability of democracy.

Rousseau's republicanism thus has a pronounced *conservative* strain. His vaunted radicalism stems from an insistence on legitimacy; however, his practical political proposals are crafted in response to the defect of political legitimacy. Consequently, Rousseau's model of popular participation is very much an exercise in "legitimation," in both its positive and pejorative senses. When it comes to the civil order, Rousseau is no anarchist, despite his essential objection to relations of rule. On the civil plane he condemns not government simply, but arbitrary and illegitimate government. His aim in books III–IV of the *Social Contract* is to show how institutional hierarchies can serve freedom rather than destroy it.

The complexity and ambivalence of Rousseau's thoughts on government derive from the vexatious problem that political inequality poses for legitimacy. His tendency is to portray inequalities as *hierarchies*, not to exacerbate their power but to mitigate it. Rousseau intuited that the sacred character of authority masks its occasional illegitimacy and softens its effect.[181] Masks are necessary insofar as the political problem is to get a free people "to obey with freedom and bear with docility the yoke of public felicity."[182] The basic dilemma is evident in the notion of "legitimate chains." Rousseau declares early in the *Social Contract* that "the social order is a sacred right," and later notes that founders are moved to attribute their wisdom to communication with the divine. In the *Poland*, Rousseau identifies Numa, who created Rome's religion, as Rome's true founder.[183] Although the fundamental legislative task is accomplished at the beginning, it must be continuously shored up: "A thousand situations for which the legislator has made no provision can arise."[184] Civil religion routinizes the activity of the Legislator, as does, to a lesser extent, the function of the Tribunate.[185] Democracy's need for civil religion is one of the most controversial aspects of Rousseau's political theory; but its rationale can be traced to the essential reliance of the free regime on authority. Rousseau proposes civil religion out of a sense that the power of the sacred could provide the "legitimate and surest way" to preserve the condition of democratic freedom.[186]

Conclusion

In Rousseau's account of civil association, the analytical task of elucidating the terms of the social contract gives way eventually to the managerial task of forming citizens who will take their contract seriously by submitting themselves to the supreme direction of the general will. The principles of political right themselves require a movement away from active or autonomous citizenship. Certainly Rousseau invests the democratic citizen with an unprecedented dignity; but at the same time, his role is carefully circumscribed and managed by a tutelary power.

I have suggested that Rousseauian freedom is ill understood as the activity of moral autonomy or self-realization, in the sense made popular by Kant. Rousseauian citizenship is similarly distorted when regarded as the *fons et origo* of participatory democracy. Rousseau's unique moral and political perspective is nicely captured in the following fragment from the *Project on the Corsican Constitution*: "I will not preach morality to them because sermons do not make one act. I will not order them to have the virtues, but I will *put them in such a position* that they will have the virtues without knowing the word; and they will be good and just without having to know what justice and goodness are."[187] Citizens will be good without knowing it, virtuous without virtue. In Rousseau's theory, virtue first appears as a way to achieve the condition of freedom at the cost of a devaluation of genuine willing, or freedom as agency. In the final reckoning, civic virtue itself depreciates.

As Rousseau thinks through the difficulties of a legitimate and reliable democratic freedom, his conception of citizenship declines from the activity of rational deliberation, to virtuous dedication to the common good, to patriotic enthusiasm for one's own. A comprehensive political art guarantees the result that citizens will the common good. And although this scheme to "determine" the will threatens to undermine its integrity, Rousseau seems convinced of its necessity. "It is not enough to say to citizens, be good. They must be taught to be so. . . . Patriotism is the most effective means. . . . for every man is virtuous when his private will conforms on all matters with the general will, and we willingly want what is wanted by the people we love."[188]

Rousseau may have regarded this formula as an adequate resolution of the aforementioned difficulty. Both virtue and freedom are served by the conformity of the private will to the general will, which is nevertheless achieved by passion. Since men can be taught to love one thing rather than another, they can be made to love their country. And because we freely will what is willed by the people we love, patriotism does not appear to offend against the legitimate principles of political obligation. This reasoning reassigns to love the legitimate capacities of will. In this model, passion is central and love of country bridges the gulf between the (internal) consent of the individual and the common good, which is external to the individual and is embodied in the *patrie*. Rousseau hopes through civic education, "[c]itizens will learn . . . to love one another as brothers, never to want anything other than what society wants."[189]

> In this way, an attentive and well-intentioned government, ceaselessly careful to maintain or revive patriotism among the people, prevents from afar the evils that sooner or later result from the indifference of citizens concerning the fate of the republic, and confines within narrow limits that personal interest which so isolates private individuals that the state is weakened by their power and cannot hope to gain anything from their good will.[190]

Just as Émile's tutor "prepares from afar the reign of freedom," government guarantees that citizens will what they ought to will.

Rousseau was fully aware of the obvious objection. "Whatever sophisms may be used to disguise all this, it is certain that if someone can constrain my will I am no longer free."[191] He distinguishes constraining the will from binding the will with its own consent. On the other hand, Rousseau forthrightly acknowledges that government involves a tutelage of the will. The true statesman extends his *respectable* dominion over wills even more than actions, and

If he could create a situation in which everyone did what was right, he himself would have nothing further to do, and the masterpiece of his works would be to remain idle. It is certain, at least, that the greatest talent of leaders is to disguise their power to make it less odious, and to manage the State so peacefully that it seems to have no need for managers.[192]

Disguised power is a continuing theme in Rousseau's writings, and many critics have duly condemned it as the seed of totalitarianism. Yet Rousseau had his reasons: it is precisely the regime of democratic freedom in which power requires the mantle of respectability. Although freedom and authority are not antithetical, for Rousseau, authority must be made respectable *in the eyes of citizens*, that is, in the greatest possible accord with legitimacy. The principles of political right exclude disguised power from the sphere of legitimacy. The defect of legitimacy occasions Rousseau's search for an "authoritarianism" that does not constrain the will. The search for a political path to freedom led Rousseau occasionally to cross (if not forget) the boundary between freedom and authority: "The most absolute authority is that which penetrates to the inner man and is exerted no less on his will than on his actions."[193]

"By what inconceivable art could the means be found to subjugate men in order to make them free?" Rousseau's political theory is an attempt to think the unthinkable, which explains its paradoxical character. The elaboration of democratic freedom begins with the kind of contract to which individuals will consent autonomously, and then shifts to the kind of community that will respect such a contract. Antinomies are generated at each stage of the argument: precivil man lacks the identification with the whole that would dispose him to generalize his will; the patriotic citizen identifies so much with the whole that his will appears to be co-opted.

While Rousseau's cosmopolitan contemporaries undoubtedly regarded his rehabilitation of patriotism as an irony, or perhaps a rustic eccentricity, it was in fact both a serious and an ingenious attempt to cope with a dilemma of the human condition as

Rousseau understood it. His model of citizenship is Janus-faced because it confronts the dichotomous requirements of contract and community, freedom and governability. The pervasive tension in Rousseau's political theory arises out of his effort to attune the political to the natural condition. The philosophic center of his political theory is the revaluation of the natural condition in protest against the conclusions of previous political thought. In the theories of Hobbes and Locke in particular, it is the *deficiencies* of the natural condition that inform the construction of the civil state; the state of nature becomes the *negative* standard for civil society. But on the basis of his revaluation of the state of nature, Rousseau makes the natural condition positively normative—as a condition of freedom. The complexity and perplexity of his thought stem from the effort to *perfect* that condition on the civil plane.

Citizenship, Community, and the Politics of Identity

4

As he expounds his "political solution," Rousseau struggles with the ineluctable principle of consent in an attempt to evade the perils of dissent and diversity of opinion without betraying the principles of right. Beyond pluralism and particularity lies a kind of citizenship in which even the primary concern for self-preservation can be subordinated to the preservation of the *patrie*. On principle, the people must legitimately (hence formally) bring themselves within that horizon; but in fact, the popular assemblies reenact the legitimation already won in communal feelings.[1]

There has been a nagging ambiguity about Rousseau's political stance. Should he be regarded as a liberal theorist of obligation or as a conservative moralist, for he employs the language of contract and also the language of the common good?[2] Is his ideal a republic of freedom or a republic of virtue? We may now say that the answer is both, not out of a lapse into contradiction on Rousseau's part but out of a judgment that the preservation of freedom requires a form of solidaristic social relations permeated by authority. Rousseau's political theory might be characterized as the search for a principled via media between the calculating spirit of the Enlightenment (which reflects, all its corruptions and distortions notwithstanding, a natural love of self) and a "romantic" expression of fellow feeling that bespeaks the spontaneous inclination for the general that is absent in the will.

The consensus found in a "union of hearts" is a political sine qua non. Rousseau declares, "As long as several men together consider themselves to be a single body, they have only a single will, which relates to their common preservation and the general welfare."[3] This amounts to saying that there must be a common interest at the bottom of the polity. When that condition is achieved, a common will can be guaranteed. But in that case the object of the general will exists prior to, and therefore independently of, public choice. The voluntaristic element of Rousseauian politics is virtually effaced when the requirement of legitimacy is fulfilled in a pale act of "legitimation." The common good is guaranteed by the solidarity of the people rather than by their will. In such a case, it seems as though there is nothing for the general will to accomplish: the common good either exists or it does not. Absent social unity, the general will cannot be expressed. One might say that the "objectivity" of the general will is promoted at the expense of its "subjectivity." Rousseau fails to show how the general will might be achieved in conditions of less than perfect solidarity. Everything seems to depend on the strength of *moeurs*, which unify the people in the first place.

The constitutional formalities on which Rousseau insists in the second half of the *Social Contract* have more to do with forestalling anticipated usurpations of sovereignty on the part of government than with declaring the general will. The popular assembly is a defensive body in which the people do not so much forge their identity in the process of establishing consensus, as *preserve* it against the inevitable tendency of partial associations, and partial identities, to displace it. The procedural forms of Rousseau's democracy are a bulwark against the "unforming" of the general will by an eruption of particularity. But if social unity is a precondition of the general will, particpatory procedures also become subordinate, or redundant. Stated differently, Rousseau does not describe for us a political process that *achieves* unity

but, rather, a political condition *of unity*, which must be preserved against erosion.

The *Social Contract* thus evinces an ultimate pessimism that
human pluralism will defeat the general will. Everything must be
arranged so that the people will have a communal identity and
acknowledge the obvious (common) good. They must be "prior
to the laws, what they ought to become by means of laws."[4] The
Legislator's soulcraft, and its routinization in *moeurs* and civil
religion, form citizens who spontaneously will the general. While
citizens cannot be denied the opportunity to declare the general
will, unless they have been shaped by civic education, they will
lack the disposition to do so.

Rousseau revealed this problem, without emphasizing it, in
his first statements about the political association. The social
contract involves a reciprocal obligation between the public and
each individual. The "public person" is formed by "the union of
all the others," that is, by private individuals.[5] At first glance,
"the public" seems to be the product of the association of previously dissociated individuals. However, the *Social Contract* subsequently reveals that the act of association is a reciprocal engagement between "the public" and all individuals. Individual
subjects *are* obligated to the sovereign, but Rousseau denies that
this is a dangerous liaison. The premise of social unity is that
one cannot harm an individual without harming the body. Duty
and interest are thus united and no further guarantee is needed,
since the sovereign cannot have any interest contrary to the
private individuals who compose it. Or, more precisely, the
sovereign acts according to the common interest shared by each.
Only concerns that have public or common significance are matters for the general will.[6]

Because the sovereign power affects all equally, there is no
ostensible motive to regulate matters that are genuinely private.
The guarantee against a totalitarian power is built into Rousseau's conception of popular sovereignty. But in order to produce citizens or patriots, no area is fenced off from civic education. Rousseau emphasized the political significance of *moeurs*,
not out of a totalitarian appetite for politicization of the private
sphere but because he denied the cogency of any rigid separation

of private and public. Only citizens can be proper subjects of the general will, and in the well-ordered democracy, citizenship will tend to be an all-inclusive identity.[7] The union of hearts is designed to reinforce the union of wills that is hypothesized on the plane of right.

Because the common interest is expressed rather than manufactured in actions of sovereignty, the sovereign must be assured of the fidelity of subjects, who are permanently liable to distinguish, and then prefer, their private interest to the common interest. The remedy is to arrange things so that the latter distinction is obscured by a communal identity.

In Book IV of the *Social Contract* we learn that "When the social tie is broken in all hearts . . . the general will becomes mute."[8] Now if the true constitution is in the hearts of citizens, then the first object of a stable polity is to maintain the integrity of *moeurs*.[9] "In every country where *moeurs* are an integral part of the constitution of the State, the laws are always more directed to the maintenance of customs than to punishment or compensation."[10]

Freedom and Custom

The operation of *moeurs* is the central theme of the final book of the *Social Contract*. In his discussion of the Roman assemblies, Rousseau shows that all was well as long as the people were not corrupt.[11] While Rousseau considers what other supports might befit a corrupt people, the centrality of *moeurs* to political health is never in doubt; they are the crucial support of the laws, the foundation of the harmonic polity. The discussion of Rome culminates, not surprisingly, in an account of censorship.[12] *Moeurs* and laws have a reciprocal influence. The censorial tribunal does not presume to compose the people's opinion, but only to declare it and apply it to particular situations. It resembles the role of government in operating on particulars only.

As to the actual source of *moeurs*, the answer appears in the next and penultimate chapter of the *Social Contract*, "On Civil Religion." The latter is "inscribed in a single country" by its laws, which give it its particular divinities, dogmas, and rituals.[13]

Civil religion works to establish the social order as a "sacred right that serves as a basis for all others."[14] Since "everything that destroys social unity is worthless," what contributes most to unity deserves to be held sacred.[15] Civil religion so melds the cult of the divine with love of the laws, that "to violate the laws is impious."[16] The sacralization of the social tie permits people to "obey with freedom and bear with docility the yoke of public happiness." "Recognizing the same power in the formation of man and of the City," the people identify civil laws with (as it were) the laws of nature and nature's God.[17]

The constitution of democratic freedom is conservative in the sense that moral forces underpin the political formalities which maintain a strategic distance between men.[18] But there is no theoretical conservatism behind the strategy of reinforcing the disposition to will the general. In this regard, it is Edmund Burke rather than Rousseau who appears as the subtle metaphysician, for the former reads a metaphysic into the customary world. Burke views artifice as part of man's nature; Rousseau sees it as a device that may *replicate* natural conditions.[19]

Because "[t]he law acts only externally, governing the actions, [and] *moeurs* alone penetrate within and direct the operations of the will," Rousseau's conservative politics of freedom strives to fulfill the principles of political right in customs.[20] This move signals a turn from stark denaturation toward at least quasi-natural forms of association. Rousseau conceived for the Corsicans a renaturing constitution in which the principles of political right would be submerged beneath deep sentiments of sociability: "Noble people, I do not wish at all to give you artificial and systematic laws that are invented by men, but to bring you under the laws of nature and order alone, which command hearts and never tyrannize wills."[21]

Customs enclose the citizen within a limited, national horizon. It is the completeness of the attachment rather than the intrinsic goodness of the *moeurs* themselves that matters. Rousseau goes Burke one better in opposing not simply the reckless assault on prejudice of the philosophes but, as it were, "Socratic criticism" as well. *Any* weakening of the hold of *moeurs* is to be resisted, even if it is produced by rational criticism, and even if the latter is oriented toward the good. Rousseau opts for the greatest possible closure for the sake of social unity. Like the prephilosophic city of Plato's *Republic*, Rousseau's "healthy society" will be spirited and xenophobic; chauvinism will prevail over *humanité*. Rousseau's rejection of the "general society of the human race" entails the conclusion that there can be no social unity beyond national unity. The conditions of freedom are located in the prephilosophic or "unenlightened" city where custom rules. In yet another paradoxical development, Rousseau's philosophic exploration of the conditions of freedom concludes with an antiphilosophic apology for custom.

Customary life camouflages the artificiality of legal systems by reducing the occasions for the explicit operation of political power, and therewith the opportunities for its abuse.[22] Even the habitat of a simple people contributes to the re-creation of the conditions of freedom:

> Thus in the midst of peaks and valleys each living on his own plot and managing to take from it everything he needs, finding himself with plenty of room, desiring nothing more. Interests and needs do not conflict and nobody depending on another, all have between them only relations of friendship and goodwill. Concord and peace would reign effortlessly in their numerous families, they would have almost nothing to regulate among them but marriages where inclination alone would be consulted, ambition would not arise, interest and inequality would never arise. This people, poor but without needs, would thus multiply in the most perfect independence in a union which nothing could alter. It would have no virtues, having no vices to conquer, to act well would cost it nothing, and it would be good and just without even knowing what justice and virtue were. . . . Corsicans, behold the model you must follow to return to your primitive state.[23]

This vision of unity in independence and simplicity powerfully calls to mind the condition of natural men.[24]

From the liberal perspective, the notion of a people habituated to a social order seems obviously incompatible with freedom.

Consider John Stuart Mill's insistence on the incompatibility of freedom and moral custom: "He who lets the world, or his own portion of it, choose his plan of life for him has no need of any other faculty than the ape-like one of imitation. He who chooses his plan for himself employs all his faculties. . . . It is possible that he might be guided in some good path, and kept out of harm's way, without any of these things. But what will be his comparative worth as a human being?"[25] It is because Rousseau reopened the question of the worth of the human being that he eventually opted for a new understanding of freedom as independence, and for a politics that would guide human beings in a good path. *Pace* the objection later crystallized in Mill's argument, Rousseau did not dichotomize spontaneous obedience and freedom. Because social unity is indispensable to civic freedom, and because *moeurs* are the impersonal custodians of that unity, he resisted the idea of an essential antagonism between moral consensus and individual freedom. Rousseau believed that once unity is shattered, the alternative is not pluralist democracy but the proliferation of private governments, or a Leviathan.[26] For Rousseau, the internalization of social norms is essential not for its own sake but as a guarantee of the general will, and he suggests that the spontaneity of consensus is an indication that the general will is truly the people's will and not something external to them.

The hegemony of custom seems to be the only form of rule that might pass for natural. Rousseau suggests that the *moeurs* of one's society are not oppressive, precisely because they are one's own.[27] These informal laws bear no trace of a state power that stands above and apart from the people, bending them to purposes which are not their own. Thus the preservation of *moeurs* is essential to a democracy that would be governable without Leviathan, and free despite the fact of social relations. A system of *moeurs* serves democratic freedom because the moral habits that unite the people dispose them to consent spontaneously to the laws. The good citizen is one who has elevated the authority of *moeurs* to the same level as the laws he prescribes to himself.

Rousseau discourages the freedom of *moeurs* that later thinkers would associate with individual liberty out of a sense that the former was incompatible with the respect for laws which guarantees freedom on the civil plane.[28] The individual must indeed be kept in a "good path" because the trajectory of social man's passions is always toward bondage. Rousseau's objection to theatrical amusements is, on one level, a defense of old-fashioned republican austerity; but his deeper critique is that the taste for diversion bespeaks a restlessness of the heart that threatens to isolate citizens from one another even as they assemble together.[29] He similarly condemns the corrosive influence of philosophy which strikes first at customs, but inevitably spreads to respect for laws.[30] The interconnectedness of custom, law and freedom explains Rousseau's defense of illiberal constraints on enlightenment. Strong customs are the token of a level of social unity which allows an easy respect for laws. Whereas a Burke might lament the stripping away of the decent drapery of life as a loss in itself, Rousseau's concern is to reinforce the sense of solidarity upon which civil freedom depends. Customary life indicates a possible junction of heart and will, feeling and reason, passion and virtue in which *freedom* as spontaneity might be recaptured.

Freedom as Spontaneity

The *Essay on the Origin of Languages* reiterates the conclusion of the *Second Discourse* concerning the relation of passion and reason. The *Essay* merits attention here because it bears on Rousseau's judgment concerning the superiority of spontaneous agreement to consensus by deliberation. In elaborating the distinction between two forms of language, Rousseau lays the foundation for that latter judgment, which, as we saw, is fraught with political consequences.

Rousseau hypothesizes that, "instead of arguments," men's first language "would have pithy phrases; it would persuade without convincing, and depict without reasoning."[31] Such a language has a power to unite that stems from the immediacy of the passions. As language develops, it becomes more precise but less passionate, more convincing but less persuasive. The root of "convaincre," "vaincre" (to conquer), implies a kind of violence or force, which Rousseau distinguishes from the art of persuasion. Interestingly, he reverts to the same distinction in describing the task of the Legislator: "Being unable to employ either force or reasoning, he must resort of necessity to an authority of a different kind, which can seduce without violence and persuade without convincing."[32] Irrational persuasion succeeds in uniting men where rational explanations of common interest fail.[33] The language of persuasion aims at producing a change of heart, if not of head.

In the final chapter of the *Essay*, Rousseau notes that force has replaced persuasion as the method of politics. Because the popular assembly is no more, there is nothing to be said to the people, and eloquence has lost its value.

> Societies have assumed their final forms: nothing can be changed in them anymore except by arms and cash, and since there is nothing left to say to the people but "give money," it is said with posters on street corners or with soldiers in private homes; for this there is no need to assemble anyone; on the contrary, subjects must be kept scattered; that is the first maxim of modern politics.[34]

Jean Starobinski's summary of Rousseau's argument is instructive. "The first languages were synthetic, passionate, warm, musical; their expressive power was maximal." However, the "progress" away from the primitive constituted a decline: "The primal unity, once split, gave way to separate and specialized progress, which heightened the practical usefulness of language, its referential precision; manners became polite and hypocritical; music cultivated the pleasures of the ear at the expense of those of the heart."[35]

In his history of language Rousseau reiterates arguments that we identified as central in the discussion of human history itself: "In proportion as needs increase, as men's dealings with one another grow more involved, as enlightenment spreads, the character of language changes; it becomes more precise and less passionate; it substitutes ideas for sentiments; it no longer speaks to the heart but to reason."[36]

The increase in needs is gradual and dependent on circumstances. The development of language is as contingent as human history generally. Rousseau reprises this story in the ninth chapter of the *Essay*. Curiously, the first men had both ferocious *moeurs* and tender hearts. They were cruel but natural; simple

needs kept them separated. Power and desire remained in equilibrium: "No one knew or desired more than was ready to hand;
his needs, far from drawing him closer to those like himself,
drew him away from them."[37]

> Assume perpetual spring on earth; assume water, cattle,
> pastures everywhere; assume men issuing from the hands of
> nature and dispersed throughout all this: I cannot imagine
> how they would ever have renounced their primitive liberty
> and left the isolated and pastoral existence that so well suits
> their natural indolence. . . . The passions that cause men to
> be restless, provident, active, are born only in society.[38]

Rousseau returns to his crucial claim that "Human associations are in large measure the work of accidents of nature." In
circumstances where human beings can do without one another,
they will.[39] Still, Rousseau alludes to rudimentary associations
that seem to arise before the complete separation from the natural. In a memorable passage recounting the origin of love, he
explains how the first language was born of pleasure rather than
of need, and how "Their seductive accent faded only with the
sentiments that had given them birth, when new needs introduced among men, forced everyone to think only of himself and
to withdraw his heart within himself."[40]

This lyrical representation of the origins of human association
and its corruption calls to mind the "golden age." Rousseau
again identifies a "natural community" based on the uncorrupted
desire of expansive hearts. As I suggested in Chapter 2, the idea
of a natural sociality stretches the concept of nature beyond
coherence and ought not to be taken as Rousseau's considered
view. But these images nevertheless suggest how Rousseau could
conceive "a renaturing" of human beings in a patriotic community. Consider the significance of the first "festivals," which
Rousseau calls "the true cradle of peoples."[41] Between the indi-
viduation wrought by *amour-propre* and the original isolated
condition stands the privileged moment of passionate unity. It is
this "sacred fire" that Rousseau later attempts to rekindle
through patriotic *moeurs*.[42] Passion produces gentler bonds than
those forged by "political right."[43] The principles of right are

expressed in the language of force, physical compulsion.[44] These principles are necessary for human beings who find themselves in the unbearable circumstances of the "late" state of nature. Such men resemble the peoples of northern climates, whose first words are "*aidez-moi*" rather than "*aimez-moi*"[45]

The decline in Rousseau's argument from citizenship to patriotism is akin to a conversion of *droit politique* into patriotic *moeurs*, or its "translation" from a "northern" into a "southern" language. In southern climates, Rousseau tells us, "the passions are voluptuous, related to love and softness," whereas in the north, the temperament is irascible. There the "natural voice" is that of anger and threats: "French, English, German are the private languages of men who help one another, who argue with one another in a deliberate manner, or of excited men who get angry; but the ministers of the Gods proclaiming the sacred mysteries, wise men giving laws to their people, leaders swaying the masses must speak Arabic or Persian."[46] *Droit politique* is inevitably harsh because it must police the relations of asocial men with a severity commensurate to their intractability. But having elaborated the legitimate principles of political right, Rousseau imagines how to moderate them without cancelling them—how to soften their operation. The fundamental law cannot but be austere and stentorian; yet, for it to endure, it must be loved. The Legislator must be "musical," for the well-ordered regime is indeed a harmonic polity. *Moeurs* have a power over the human heart that reason cannot approximate.[47]

The movement from civic virtue to patriotic *moeurs* testifies to Rousseau's ultimate fidelity to the modern principle of *humanité*, which he encountered especially in Montaigne and Montesquieu. While he rejected the easygoing cosmopolitanism of Diderot, Rousseau understood that his own Spartan-Roman ideal, while more "politic," remained repressive and inhumane. Montaigne, Montesquieu, and the modern political philosophers generally, rejected this Plutarchian heroism as inconsistent with human nature. They were inclined to defend the desire for security and comfort and the absorption in *divertissement* (amusement) as truer to man's natural bent.[48] It was the terminus of this modern reasoning that Rousseau could not accept, for he saw (in the forceful expression of Allan Bloom) that a true theoretical insight had given rise to a low human consequence.[49]

Calling to mind the festivals of his youth, Rousseau describes an experience of spontaneity and suspension of duty within the political order. "The only pure joy is public joy," he exclaims at the conclusion of the *Letter to D'Alembert*, as though the sentiment of existence itself could somehow be collectivized. As Rousseau evokes his communitarian ideal, he implicitly reverts to the norms of nature. Sincerity, transparency, simplicity might replace the deceitful veil of politesse that drapes the present age. In a true community, citizens appear to recover the natural concerns of preservation and well-being, this time as "la commune preservation" and "bien-être général."[50]

The good patriot may be hard hearted toward foreginers, but he will be sensitive toward his countrymen. Under the pressure to bridge will and generality, Rousseau redefines citizenship as a habit of the heart so that social men might find themselves at least in the vicinity of the natural. As George Kelly has written,

> To be "beneath the laws of nature and order" is somehow to recapture that symmetrical distance between instinct and reason which verified man's orderly place in the cycles of nature and yet already bespoke his privileged position in the creation. Custom now becomes the spring of the will, and the will is so conditioned that it ceases to aspire beyond the rectitude of custom.[51]

The legitimate constitutional forms of civic association are necessary but insufficient conditions of democratic freedom, because "There will never be a good and solid condition unless the law rules over the hearts of the citizens."[52] In contemporary parlance, Rousseau indicates the priority of political culture to political institutions. *Droit politique*, as Kelly observes, "reasserts men's independence *vis-à-vis* each other while binding them equally beneath laws of adoption and application."[53] Political right reestablishes the distance between men that obtained in the state of nature, but citizens must also be attached; hence the need for patriotism, which unites hearts in an emotional solidarity. Democratic freedom accomplishes "the assimilation of the independence of nature to the mutuality of communal life."[54]

In his brilliant interpretation of the meaning of the festival, Starobinski writes: "The festival expresses on an 'existential' level of emotion everything that the *Contract* formulates on the level of the theory of right."[55] I would amend Starobinski's point as follows: The festival expresses a unity that is contemplated in the theory of right but that cannot be actualized by a juridical framework alone. In the festival, the people actually experience themselves as a *moi commun* and recover, however imperfectly, their natural sentiments.

The Rousseauian turn in political theorizing could be described as an effort to relieve the tension between independence and community that has bedeviled modern political thought. The fundamental argument between Rousseau and his liberal critics would appear to be over whether this dilemma can be resolved, or merely managed. The latter strategy seems more sober and responsible only if one disregards Rousseau's insistent assertion that the tension is unbearable. Rousseau declares that men, as they are, will be condemned to unhappiness so long as the freedom they enjoyed outside of community is unavailable within. The failure of democratic freedom is tantamount to the failure of humanity. It would be difficult to fathom Rousseau's intense concern with political questions apart from this consequence.

Rousseau's "complete" political solution includes the denaturing of man into citizen, but also his "renaturing" through patriotic attachment to a set of quasi-natural *moeurs*. Custom becomes man's second nature.[56] There is nothing genuinely "progressive" about democratic freedom. Rousseau's political vision is fixed backward, toward origins, toward nature, and even toward the darkness of national customs and prejudice, which the philosophes had hoped to uproot once and for all.

Yet, as Bertrand de Jouvenel observed, Rousseau is pessimistic about insulating *moeurs* against the degenerative effects of commerce and enlightenment, and he is positively dismissive about the possibility of rehabilitating a corrupt people: "The *moeurs* of a people are like the honour of a man, a treasure to be preserved, but one which, when lost, can never be recovered."[57] Rousseau turned against the philosophes because their project of eradicating superstition and spiritual oppression involved a crusade against *moeurs* as such. He insisted that a good society required healthy *moeurs*, and he denied that the criterion of health is rationality or universality. He finds an invincible heterogeneity in the political world: "Man is one, I admit it! But man modified by religions, governments, laws, customs, prejudices, and climates becomes so different from himself that one ought not to seek among us for what is good for men in general, but only what is good for them in this time or that country."[58]

Since *moeurs* constitute the moral life of a community, "As soon as men cease to respect them, there is no rule but the passions, no restraint but the laws. And though these may occasionally deter men from evil, they can never make men good."[59] *Moeurs* mediate men's passions and the law, preserving the naturalness or spontaneity of the one and the formality and discipline of the other, simultaneously guarding against both disorder and the yoke.

The political instincts of the philosophes were correct. They had to drive Rousseau out of public discourse, because his plan was designed to leave citizens in a Platonic cave. Indeed, Rousseau's resistance to the cosmopolitanizing efforts of the philosophes could be described as an attempt to seal the cave shut, to fix the citizen's gaze on nothing but the *patrie*.[60] Rousseau judged that cavelike ethnicity was closer to nature than the sunlit cosmopolitanism of the philosophes.[61]

However, Rousseau always understood that customary life is ultimately something legislated, hence artificial. He may have inspired the Romantic reaction to Enlightenment politics, but those who later celebrated the "expressiveness" of each particular *volksgeist* neglected the ineluctable artificiality at the bottom of community, which Rousseau never forgot.[62] *Moeurs* clearly do not exist apart from society. They, too, are a product of man's departure from the state of nature.[63]

Rousseau's extraordinary account of citizenship is "exoteric." The effectiveness of patriotism in preserving the condition of independence requires that the truth about freedom be kept from view. This fact can be glimpsed in the dialogue that serves as a denouement in *Émile*.[64] The tutor asks Émile to choose his course, to engage in the act of will that had been deferred by his separation from Sophie and his education in "civil relations."

Émile's answer exemplifies the central problem of Rousseau's political teaching: " 'What course have I chosen! To remain what you have made me and voluntarily to add no other chain to the one with which nature and the laws burden me.' "[65] With his decision Émile ratifies the work of the tutor and thereby renders it legitimate as well as reliable or "sure." Émile has already been properly "constituted"; his choice now is to remain what he ought to be. His act of volition is indistinguishable from one of submission; but his expression of consent remains *de rigueur,* despite the fact that it is a wholly predictable compliance with authority.

Note that the chain with which "nature" and "the laws" burden Émile appears to be one and the same. One can explain this singular subordination by reference back to the tutor's educational plan.[66] The tutor has followed the road of nature, knowing that it will lead Émile to happiness. Owing to the continual exertions of the tutor's artifice, Émile has been "free and contented," but also "just and good." Émile's desires have not led to his undoing because they have been carefully limited; his freedom has been preserved because he has been subject only to necesssity. To preserve this state, the tutor enjoins Émile to "let your condition limit your desires." Freedom will be maintained objectively rather than subjectively, but Émile must consent to the reimposition of the condition of freedom. This is the meaning of the tutor's instruction "to extend the law of necessity to moral things," which is to say, to Émile's relations with others. Since Émile has no choice but to live among others, he must ensure that his moral relations imitate the necessity of natural relations, or his relations to things. Émile himself seems to have achieved a philosophic awareness that rivals his tutor's:

> The more I examine the work of men in their institutions, the more I see that they make themselves slaves by dint of wanting to be independent and that they use up their freedom in vain efforts to ensure it. In order not to yield to the torrent of things, they involve themselves in countlesss attachments. Then as soon as they want to take a step, they cannot and are surprised at depending on everything. It seems to me that in order to make oneself free, one has to

do nothing. It suffices that one not want to stop being free. It is you, my master, who have made me free in teaching me to yield to necessity. Let it come when it pleases. I let myself be carried along without constraint, and since I do not wish to fight it, I do not attach myself to anything to hold me back.[67]

However, while Émile has evidently grasped that the structure of natural independence endures in the social state, he errs in pressing the logic of freedom to its conclusion: "I shall be free everywhere on earth. All the chains of opinion are broken for me; I know only those of necessity. . . . What difference does it make to me what my position is on earth? What difference does it make to me where I am?"[68] The tutor must draw Émile back from this conclusion, for, while true, it threatens to undermine his identity as a citizen and, more precisely, to steel him against the affective bond that will guarantee his dutiful conduct. Reconstructing the condition of freedom within society logically requires that duty be given precedence over inclination, since the crucial issue has become precisely *how* one will be attached to others in the social condition. As we saw, political freedom requires moral freedom; but the ethic of duty must still be infiltrated by love if virtue is to rule reliably. In his desire to maintain his independence, Émile is prepared to rush headlong past all attachments and risks a posture of sovereign disregard toward his fellow men. The tutor must bring him up short:

If I were speaking to you of the duties of the citizen, you would perhaps ask me where the fatherland is, and you would believe you had confounded me. But you would be mistaken, dear Émile, for he who does not have a fatherland at least has a country. . . . O Émile, where is the good man who owes nothing to his country? Whatever country it is, he owes it what is most precious to man—the morality of his actions and the love of virtue. If he had been born in the heart of the woods, he would have lived happier and freer. But he would have had nothing to combat in order to follow his inclinations, and thus he would have been good without merit; he would not have been virtuous; and now he knows how to be so in spite of his passions. The mere appearance of order brings him to know order and to love it. The public good, which serves others only as a pretext, is a real motive for him alone. He learns to struggle with himself, to conquer himself, to sacrifice his interest to the common interest. It is not true that he draws no profit from the laws. They give him the courage to be just even among wicked men. It is not true that they have not made him free. They have taught him to reign over himself.

Do not ask, then, "What difference does it make to me where I am?" It makes a difference to you that you are where you can fulfill all your duties, and one of those duties is an attachment to the place of your birth. Your compatriots protected you as a child; you ought to love them as a man.[69]

The citizen must engage in acts of moral freedom (which amounts to doing his duty) if he is to extend the realm of necessity to moral things and maintain his own independence. But the tutor recognizes that an "extravagant disinterestedness" threatens to preclude the very possibility of relations with others.[70] So it is that he designs to temper Émile's "stoic" disposition with love of country. It is an awkward moment. Émile is technically correct about the conditions of freedom in the social state; the tutor's response (without others, moral relations and, a fortiori, virtue and moral freedom would be impossible) is a red herring, since moral relations are only a means, and Émile desires the end in itself. But the tutor then builds upon this point and elevates attachment to the level of a positive injunction; it becomes a duty in its own right rather than the precondition for duty altogether. One ought to love one's compatriots, and for a reason that transcends the banal fact that one cannot be moral in a vacuum: extravagant disinterest or heroic virtue is excessive, painful, too unnatural.[71] As Jouvenel astutely observes, Rousseau is "intoxicated by sublime things" but "their difficulty repels him," and consequently, "he seeks an easy way."[72] Patriotism is the short cut to civic virtue. The realm of necessity can best be extended to moral relations if painful duty is transmuted into a commandment of love.[73]

Before Tocqueville, Rousseau discovered that citizenship must be a habit of the heart; and in relations of the heart, the language of will and contract loses its meaning. The adamantine principles of political right present an insuperable obstacle to political prudence and visibly tax Rousseau's ingenuity. Their intractability eventually forces him to turn the art of politics against the principles of politics. And as this theoretical labor proceeds, the dilemmas of democratic freedom are dissipated in what one might call "a politics of identity." The self-forgetting of the patriot requires, finally, the oblivion of the will.

One might mount a defense of Rousseau's framework as the result of a superior, practical reason. But whose? Certainly not Émile's, and not the democratic citizen's. But that question aside, Rousseau's plan involves more than the application of rational principles to changing circumstances; it extends to modifications of the will in which the ostensible result of practical reason is guaranteed in a life of passionate commitment. What Rousseau instinctively sensed (and communicated rhetorically in the *First Discourse*) and subsequently reasoned through (in the *Second Discourse*, *Social Contract*, and *Émile*) is that full clarity about the principles of political right undermines the achievement of the good society. The truth of those principles—enucleated in the recognition that "man is born free"—threaten (as they did for Émile) to break all the chains of opinion, including those that forge the new order of freedom.[74]

The Rousseauian response to the prima facie contradiction between freedom and any dilution of the will is to stress the negativity and passivity of freedom. The requirements of legitimacy and reliability, which pull in opposite directions, necessitate such a dilution: political art must "subjugate men in order to make them free."[75] While Rousseau could not follow Hobbes in obliging the citizen to blindly authorize all future acts of the sovereign as his own, he sought the closest approximation to an a priori determination of the will: the spontaneous willing of the public good by each individual. In practice, however, the act of willing gives way to a spontaneous *feeling* of identification with the common good that circumvents the problem of consent altogether. A spontaneous community of transparent hearts can dispense with the mediation of ordinary political deliberation in reaching decisions. In such circumstances, "One follows one's heart and everything is done."[76] Spontaneous unanimity crosses the hurdles of consensus-building and rational agreement; but in transcending the realm of contingency it leaps over politics, too.

It is not surprising, therefore, that Rousseau's most compelling vision of the *moi commun* pertains to the festival rather than to the public assembly. The essence of the festival is utter spontaneity, an eruption of feeling, sheer participation. At the festival no one is a mere spectator; each is an actor who identifies himself with all. The festival is an improvisation; it commemorates nothing.[77] Yet while it is devoid of purpose, the festival does have political significance. As Starobinski puts it, "The exaltation of the collective festival has the same structure as the general will of the *Social Contract*. The description of the 'public joy' presents to us the lyrical aspect of the general will, the aspect which it assumes in Sunday habits."[78] The festival accomplishes on the level of feeling what the general will aims at on the level of political right.[79] In Rousseau's dream of the best community, the citizens do not fly to the legislative assembly—they take to the streets.[80]

The passivity of democratic citizenship is traceable to Rousseau's understanding of the soul. The latter is by nature weak. While the first movements of nature (and the nature of the soul) are always good and right, tending directly toward our preservation and happiness, these inclinations lack the force to maintain their original direction. The soul aimlessly follows its natural path until it encounters an obstacle. The most difficult obstacles stem from relations with other human beings; the free movement of nature is thwarted in the traffic of society.[81] Rousseau's reflection on his own soul led to the discovery that he was not made for civil society. His idiosyncrasies aside, the problem of Jean-Jacques is the problem of the soul itself. It is also the problem of freedom:

> As long as I act freely I am good and I only do good; but as soon as I feel the yoke, either of necessity or of men I become rebellious, or rather restive, and then I am nothing. When it is necessary to do the opposite of my will, I do not do it at all, regardless of anything; I no longer even do my

own will, because I am weak. I refrain from acting: because my whole weakness is for action, all my strength is negative. . . .[82]

The essence of freedom is the listless meandering of our natural inclinations. The free man does not rule his soul, he succumbs to it. This essential passivity seems to reappear in the ideal community, where "one follows one's heart and everything is done."

Were the operation of *moeurs* to be so perfected, the formal expression of the general will would be a kind of benediction required by the principles of right, but it would otherwise be redundant to the rule of custom. When the informal rule of *moeurs* is strong, the polity is immunized against the politics of difference. The Legislator and civil religion bathe democracy in a Styx of morals, customs, and opinions, leaving no substantive task for the general will to accomplish. The conditions of freedom are already established.

Individuals begin with no natural feeling for the common good; and even if they can conceive an idea of justice, it will fail to move them.[83] Rules of natural right remain ineffective without a passionate attachment to them. A sound political order must sink its roots in the hearts of its citizens. The question becomes "How can one reach those hearts?"[84]

When Rousseau is faithful to the standard of nature, he is candid about the problem of civic virtue. Pondering the question of whether one would do his duty if he had to combat his deepest desires, Rousseau concludes: "I doubt it. The law of nature, or at least its voice, does not extend so far. Another voice would have to command, and nature remain silent."[85] Rousseau acknowledges time and again that nature never truly stops speaking to man. It is impossible to perfect the political art because men cannot wholly forget themselves and live only for the city.

> The difference between human art and the work of nature is felt in its effects. Citizens may call themselves members of the state, but they cannot unite themselves to it as true members are to the body. It is impossible to prevent each of them from having an individual and separate existence,

by which he could attend to his own preservation.[86]

Because the political order has only an artificial existence, because individuals have no feeling for justice, because politics cannot work on the basis of calculating reason, Rousseau considered, by turns, the rule of virtue and patriotism.[87]

Rousseau found in Plutarch's heroes an alchemy that surpasses the modern achievement of asocial sociability: civil man's dangerous propensity to prefer himself, from which all his vices arise, might be transformed into the most sublime virtue, if the citizen could be denatured. But the very term "denaturation" signals its essential flaw as a *Rousseauian* strategy, and consequently Rousseau stops us, as Jouvenel puts it, on the road that leads to Sparta. Patriotism seems closer to authentically natural sentiments. Patriots are bound together in an affective unity that seems to mitigate the violence toward oneself characteristic of denatured virtue. The patriotic citizen is capable of the sacrifices involved in making his private will conform to the general will, not because he has iron in his soul but because "we willingly desire what is desired by the people we love."[88]

This solution to the problem of freedom and subordination, will and authority, has a coherence that bespeaks more the mind of a genius than the neurosis of a tortured soul. But that coherence obtains, as Rousseau never forgot, only in the realm of possibility, as a simulation of the natural condition. Its artificiality was irreducible, for the fact remained that the city is not really a family, and human beings are not really brothers and sisters. Nature causes an individual to love only himself. Every reader of Rousseau is struck, as Kant was, by the poetic account of the state of nature.[89] Yet it is Rousseau's account of democratic freedom that is truly a fabrication.

At the beginning of this study I suggested that Rousseau's political theory might assist us in our efforts to sort out the vexing questions of individualism and community, freedom and authority, rights and duties. Critics of contemporary liberalism move beyond its intellectual confines into the territory that Rousseau explored. Two separate paths have been marked by "communitarians" and "participatory democrats."[90] Although the paths cross at more than one point, they are distinguished by opposed understandings of citizenship. Communitarians point toward a politics *of identity*; strong democracy is a politics of difference in which identity formation is (to borrow a phrase from John Rawls) political, not metaphysical. According to the communitarian view, the activity of citizenship consists in "living out" shared meanings or traditions; strong democrats worry that this vision contains an implicit appeal to "order" and threatens to sublimate politics into community.[91] One might say that while each theory rejects the "atomistic" ontology of liberalism, the issue dividing them is the proper construction of the "we-identity" that would replace the "I-identity" fathered by liberal metaphysics.[92] The strong democratic view insists on the priority of the political to the communal and defends the *civic* personality against all authoritative conceptions of communal identity.

While participatory or strong democracy has been viewed by most of its defenders and critics as an offshoot of Rousseau's theory, I will argue that the two are, in fact, incompatible.[93] Communitarianism, on the other hand, has an affinity with Rousseau that has generally gone unnoticed.[94] It turns out that communitarian theory argues for a form of communal life very much like the one Rousseau envisaged; the difference is that communitarian theory tends to "ontologize" that result, whereas for Rousseau it remained an artifical construct. On the other hand, it seems to me that strong democracy is closer to Rousseau (and even to contemporary liberal theory) in accepting as an ontological fact the separateness of persons, or an irreducible human plurality. Whereas Rousseau conceived democracy as the overcoming of difference (which finally required that democracy be sunk in strong community), strong democracy sees plurality as the indispensable source *for* the construction of political community.

My procedure will be first to sketch the communitarian critique of liberalism and then consider it in the light of Rousseau's theory. I will then turn to what I take to be the essence of the strong democratic objection to communitarianism. Finally, I will take up the assertion that strong democracy must dispense with strong *community* or deep consensus for the sake of politics, and argue that such a view cannot be grounded, as it is now, in Rousseau's theory.

The Communitarian Critique of Contemporary Liberal Theory

As is by now well known, contemporary liberalism is justified not by any substantive account of the human good but by a strict neutrality toward all such claims. Its central principle is the priority of freedom to all assertions that a certain way of living should be authoritative for the community. Its precise political corollary is the priority of individual rights to the common good. Indeed, liberals characteristically suspect that the latter notion is a fiction masking the imposition of an allegedly superior and deeply partisan way of life on the political community. From the liberal perspective, communitarian values seem to be inherently at odds with freedom. Consequently, pluralism and individual rights (and the policy of tolerance to which they naturally point) are held to be the best fence to negative freedom.[95]

Liberal justice is informed by principles that are not derived from any particular or substantive conception of the good; the right is understood to be prior to the good. This conclusion has implications for the nature or possibility of community, for all communities are particular communities; their bases may be said to be a shared view of the good life that is authoritative, that is, it takes precedence over considerations of abstract justice. For the liberal, the priority of the right to the good (or the priority of justice) means that the public realm must be purged of all such deep identifications or ultimate claims. The polity is fundamentally a framework of laws or neutral procedures within which individuals pursue their private interests.

There is a philosophical and a practical justification for liberal neutrality. At the philosophical level, liberalism subscribes to the view that reason is unable to rank the ends of life. The preferred consequence of this epistemological difficulty (summarized in the infelicitous expression "value noncognitivism") is toleration of competing conceptions of the good, or pluralism. The contrary view, that reason can disclose a hierarchy of human purposes, appears to encourage the dogmatic imposition of a particular conception of the good on society, the establishment of an authoritative common good. The liberal tradition began as a reaction against just such a view and its institutional expressions.[96] Contemporary liberals have not lost their ancient fear of strong conceptions of the common good, whether of the right or left. Such understandings of individual and society were based on a purported apprehension of a natural order, or a utopian one, and all such views, according to liberals, have been shown to be untenable. If society is directed by an authoritative account of the good—whether natural, socially constructed, or implicit in shared meanings—individual choice is demoted. Since conceptions of how human beings should live are essentially contestable, the political order should remain neutral toward them; politics is not the appropriate arena for the settlement of ultimate questions. The practical justification for neutrality is related to the latter point by way of confirmation: as a matter of fact, we do not happen to agree on ultimate questions. There may have been societies in the past that did, and our own society may at one time have enjoyed such a consensus about "the good," but there is manifestly not one now.

Various communitarian critics assert that liberalism boasts a spurious neutrality. Some argue that behind the façade of toleration and pluralism lurks a metaphysic that advances a mistaken understanding of the self, one that necessarily undermines political community. Others find the liberal polity to be caught in a crisis caused by the inadequacy of its theoretical underpinnings, which in turn weakens its practice. The state is increasingly "ungovernable," suffering from hypertrophy and delegitimization.[97] The root of the crisis is that liberalism's very premises render it unable to secure commitment to the common good, whereas such commitment is the only way to stave off social dissolution. Alasdair MacIntyre warns: "In any society where government does not express or represent the moral community of the citizens, but is instead a set of institutional arrangements for imposing a bureaucratized unity on a society which lacks genuine moral consensus, the nature of political obligation becomes systematically unclear."[98] William Connolly argues that the modern polity can be governed only if it summons forth a civility rooted in an awareness of and commitment to a common good; mere law-abidingness will not suffice. A threat of a fascist suppression of politics looms on the horizon.[99] Disparate commentators agree that liberal neutrality is the cancer of liberalism, eroding community where it exists by failing to contain the aggressive expansion of individual rights, and interfering as a matter of principle with remedial efforts to generate civic virtue.

There is a strong element of irony in this "crisis." The liberal strategy was always to stress human rights over any substantive account of the good (what Rawls now calls "perfectionism") as a way of staving off or defusing social antagonisms. Controversies about "ultimate questions" (especially theological ones) would be relegated to the private sphere. If value conflicts could be kept out of the formal public sphere, the raw tensions of a moralized politics would be assuaged naturally as human beings pursued a "lifestyle" in an atmosphere of tolerance or mutual indifference. Liberals had a sense that if questions of ultimate value worked their way onto the public agenda, liberal institutions would be unable to treat them, and the body politic would be poisoned by partisan rancor. Surveying the contemporary political scene, communitarians announce that the chickens have come home to roost.

Dissatisfaction with "rights talk," with liberalism's dominance of moral and political discourse, is widespread.[100] The late George Grant wondered whether the absorption in private life, the retreat from the public realm as something alien, is not a symptom of a deep yearning for a more comfortable place, where relations are not contractual: "The omnipresence of contract in the public realm produces a world so arid that most human beings are unable to inhabit it, except for dashes into it followed by dashes out."[101] Bertrand de Jouvenel made the similar observation that people have

> a tendency to classify as "personal relations" those which please them and convey an emotional warmth and as "social relations" any which they dislike and find a burden. It is often said nowadays: "I cannot dine with friends, I have a social engagement." Thus social relations means for us the unpleasing remnant from which the pleasing ones have been extracted. For this reason society affects us as a burden even when it is in reality carrying us.[102]

According to Michael Walzer, "The state has simply outgrown the human reach and understanding of its citizens. It is not necessarily monstrous, divided, or subjugated, but its citizens are alienated and powerless. They experience a kind of moral uneasiness."[103]

One cannot fail to be struck by these insights, which derive from competing traditions yet reiterate a single theme. The three authors cited are prominent representatives of conservatism, liberalism, and democratic socialism, respectively; and they all conclude that *the* problem of liberalism is its thin theory of citizenship and its failure to generate a sense of community. Since liberal contractualism aims at nothing more than an interest association, it is no wonder, say the critics, that it has difficulty calling for self-sacrifice. Even in liberal society, the characteristic disinclination for commitments to others must occasionally be overcome, but self-interest is an incongruous and ineffective incentive. An adequate social bond must be sought elsewhere. Given the predicament, it is not surprising that "lacking an alternative, presidents term every major civic need 'the equivalent of war.' "[104]

The communitarian critique of liberal neutrality has a theoretical as well as a practical dimension. Michael Sandel argues that liberal metaphysics (it would be more accurate to say Rawlsian metaphysics) illicitly detaches human beings from their social context.[105] The liberal understanding of the person is that of a self unencumbered by nature, or community. For Rawls, "The self is prior to the ends affirmed by it."[106] But, Sandel counters, our selfhood is inextricably bound to some conception of the good, which is in turn given authoritative expression in a particular community.

In Sandel's view, Rawls arrives at pluralism on the social level by assuming it in his very definition of selfhood. For Rawls, "The plurality of distinct persons with separate systems of ends is an essential feature of human societies."[107] What confers distinctness is our individuating characteristics, which are given empirically. Why might not these same empirical characteristics be a foundation of unity, assuming a sufficiently homogeneous society? Rawls's answer is that any possible "social traits" cannot *constitute* who we are; the self is always detachable from the ends it chooses. It stands toward those ends as a subject of possession, never as an object of identification. The latter perspective is incompatible with the assumption of human autonomy.[108] As Sandel puts it, according to Rawls, "I must be a subject whose identity is given independently of the things I have, independently, that is, of my interests and ends and *my relations with others*."[109] Because the self is prior to its ends, the right must be prior to the good, and the proper arrangement for a society of independent selves is a neutral framework that resists the rank-ordering of competing human purposes. But Sandel suggests that we conceive of the self as at least partly "situated." He means that the community in which we live is in some measure constitutive of our identity. We cannot stand apart from our attributes, interests, or aspirations, and to some extent these are given to us by our social context. Rawls's conception of a self complete, independent, and prior to its ends is wildly implausible and yet, according to Sandel, it is the ground of Rawls's entire argument for the priority of justice over, among other things, community. Members of Rawls's well-ordered society cannot possibly share a common identity constituted by a pattern of social life.

The philosophical issue between communitarians and liberals is profound. It involves what it means to be a human subject, to be free; it raises the question of whether our identity is chosen or given. Now, if the conditions of identity are inherently social, the dominant moral paradigm of our age must be rethought. According to Charles Taylor,

> The crucial point here is this: since the free individual can only maintain his identity within a society/culture of a certain kind, he has to be concerned about the shape of this society/culture as a whole. He cannot . . . be concerned purely with his individual choices and the associations formed from such choices to the neglect of the matrix in which such choices can be open or closed, rich or meager.[110]

At this point Rousseau's theory becomes a useful framework for situating and adjudicating the competing claims of contemporary liberals and communitarians. Rousseau shares the Rawlsian assumption that "the plurality of distinct persons with separate systems of ends is an essential feature of human societies." It was on that basis that he rejected Diderot's notion of "a general society" of the human race. But at the same time, that feature of society is pathological and must be overcome. Thus, if Rousseau begins like Rawls, he ends with something like Sandel's position *as a goal* of his political theory. Human relations must become constitutive of our identity, but only after they have been reformed or "moralized" through civic education. Rousseau is very conscious that his "remedy" draws on the disease itself.[111] Naturally, human beings are not so constituted; the social identity is a historical acquisition that must be corrected if individuals are to recover independence. Interestingly, Rousseau's prescription is quite precisely echoed in Taylor's call for a new paradigm, with one important difference. For Rousseau, because the conditions of identity are not originally social, the new matrix must be carefully constructed and prepared so that it becomes virtually the exclusive concern of the citizen; the social matrix is promoted from neglect to sacred reverence.

Theorists such as Taylor, MacIntyre, and Sandel begin from the premise that political theory is inextricably bound to the world of practice. Political theories are articulate, systematic versions of the often inarticulate and unsystematic interpretations that ordinary citizens have of their own experience. Sandel suggests, paradoxically, that it is a false theory (liberalism) which today rules out "the possibility of membership in any community bound by moral ties antecedent to choice; the unencumbered self cannot belong to any community where the self *itself* could be at stake."[112] Such a community would be "constitutive" rather than cooperative. It would engage the *identity* as well as the interests of its participants. Once again, we see reflected the political concerns of Rousseau: the relation of morality and choice, the construction of the social self, the relation of interest and identity (*moi particulier* vs. *moi commun*). But whereas Rousseau problematized this social "ontology" and struggled over its theoretical-practical realization, communitarian theory seems merely to adopt it as a point of departure for the critique of liberalism.

From the communitarian perspective, politics is *naturally* a matter of identity formation and affirmation. As Taylor explains it, the conditions of our identity are indispensable to our being full human subjects: "The conception of identity is that outside of the horizon created by some master value, or some allegiance, or some community membership, I would be crucially crippled, would be unable to ask and answer effectively these questions, would thus be unable to function as a full human subject."[113] Because our particular culture and community constitute the crucial pole of our identity, we have a right to demand respect for whatever is indispensable to that community's integrity.[114] Rousseau himself endorsed the latter conclusion in arguing that the community could police its integrity by forcing to be free those who would violate it. But for Rousseau, our particular culture and community are crucial to a *new* identity that is now incompatible with an original human subjectivity which was indeed independent of any social matrix. The latter still casts a shadow over Rousseau's polity and accounts for the fact that he struggled to maintain a role for the principles of right. One significant consequence is that law is limited to the establishment of exclusively general or strictly impersonal standards; in Rousseau's own words, law is confined to matters of "rigorous right." The law would apply only to actions; the people (as the custodian of *moeurs*) would remain the judge of personal worth or character.[115]

Thus Rousseau arrived at his own separation of law and morals, which is the hallmark of liberal legal theory. But if the law had to be confined to actions, Rousseau argued that the moral force of public opinion should nevertheless make itself felt within the polity.[116] On the basis of Rousseau's individualistic assumptions, social identity is a means to an individual end. His polity consequently can incorporate something of the liberal standard of impersonal justice and the separation of law and morality while still finding an authoritative role for "conservative" community values. Contemporary communitarians (for the most part) show no enthusiasm for *legislating* a social identity, but their critics could have a point in suggesting that their ontological assumptions throw up no *principled* barrier to the emergence of a moral majority that would actively engage in legal discrimination on behalf of its way of life, which is, after all, no mere preference but something constitutive of its identity. The ideal policy would seem to be something like a moderated liberalism in which procedural justice operates against a backdrop of communitarian assumptions about the essentially social identity of individual human beings. If this arrangement could be won, presumably liberal justice would be cured of its corrosive antagonism to legitimate community needs. Rights talk might be cured of its "near aphasia concerning responsibility."[117] But can communitarianism ground such a (positive) double standard in *its* ontology?[118]

At the center of the communitarian political vision is an ideal of consensus, understood as a system of shared meanings.[119] Virtually all theories of consensus presume that the sharing of ideas, values, feelings, or attitudes is essential to the well-being, if not to the very survival, of a society.[120] In the words of Edmund Burke, "The only firm seat of all authority is in the minds, affections and interests of the people."[121] A similar view informs the "neoconservative" perspective of Samuel Huntington: "The extent to which a society or a political system is harmonic or disharmonic depends as much upon the values of its people as upon the structure of its institutions."[122] Despite the difficulty in attaching a precise definition and application to the concept of consensus, it is one of the principal phenomena with which political theorists and political actors grapple, and it is routinely evoked in the communitarian vision. Michael Walzer asserts that "a given society is just if its substantive life is lived . . . in a way faithful to the shared understandings of its members."[123] In other words, the foundation of society is not rights but meaning or "values." Political theory, consequently, should mirror social meaning rather than ground privileges and immunities.[124] Everything seems to hinge on whether a society has such shared meanings, and whether they are sufficiently beyond controversy.

The question arises of whether consensus is something that is discovered or produced, and if the latter, what its mode of production is. To raise the question of consensus is to broach the character of democratic politics itself. There seem to be two possibilities. Politics may be the *expression* of an existing consensus, which would indicate the priority of community. Alternatively, politics may be an *instrument* of community, a kind of "art" that can bring about a consensus where none previously existed. It is crucial to know whether a consensus exists *because* a community exists, or whether politics builds community by crafting consensus. Is democratic politics to be understood as the expression or the design of consensus or, perhaps, a mixture of both?[125]

Strong Democracy in the Light of Rousseau

Benjamin Barber defines strong democracy as the antithesis of a politics of consensus. In his view, the communitarians err in the belief that the conflict and dissensus of modern life can somehow be sloughed off in a recovery of community. In his judgment, to privilege consensus is to vitiate politics, because "where consensus stops, politics starts."[126] He underscores the political inutility of the one piece of political counsel that Alasdair MacIntyre offers toward the end of *After Virtue*: construct "local forms of community within which civility and the intellectual and moral life can be sustained through the new dark ages which are already upon us."[127] Barber observes, "What [MacIntyre] can possibly mean in an era of multinational corporations, economic interdependence, irredentist nationalism, religious fundamentalism, and the constant threat of nuclear oblivion is not spelled out."[128]

Communitarianism points implicitly (if not explicitly) toward a unitary democracy in which citizenship is largely a matter of reaffirming a common and given identity. Barber judges that unitary democracy betrays "the democratic impulse."

> The unitary form of democracy is defined by politics in the consensual mode and seems at first glance to eschew representation (if not politics itself) in pursuit of its central norm, unity. It calls for all divisive issues to be settled unanimously through the organic will of a homogeneous or even monolithic community. . . . [T]he individual citizen achieves his civic identity through merging his self with the collectivity, that is to say, through self-abandonment.

> Although this surrender assures a certain equality . . . it is obviously corrupting to autonomy and thus ultimately to citizenship itself.[129]

The danger Barber sees is that "if one claims that the condition of unanimity and consensus that politics wishes to achieve by art already exists by nature, then politics loses its purpose and becomes superfluous."[130]

Now although Rousseau emphatically denies that such a consensus exists by nature, his theory is devoted to how consensus can be generated and guaranteed. As we have seen, he explores the ways in which civic life could literally become an exercise in *consentir*—a feeling together. Barber's strong democracy aims to be genuinely political, which is to say, its politics is concerned with the generation of procedures for coping with conflicting conceptions of the good. But Rousseau's model provides no harmonizing principle or procedure to resolve conflicts other than the appeal to a consensus. Genuine politics does indeed disappear from Roussseau's regime. He writes:

> As long as several men together consider themselves to be a single body, they have only a single will, which relates to their common preservation and the general welfare. Then all the mechanisms of the State are vigorous and simple, its maxims are clear and luminous, it has no tangled, contradictory interests; the common good is clearly apparent everywhere, and requires only good sense to be achieved.[131]

The "antipolitical" nature of Rousseau's democracy emerges quite clearly in his discussion of the popular assembly. The conduct of the assembly provides a measure of "the actual state of the *moeurs* and health of the body politic."[132] The more harmony reigns in the assembly, the more the general will is dominant. Clearly the general will itself is not the cause of harmony. Long deliberations, dissensions, tumults do not represent the working out of the general will but, rather, the ascendancy of particular interests and the decline of the state.[133] "The law of order in public assemblies is not so much to maintain the general will therein as it is to be sure that it is always questioned and that it always answers."[134] But division in the community silences the general will; and no set of decision procedures can repair the damage of dissensus. Realizing that unity is always subject to erosion, Rousseau does not insist that an assembly produce a unanimous declaration of the general will. Outside of the social contract itself, the vote of a majority obligates all the others.[135]

The common good is the object of the general will, but the common good must nevertheless be willed. What disposes men to do so? This is the stumbling block that Rousseau's theory confronts with a forthrightness unequaled in contemporary treatments of democracy. The latter tend to assume the very disposition that Rousseau problematizes.[136] It might be supposed that because the common or general good is intrinsically attractive, one could count on its being either discovered or generated in a process of deliberation.[137] But, to mention only one difficulty, deliberation is vulnerable to an "aristocratic" problem: in an open forum, the best speakers, the wisest minds, or (in the worst case) the most cunning may dominate.

Voting is a strictly democratic alternative to deliberation. It factors out all inequalities that might enhance the persuasive abilities of some over others. In a vote, participants really are equal.[138] Rousseau's choice of voting over deliberation seems to signify the primacy of will over reason. Rousseau might have conceived a system in which deliberation about the common good would proceed until a consensus had emerged. Instead, the question is put to a vote, subject to certain strictures that compensate for the apparent deficiencies of voting versus deliberation as a method of "finding" the general will: (1) everybody's vote must be counted; (2) the general will obligates everyone, no matter how each voted; (3) the general will concerns itself only with matters of common or general interest—no individual can be discriminated against; (4) the general will must be expressed by voters who follow the spirit of rule (3).[139] The general will can be declared only by suppressing regard for personal interest. Hypothetically, citizens might regard their personal interests and still achieve a unanimous vote; but the latter would not amount to an authentic expression of the general will.

As we have seen, the general will can be expressed in the

popular assembly if and only if decisions are made in pursuit of the common interest rather than of individual interests. The role of procedures is to ensure that the decision process is not deflected from the path to the common good. The superiority of voting to deliberation is that it forestalls the introduction of myriad perspectives, which might subtly turn the question, "Is Proposal X advantageous to the state?" to some more particular end. As Bernard Manin has convincingly argued, Rousseau intended to exclude from democracy the effects of rhetoric and the power of persuasion. The result is that deliberation is excluded altogether. By "délibération publique" Rousseau refers not to an exchange of views or some antecedent process of opinion formation that eventually determines the public choice but to the decision itself.[140]

Since the act of voting is the registering of opinions about what the general will is, one can be confident that the majority opinion will be closest to the truth. The perception of a majority would be more reliable than the perception of the few.[141] Rousseau qualifies this maxim, however: "This presupposes, it is true, that all the characteristics of the general will are still in the majority. When they cease to be, there is no longer any freedom regardless of the side one takes."[142] Now "the characteristics of the general will" to which Rousseau refers are the very qualities that *moeurs* instill. "Upright and simple men are hard to fool because of their simplicity"; they will never be duped into a misidentification of the general will as long as they remain so.[143] One might say that simple *moeurs* are Rousseau's democratic analogue to the Aristotelian ethical discipline that cultivates the *spoudaios*, the morally serious citizen who is prepared for the exercise of "practical reason."[144]

Another reason Rousseau opts for voting is that the common good must indeed be willed in order to satisfy the criterion of legitimacy.[145] But while the will must be "consulted," it must nevertheless be confined to what is truly general. Provided that the general will is so "conditioned," it is "toujours droite" (always right) and unerringly hits its mark.[146] Civic education establishes the condition in which the general will can be declared by encouraging the civic disposition, which is to say, by effacing the "contrary will" that each individual has "as a man."[147] Voting testifies to the "strength of soul" (*vigueur d'âme*) in individual citizens rather than to the strength of democratic procedures.[148] It serves as a barometer of corruption in that its result informs each citizen as to whether his private will or the general will prevails in his heart.[149]

The conditioning of the people and the limitation of their role to voting are, for Rousseau, the reasoned requirements of political freedom. To evaluate the latter in terms of substantive popular participation is to apply the wrong standard. Rousseau makes no case for self-development through political activity, at least as that notion is currently understood.[150] His principles do justice to the legitimate rights of the people, but his prudence circumscribes their exercise out of the belief that untutored *volonté* cannot produce *généralité*. Will and the common good must be mediated by civic education so that the disposition to generality or the common good will itself informs the act of willing.[151] Rousseau's reasoning makes sense only on the assumption that democratic politics is a bulwark against domination rather than an end in itself.[152] That defensive purpose is signified by his remark that the popular assembly is "the aegis of the body politic."[153]

Because Rousseau regards real deliberation as an invitation to express particular opinions about private interests, he proposes a ban on communication.[154] The fragility of the general will is underscored by the extraordinary measures that must be taken to suppress the emergence of factions.[155] The very distinction between acts of sovereignty and of government is meant to insulate the people from the temptation to consider particular objects. "Nothing is more dangerous than the influence of private interests on public affairs."[156]

The procedural forms of the Rousseauian assembly serve the legitimacy criterion by fixing the collective perspective on what is exclusively general. But since citizens must "feel" the common interest as well as "see" it, reliability requires a renaturing connection with sentiment.[157] The phenomenon of patriotism demonstrates that men can be lovers of their country, disposed to sacrifice for it and each other.[158] Passionate attachment to one's fellow citizens is the surest means of submerging private wills in the general will.[159] In the community of hearts, citizens will indeed "feel together."

The social contract is the original expression of consent, and the popular assembly subsequently maintains its integrity. Rousseau considers how to ward off any recrudescence of pluralistic dissensus. The need to achieve consensus and avoid dissent produces a shift from contract to community, which is already expressed in the terms of the social contract itself.[160] It is Rousseau's attention to the obverse of consent that accounts for his unique approach to the role of the assembly. Whereas Hobbes and Locke provide for consent, the latter is a prelude to the citizen's subjection to power in a form that Rousseau rejects.[161] We have already seen that the Rousseauian democracy does not establish a relation of ruler and ruled in the traditional sense, since each continues to obey only himself and "gives himself to nobody."[162] But democratic freedom must be kept from undermining its own foundation in civil obligations, which is to say, the democratic citizen must be governable. The will must be "steered" because human beings have no natural compass orienting them toward the general. Dissent can be taken as a sign that the community has lost its way and is heading down the path of *volonté particulier*, where men do nothing but "obstruct, supplant, deceive, betray and destroy one another."[163]

In Rousseau's theoretical reformation of the popular assembly, the problem of legitimacy reduces to the problem of ensuring consent, and the legislative role of the people is consequently limited.[164] Far from participating in the design, revision, and compromising of legislative proposals, the citizen casts a vote in a kind of referendum. As David Gauthier remarks, Rousseau's citizen does not really practice the political art in any substantive sense.[165] The latter would seem to belong, in the first place, to the Legislator who frames the constitutional order and, next, to the magistrates who govern. Rousseauian democracy is government for the people, but not truly by the people or of the people.[166] Although as a matter of *right*, government is subordinate to the sovereign people, its role is substantial and its powers are considerable. Government initiates, and the people ratify as a punctuation of the political process. According to Rousseau, this division of roles between the people and the magistrates does not entail a separation of power to the disadvantage of the people. The latter always remain masters of the government, periodically choosing or reconfirming it.[167] While Rousseau's plan does not require the people to be powerless, it does seem to reduce them to passivity.

As we saw, the act of voting, as Rousseau conceives it, presumes that "all the characteristics of the general will are still in the majority." This perspective is at odds with the recognition of human plurality, and indicates the presence of a strong subterranean current in Rousseau's theory that can only be called antipolitical.[168] If, as Robert Dahl has suggested, "the dilemma of politics is the dilemma of pluralism," Rousseauian democracy would resolve the dilemma only by transcending it.[169] For it is difficult to resist the conclusion that Rousseau conceives "the facilitating conditions of citizenship" in such a way as to overwhelm its practice.[170] Rousseau breaks through the dilemma of democratic politics and betrays the cause of strong democracy by appealing to, in effect, a preexisting or "hidden consensus." Democratic freedom is too fragile to survive the encounter with difference, too weak to fulfill the mandate of "a permanent confrontation between the me as citizen and the 'Other' as citizen."[171] Rousseauian citizenship abolishes the distance between self and other in the *moi commun*. The encounter of "each" with "all" is consummated in an act of identification so that the individual becomes an indivisible part of the whole.

We are now in a better position to appreciate why democratic freedom is geared toward avoiding factions rather than the positive experience of political participation, and why the people's role consists in *consent* rather than in initiative. Nothing can legitimately deprive the people of their right to make sovereign decisions, but that participation is carefully channeled by a rigorous proceduralism designed to filter out the fractiousness associated with genuine popular deliberation. The value of majority decision is not bound up with wider opportunities for participation; it is simply the case that majority decisions are more likely than anything else to reflect the constant unanimity in favor of the general will.[172]

Rousseau assumes that unanimous consent to the general will is always present. Schemes of voting may or may not reveal it perfectly, but the majority vote remains an instrument rather than an end in itself. Votes are not only counted but *interpreted*; and they are always to be interpreted as a correct reflection of unanimous consent.[173] For the general will to operate, individuals must regard themselves as part of the *moi commun*. Only those who transcend their own interest in favor of the collective can be relied on to express the general will; and as we have seen, "civic education" is the ultimate guarantor that the moralization of individuals achieves the conquest of the self.

There would seem to be no question that Rousseau's is a theory of consensus.[174] Yet Barber draws a message quite different from Rousseau's:

> Wise political judgement demanded no special cognitive faculty, no virtuous altruist, no universal imperative; it required only that all members of a community participate in a political process of deliberation and decision making aimed at disclosing what they shared in common and thus what constituted their being as a community. . . . Those political judges whom we call citizens cannot impose cognitive consensus as a solution to the collision of interests. The problem is not one of knowledge but one of interests in opposition, and interests in opposition can be adjudicated only by such political means as bargaining and exchange or—better from the perspective of strong democracy—the artificial creation of civic communities that transform how individuals perceive themselves and their particular interests.[175]

While Barber is right in emphasizing that Rousseau eschews a cognitive consensus and a universal imperative (for reasons that emerged in the quarrel with Diderot), he seriously misconstrues him. The nub of the problem is Barber's substitution of his own notion of participation (with its corollary of self-transformation through the encounter with others in deliberative discourse) for what Rousseau actually had in mind. It is this misinterpretation that allows Barber to invoke Rousseau to attack the politics of consensus. In Barber's reading, Rousseau

> anticipates and remonstrates with enthusiasts who would imagine that the General Will not only achieves an artificial

community but is engendered by and acts as a mirror to a natural consensus. "If there were no different interests," he writes, "the common interest would be barely felt, as it would encounter no obstacle; all would go on of its own accord, and politics would cease to be an art." Where there is natural consensus there cannot be conflict or power or need for reasonableness.[176]

The passage from the *Social Contract* quoted here serves as a touchstone not only for Barber's interpretation of Rousseau but also for his conception of "politics in the participatory mode."[177] It is *the* text that "authorizes" the strong democratic model of citizenship qua transformative membership. This "genuine politics" "enables individuals to transcend their private interests through membership in the civic community."[178] The general will is disclosed in "the collision of interests" in the public arena. For Barber, it is the *encounter* as much as anything else that matters. He finds in Rousseau "a portrait of political judgement in which politics was much and reason little."[179] Again, the crucial passage of the *Social Contract* is cited in support:

> "There is often a great deal of difference between the will of all and the general will; the latter considers only the common interest, while the former takes private interest into account, and is no more than a sum of particular wills: but take away from these same wills the pluses and minuses that cancel one another, and the general will remains the sum of the differences." What citizens share is the residue precipitated by the clash of their private interests publicly confronted.[180]

The *public* confrontation of private interests is the essence of strong democracy. In the political space created by democratic procedures there can be an encounter between self and other as citizens. I have already suggested that to unpack Rousseau's notion of citizenship is to reveal a strategy for *overcoming* the encounter with otherness. But it is worth noting again, with the help of the text in question, that for Rousseau the "artificial creation of civic communities" consists not in the public, political encounter with difference but in the suppression of particularity through a stance of moral asceticism toward one's self. The social tie is forged in the hearts of citizens rather than in their common public space.

The citizen indeed undergoes a profound transformation; he comes to regard himself under a new aspect, as a member of an indivisible whole. Such a citizen no longer experiences his particularity in the same way. Qua citizen, he subordinates himself to an assessment of a good that, being indivisible, cannot be open to the variety of individual claims. Such a good remains outside the purview of those who are still oriented by their own particularity, who are propelled by their interests. As William Connolly has suggested, the common good is not an aggregative notion, because aggregates can leave some interests out. For the true citizen, one might say, an aggregative concept is incomprehensible, since he has passed beyond the horizon of particularity altogether.[181] But, and this is a crucial point, the citizen transcends his particularity by internalizing customary norms rather than through substantive participation in political decision making.[182]

Hannah Arendt is another who appreciated the antipolitical nature of the general will. To rely on will, she wrote, "essentially excludes all processes of exchange of opinions and an eventual agreement between them. The will, if it is to function at all, must indeed be one and indivisible."[183] Arendt captures Rousseau's intention so precisely that it is worth quoting her account at length. Noting that common experience taught that conflicting interests within a nation could be unified by confronting them with an *external* opposition, Rousseau took a further step:

> He wished to discover a unifying principle within the nation itself that would be valid for domestic politics as well. Thus, his problem was where to detect a common enemy outside the range of foreign affairs, and his solution was that such an enemy existed within the breast of each citizen, namely, in his particular will and interest; the point of the matter was that this hidden, particular enemy could rise to the rank of a common enemy—unifying the nation from within—if one only added up all particular wills and interests. The common enemy within the nation is the sum total of the particular interests of all citizens.[184]

At this point Arendt refers to the note in which Rousseau endorses the idea of the Marquis D'Argenson that "the agreement of all interests is formed by opposition to that of each." She again grasps Rousseau's meaning exactly: "If only each particular man rises against himself in his particularity, he will be able to arouse in himself his own antagonist, the general will, and thus he will become a true citizen of the national body politic. . . . To partake in the body politic of the nation, each national must rise and remain in constant rebellion against himself."[185] Rousseauian politics is predicated on a polemical confrontation *within the self*; only in that way could the encounter with difference be avoided. For Rousseau, this dualism within the soul was wholly passional and did not bespeak the dualism of reason and passion posited in the classical understanding of the soul.[186]

I argued above that careful scrutiny of Rousseau's "reform" of the popular assembly reveals an antipolitical attitude. It is significant that his perspective on the political assembly was fixed in his discussion in the *Second Discourse* of the first human assemblies:

> People grew accustomed to assembling in front of the huts or around a large tree; song and dance, true children of love and leisure, became the amusement or rather the occupation of idle and assembled men and women. Each one began to look at the others and to want to be looked at himself, and public esteem had a value. The one who sang or danced the best, the handsomest, the strongest, the most adroit, or the most eloquent became the most highly considered; and that was the first step toward inequality and, at the same time, toward vice.[187]

That this moment is fraught with political consequence emerges in a later passage in the same work, after Rousseau has chronicled "the progress of inequality" through the various "revolutions" in the natural condition:

> If this were the place to go into details, I would easily explain how, even without the involvement of government,

inequality of credit and authority becomes inevitable between individuals as soon as, united in the same society [*les
Particuliers sitôt que réunis en une même Société*], they are
forced to make comparisons between themselves and to take
into account differences they find in the continual use they
have to make of one another. These differences are of
several kinds; but in general wealth, nobility or rank, power,
and personal merit being the principal distinctions by which
one is measured in society, I would prove that the agreement or conflict of these various forces is the surest indication of a well- or ill-constituted state.[188]

The fatalistic tendency of social relations is once again underscored ("as soon as individuals are united in the same society
. . ."). The "forces" that must be brought into agreement [*accord*]
are the particular interests or wills of individuals or, in Rousseau's more compact language, *les particuliers*. Rousseau takes up
the details that he could not address in the *Discourse* in the *Social
Contract*:

Each interest, says the Marquis d'Argenson, *has different
principles. The agreement of two private interests is formed in
opposition to the interest of a third.* He could have added that
the agreement of all interests is formed in opposition to the
interest of each. If there were no different interests, the
common interest, which would never encounter any obstacle, would scarcely be felt. Everything would run smoothly
by itself and politics would cease to be an art.[189]

What Rousseau means in this note is that the agreement or
union of "les particuliers" (which will be a "moral whole" in
Rousseau's sense) arises out of the opposition of the "interests
of all" to *the particular interest of each*. He does not mean that
the mere clash of interests *among themselves* gives rise to the
common interest, as Barber's reading suggests. (One can avoid
misunderstanding by noticing—as Hannah Arendt does—that
Rousseau uses "will" and "interest" synonymously in this discussion.) We have already seen how the polemical confrontation of

"tous" and "chacun" occurs within the breast of each individual in the activity of moral freedom. In the chapter under examination, Rousseau restates the argument in more straightforwardly political terms. "If there were no different interests, the common interest, which would never encounter any obstacle, would scarcely be felt. Everything would run smoothly by itself and politics would cease to be an art." That is to say, if there were no particular wills, the general will would scarcely be felt (painfully!) because it would encounter no obstacle. But there *are* such particular wills because there is human plurality; the obstacle the latter throws up before the general will consists in the fact that the particular will "tends by its nature toward preferences"—toward the *preference for oneself* that Rousseau saw, from first to last, as the tendency of social relations whenever human beings are "assembled" and confront one another.[190]

There is indeed a great difference between the will of all and the general will. The former considers particular interests. The will of all is the aggregation of the different interests of each particular individual *vis-à-vis the general will of each individual.* Each individual can, and does, have different reasons (reflecting different interests) for opposing the general will within himself. "But take away from these same wills the pluses and minuses that cancel each other out, and the remaining sum of the differences is the general will." Once each individual has overcome his own particular (idiosyncratic) reason for opposing the general will, the "remaining sum" is indeed the general will, now unobstructed by "difference." This result (difficult in its own right) faces an even greater impediment:

> If, when an adequately informed people [a people that has not been deceived][191] deliberates, the citizens were to have no communication among themselves, the general will would always result from the large number of small differences, and the deliberation would always be good. But when factions, partial associations at the expense of the whole, are formed, the will of each of those associations becomes general with reference to its members and particular with reference to the State. One can say, then, that there are no longer as many voters as there are

men, but merely as many as there are associations. The differences become less numerous and produce a result that is less general.[192]

The obstacle that difference throws up becomes almost insurmountable when individuals coalesce into factions. The particular interest enlarges to become a group interest. There are indeed fewer "voters"; and there are fewer, but larger and more intractable, "differences." Rousseau foresaw the problem that is said to be the malaise of contemporary democratic life: the insidious operation of "special interests" whose force seems to suppress the "public interest" that would otherwise be close at hand. Inside the "interest group," the struggle against particularity is confounded since the individual must now prefer one general will to another: the general will "of the State" to the general will of his association, the latter being for him simultaneously general and particular. Rousseau's point is that simple self-interest is "thinner" than group interest; consequently, the citizen can "overcome" the former much more easily than the latter. If one cannot avoid interest groups, then it is better that they proliferate, for the corporate interest of each one will be diluted as differences multiply.[193] In conclusion, Rousseauian politics is not about the encounter with difference but about the *overcoming* of difference. As such, it is the antithesis of strong democracy.

Barber is too perceptive a critic of "antipolitics" in all its forms simply to miss this conclusion. His writings reflect, if one may say so, a love-hate relationship with Rousseau. Both because of his deep conviction of the worth of political life and because of his lifelong encounter with Rousseau's ambivalent works, he notices the tendency (which I have emphasized) for the politics of identity to overwhelm democratic self-rule:

> As Rousseau expressed it, the problem is that individuals cohere into a community through the process of communally resolving conflict but that, at the same time, the ability to resolve conflict seems to depend on the community's prior cohesion and on a generic commitment to common values. In addressing this problem, democratic theorists have always shown a strong impulse to imitate Rousseau

and burn the candle at both ends. At one end, they have designed procedures that will work in the most individualistic and pluralist (conflict-ridden) circumstances, where community is a peripheral byproduct of participation. At the other, they have designed procedures aimed at building community, procedures that mitigate conflict from the outset and give to participatory activity the support of a prior consensus.[194]

But because Rousseau in fact held no brief for participation, it would be best to let strong democracy out from under his shadow. In his most philosophic work, Rousseau remarked that the citizen is the antipode of natural man, who breathes only freedom and repose.[195] Outside the natural condition, freedom is inherently problematic. Rousseau's political theory aims at a *reconciliation* of freedom and citizenship, but the latter's goodness derives *exclusively* from its role in the new framework of independence. Citizenship comes to light as a potential solution to the problem of the loss of freedom. By elevating citizenship itself as the good, the theory of strong democracy inverts Rousseau's argument and distorts his understanding of freedom even as it invokes them. It does an injustice to Rousseau, and to itself.

Barber invokes Rousseau as he argues against that negative definition of freedom which "produces a conception of political liberty as entirely passive. This freedom is associated with the unperturbedness of the inertial body, with the motionlessness of the inertial frame itself. It stands in stark opposition to the idea of politics as activity, motion, will, choice, self-determination, and self-realization."[196] But as I have argued throughout this book, that is Rousseau's own understanding of freedom. Barber's purpose in articulating a theory of strong democracy is to restore political activity itself as the antidote to a culture that has forgotten the value of self-government. It is a cause that deserves a respectful hearing in its own voice. It is confounded by association with Rousseau, who was concerned to restore the natural condition of independence, and who was prepared to bend authentic democratic values to that purpose precisely because they had no intrinsic worth for him. Barber is quite right when he remarks, "The garden where there is no discord makes politics unnecessary."[197] But Rousseau yearned for such a place. And that is why his political theory betokens the most thoroughgoing conquest of politics.

Conclusion

In his rebellion against the conquest of politics by a certain kind of philosophy, Barber made Rousseau the model of the "politically minded" philosopher. As the champion of political autonomy (and, by entailment, the autonomy of the political), Rousseau seemed to avoid the error of philosophical didacticism, which would redeem the world of practice by reforming it in the image of philosophy.[198] But he also is a "foundationalist," even a radical one, in the sense that his philosophical standard is the original condition of the human soul. Rousseau's ironic democracy is a means to simulate the natural and best relations of human beings, independent relations of low intensity, appropriate to people who may need, but ought not to care much about, one another, since their very connectedness is designed to prevent encroachment.

Rousseau's political order aims at freedom, but it is not a sphere of rational freedom in the sense that citizens do not themselves deliberate and choose the means that will promote it. Their task is to keep the tablets, both of constitution and of customs, which are, of course, in reality neither perpetual nor immemorial.[199] The democratic citizenry easily tolerates this ambiguity concerning its own sovereignty so that the yoke of the laws is, indeed, lightly worn. But at some point it becomes impossible to distinguish a spirit of reverence from the spirit of liberty, which sheds light on the curious fact that Rousseau has been regarded as a conservative and a libertarian. It is one thing to suggest that a free constitution requires the support (perhaps obliquely stated) of custom, religion, morality; one finds such thoughts in the writings of the founders of the American republic. But Rousseau's democratic freedom erases the distinction between ends and means, for reasons that we may now appreciate. Unlike the American Constitution, which forbids religious establishments, Rousseau's social contract would legislate civil religion. Such laws bear a burden beyond the capacity of a liberal democracy, striving as they do not only to demarcate what is legitimate but also to guarantee what is best. Yet in this scheme, the virtues of democratic citizens themselves are ignored or underrated. Rousseau seems to have had little confidence in a citizen's capacity for self-restraint, for respecting forms and limits, for distinguishing short-run desires from long-range interests. The problem of politics is, at bottom, the futility of moral relations as such:

> Here we are in the moral world; here the door on vice opens. With conventions and duties are born deceit and lying. As soon as one can do what one ought not, one wants to hide what one ought not to have done. As soon as an interest causes a promise, a greater interest can cause the violation of the promise. The only concern now is to violate it with impunity. The means are natural; one conceals and one lies. Not having been able to forestall vice, we are now already reduced to punishing it. Here are the miseries of human life which begin with its errors.[200]

It is a somber thought, and reflection on Rousseau's ingenious yet dismal political vision should lead us to reconsider his pre-suppositions concerning human nature.

Arthur Melzer forcefully argues that the *Social Contract* can be understood exclusively as a strict consequence of the principle of the natural goodness of man, notwithstanding the fact that the latter term is never mentioned there.[201] I agree with Melzer's conclusion that Rousseau's political plan intends to prevent men fom ruining one another through mutual dependence. That is to say, the *political* goal remains the preservation of the naturally good self.[202] In this way, Rousseauian political freedom is essentially negative, an attempt to stave off, primarily, the corruption of the social and economic interdependence of modern commercial life, and yet, ultimately, of social relations as such.

By fitting Rousseau's response to the Enlightenment project into the larger historical movement of Western thought, Melzer persuasively characterizes Rousseau's thought as "a study in the pessimistic consequences of humanism," a more penetrating installment of what Melzer aptly calls "idealistic realism," the armature not only of Rousseau's system but also of the whole modern attack on the transcendent idols of classical and Christian morality. Rousseau's "philosophical move" is to radicalize Hobbes's defense of the "low" against the "high," the body and the passions against the claims of the spirit and virtue. By "lowering" man even further than Hobbes did, Rousseau "discovers a new, bodily route back to the transcendent heights of Christian and classical thought."[203]

But the question arises of what these transcendent heights can be, given Rousseau's assumptions. Certainly not those of Christian and classical thought per se. What is *positive* about the Rousseauian soul? Apart from its ability to fend off corruption, is there genuinely a structure to the soul that might indicate a positive standard for its development? For if, as I have suggested, the Rousseauian soul is inherently passive, negative, and defensive, what conception of human life is imaginable on this basis? To live in such a way as to be good for ourselves and harmless (but also useless) to others would seem to consign us to a life of desire whose principal features are narrowness and velleity. Natural goodness seems to involve not so much an ordering of the soul as a simple circumspection in its operations. But there is no internal governance of those operations; they are an automatic response to the natural condition. Rousseau indicates that this limitation is the natural consequence of the free sway of the soul's prerational disposition to seek its own good. Natural goodness is literally the seeking of one's own good; and since the latter is minimal (not to say primitive), a solution is available in principle to the problem of human conflict. All that is required is that each individual sincerely pursue his own good, a policy that will automatically confine his will within the tight circle of self-regarding passions, and guard it against domination of and by other wills. Thus natural goodness appears synonymous with freedom.[204]

But can nature so conceived be regarded as providing the sufficient condition for the good life?[205] The good is now emptied of all content, because the latter would amount to an *external* imposition, a given, something not self-imposed and therefore something beyond the willing self.[206] When the human good is viewed as authoritative for the will—when, that is to say, it becomes the object of choosing rightly—human freedom is again subordinated to something higher than itself. Whether this link is to God or to the common good, the existence of a good that the will ought to will amounts to a chain on human freedom.

Natural goodness appears to be indistinguishable from the circumstances that not only conduce to but actually accomplish the self-sufficiency of natural man. Just as Rousseau insists that his faults "came to me more from my situation than from myself," so the goodness of natural man derives more from his situation than from himself.[207] And when he remarks in a rhetorical flourish that "all these disorders stem more from the constitution of societies than from that of man," Rousseau refers not to some natural structure of the soul but, rather, to "the natural constitution of things," to the natural condition.[208]

Thus it is that the Rousseauian self seems to disintegrate into a patternless amalgamation of "conditioned" responses, and human nature is displaced by a human history. For what can the sentiment of existence be except subservience to some given state of affairs? In the silent ratification of the present and the unified recollection of the past, one might "feel life" as an undivided whole, but such experience would seem to be entirely fortuitous, not something to be consciously achieved. Unity is natural, but that experience becomes shattered in history. For that very reason, the natural condition itself appears retrospectively as a historical moment.[209] The cause of the human condition, strictly construed, is at the same time its curse. In his prehistory, man is good because he is not evil, because he exists prior to (rather than beyond) good and evil, because he is fully ensconced within a natural order.[210] Natural goodness is the faint residue remaining after Rousseau's thorough deconstruction of human attributes. Is there some essential foundation to this being whose character seems wholly adventitious? Can anything positive be established on the basis of this cipher?

Melzer argues for a positive meaning of natural goodness, from which one might extrapolate correspondingly positive aspects of natural freedom. Because the naturally good man's "deepest self is absolute and self-sufficient," he is a being at rest. Consequently, he poses no threat to others and can be said to be good for them. Melzer then suggests that this man's natural goodness for others has a positive dimension as well, deriving from " 'the expansiveness' of his contentment and love of existence." "Under the right circumstances this natural expansiveness inclines men to a positive goodness or benevolence."[211] Here we might imagine a kind of "rapport" with others that would invest freedom with positive significance. But the argument is not persuasive. At most, the naturally good man avoids feelings of hatred because they are incompatible with his own intense self-love. It is hard to see how this "benevolence" rises above a posture of benign neglect. The very passage that Melzer cites (from *Reveries* VI) to document positive natural goodness refers to the solitary's "repugnance" for others, one that stops short of aversion, again for self-interested reasons. But, more revealingly, when Rousseau adverts to the effects on his "moral being" of acts of justice and injustice, he adopts the perspective of a *spectator* rather than an agent. *He* will be neither virtuous nor vicious; rather, his heart will register, from a distance, an emotional response to the deeds of others. There is something narcissistic and (literally) voyeuristic in this pose, and it seems both more finely wrought and less benevolent than the sentiment of pity attributed to natural man. Whereas the latter had a natural repugnance for the suffering of other men, the former admits to a repugnance for other men themselves.[212]

Melzer's exposition of Rousseau's reconstituted theory of self-love and self-preservation (achieved in juxtaposition to its classical-telelogical and Hobbesian-naturalistic antecedents) issues in something like the following conclusion: the positive experience of natural goodness depends on our separating ourselves "from all that is not part of us."[213] Our intense love of life ordains a neutrality or indifference toward others, which is a far cry from the posture of mutual antagonism found in the Hobbesian conception. As Melzer puts it, Rousseau's insight is that "a man exists not through his relation to God or to the essence of man but through a relation to himself." The sentiment of existence *is* our being, and the completion or perfection of our existence is located in our source rather than in our end.[214]

Contemplating the political ramifications of this doctrine, one appreciates how discordant the notion of a self-legislating subject is with Rousseau's passive ontology. Human satisfaction is not achieved by carving out a space for human agency with claims of right, nor by pursuing power after power. Its direction is inward rather than outward toward the world and others; its tendency is toward withdrawal and separation from all that is not a part of oneself.[215] Such a radical individualism stands opposed to reason and the common life the latter makes possible; it is bound up with private feeling, with what Melzer calls the "power of the inner."[216] It is difficult to see how the goodness of this power can be anything other than negative.

In the final analysis, Rousseau offers us a genealogy of the moral life, but no pragmatic guidance is forthcoming from that reconstruction. While the lack of content in Kant's transcendental conception of freedom has been widely and rightly remarked upon, there is a sense in which Rousseau's conception of freedom is similarly incompatible with any empirical account of human life, and thus equally vacuous.[217] The pure state of nature does seem to function in Rousseau's thought as a transcendental hypothesis, but it removes human beings even further than does Kantian freedom from the contingent and messy business of moral deliberation.

While nature may have made man happy and good, it is difficult to accept the thought that nature provides the sufficient condition for the good life. The pristine desires of man in the natural condition (as stipulated by Rousseau) require neither justification nor moderation, for they conflict neither among themselves nor with the desires of others. But that natural condition was itself fragile and contingent, and therefore essentially imperfect. Rousseau's fidelity to "naturalism" produces a political logic that culminates in impossible or inhuman procedures of renaturing. Once again Rousseau puts us in mind of Plato, and the *Republic*'s inhuman unity. Does not the extraordinary manipulation of the self that Rousseau's philosophy requires *on behalf of freedom* bespeak a terrible anomaly, and indicate the need for another view of human nature, and of freedom?

Notes

Abbreviations

CGP   *Considérations sur le gouvernement de Pologne*
CS   *Du contrat social*
DI   *Discours sur l'inégalité*
DSA   *Discours sur les sciences et les arts*
E   *Émile*
EOL   *Essai sur l'origine des langages*
EP   *Discours sur l'économie politique*
MG   *Manuscrit de genève*
R   *Les rêveries du promêneur solitaire*
O.C.   Jean-Jacques Rousseau, *Oeuvres complètes*, Bernard Gagnebin and Marcel Raymond, eds., 4 vols. (Paris: Pléiade, 1964–). Roman numeral after abbreviation indicates volume number. The works listed above, with the exception of EOL, are found in this edition.

Citations are normally first to the Pléiade edition of the *Complete Works,* followed by page reference to an English translation, if available. For example, EP 242/210 refers first to the Pléiade text and then to the corresponding page in the Roger Masters translation of *Political Economy.* Quotations in the text are from available translations in the editions cited below. I have occasionally modified them for greater literalism. Other translations are my own. I have used the following translations of Rousseau's works:

Émile or On Education, Allan Bloom, ed. (New York: Basic Books, 1979).
The First and Second Discourses, Roger Masters, ed. (New York: St. Martin's Press, 1964).
The First and Second Discourses and the Essay on the Origin of Languages, Victor Gourevitch, ed. (New York: Harper & Row, 1986), for EOL and preface to *Narcissus*.
On the Social Contract, with Geneva Manuscript and Political Economy, Roger Masters, ed. (New York: St. Martin's Press, 1978).
Politics and the Arts: Letter to D'Alembert on the Theatre, Allan Bloom, ed. (Ithaca, N.Y.: Cornell University Press, 1960).
The Reveries of the Solitary Walker, Charles Butterworth, ed. (New York: Harper & Row, 1979).

Chapter 1: The Problem of Freedom

1. "Behold all our faculties developed, memory and imagination in play, *amour-propre* aroused, reason rendered active, and the mind having almost reached the limit of the perfection of which it is susceptible. . . . Having formerly been free and independent, behold man, due to a multitude of new needs, subjected so to speak to all of nature and especially to his fellow men, whose slave he becomes in a sense even in becoming their master." DI 174–75/155–56. Cf. the following, from the *Social Contract*:

> This passage from the state of nature to the civil state produces a remarkable change in man, by substituting justice for instinct in his behavior and giving his actions the morality they previously lacked. Only then, when the voice of duty replaces physical impulse and right replaces appetite, does man, who until that time considered only himself, find himself forced to act upon other principles and to consult his reason before heeding his inclinations. Although in this state he deprives himself of several advantages given him by nature, he gains such great ones, his faculties are exercised and developed, his ideas broadened, his feelings ennobled, and his whole soul elevated to such a point that if the abuses of this new condition did not often degrade him beneath the condition he left, he ought ceaselessly to bless the happy moment that tore him away from it forever, and that changed him from a stupid, limited animal into an intelligent being and a man. CS I.8.1.

2. CS I.8.2–3.
3. CS I.4.6, I.7.8.
4. At the outer limit of sensible judgment, Bertrand Russell exclaimed that Hitler was an outgrowth of Rousseau. *History of Western Philosophy* (New York: Simon and Schuster, 1945), p. 790.
5. According to Arthur Melzer, "Rousseau is the first philosopher to have found in freedom and law as such the means to the most comprehensive human good, to men's highest as well as most elementary ends." "Rousseau's Moral Realism," *American Political Science Review* 77 (September 1983), 634.
6. Raymond Polin, *La Politique de la solitude* (Paris: Éditions Sirey, 1971), p. 5.
7. CS I.4.6.
8. Charles Taylor, *Hegel* (Cambridge: Cambridge University Press, 1974), p. 15. Cf. Leo Strauss, *Natural Right and History* (Chicago: University of Chicago Press, 1953), p. 279: "Rousseau may be said to have originated the philosophy of freedom."
9. Benjamin Constant, "De la Liberté des anciens comparée à celle des modernes," in his *Oeuvres* (Paris: Pléiade, 1964). See also Stephen T.

Holmes, *Benjamin Constant and the Making of Modern Liberalism* (New Haven: Yale University Press, 1984), pp. 79–103; cf. Thomas Hobbes, *Leviathan*, C. B. Macpherson, ed. (London: Penguin Books, 1968), ch. 21.

10. Jouvenel identifies the options and correctly rejects them in favor of a Rousseau who is sensitive to the need to distinguish different situations. "Essai sur la politique de Rousseau," in his edition of *Du contrat social* (Genève: Éditions Cheval-Ailé, 1947), p. 97.

11. See preface to *Narcissus*, pp. 104–05. This edition contains references to the Pléiade text.

12. John Plamenatz, "Ce qui ne signifie autre chose qu'on le forcera d'être libre," in Maurice Cranston and R. S. Peters, eds., *Rousseau and Hobbes: A Collection of Critical Essays* (Garden City, N.Y.: Anchor Books, 1972), p. 319.

13. *Letter to Malsherbes*, O.C. I, 1135–36. See also *Letter to Beaumont*, O.C. IV, 935–36, 945; and *Rousseau juge de Jean-Jacques*, O.C. I, 934. The most thorough examination of this principle is Arthur M. Melzer, *The Natural Goodness of Man: On the System of Rousseau's Thought* (Chicago: University of Chicago Press, 1990).

14. DI 181/163. Cf. O.C. I, 1019: "I love freedom; nothing is more natural. I was born free; . . . I detest servitude as the source of all the evils of the human condition." As Arthur Melzer notes, Rousseau's reduction of evil to the effects of dependence amounts to a radical simplification of the human problem. "Rousseau's Moral Realism," p. 634. Cf. Charles Taylor, *Philosophy and the Human Sciences: Philosophical Papers,* 2 vols. (Cambridge: Cambridge University Press, 1985), vol. 2, pp. 320–21.

15. "Préface d'un seconde lettre à Bordes," O.C. III, 105. Cf. O.C. I, 1115, "I studied man himself and I saw, or thought I saw, finally in his constitution the true System of nature. . . ."

16. The difficulty of making this conjunction of nature and freedom is evident in Alfred Cobban's struggle to grasp the foundation of Rousseau's thinking:

> [T]o appreciate the inspiration of [Rousseau's] political writings and understand their underlying unity, we must discover what more general principle is hidden behind his political thought. One might suggest that his ideal is freedom. Yet in the *Contrat Social* we find the primitive idea of freedom greatly restricted, and in fact natural liberty, as he recognizes, cannot exist once men have agreed to live together in a state. . . . We can hardly accept the idea of liberty as by itself a sufficient explanation of his political system. Indeed, the note which is sounded throughout Rousseau is the very opposite of unrestrained freedom. *Rousseau and the Modern State* (London: Allen

and Unwin, 1964), p. 142.

Cobban might have pursued his initial supposition. He allows himself to be diverted by the mistaken perception that Rousseau celebrates unrestrained freedom, as though he were the apostle of anarchy. The idea of liberty is indeed the explanation of Rousseau's political system.

17. The striking thesis of the *Second Discourse* is that solitude is the natural condition of man. Rousseau is driven to that conclusion because "freedom finds its perfect, immediate or natural expression only in solitude." Polin, *La Politique de la solitude*, p. 5.

It is unclear whether Rousseau's faith in freedom shapes his anthropology, or whether the latter independently establishes the primacy of freedom. If one begins with a conception of freedom at odds with bourgeois society, one is pushed back to the state of nature. If one investigates the state of nature and discovers freedom there, freedom can become a constitutive norm of humanity.

18. Cf. CS II.3.1 with *Lettre à Franquières*, O.C. IV, 1137.

19. Bertrand de Jouvenel, "A Discussion of Freedom," *Cambridge Journal* 6 (September 1953), 69.

20. Marvin Zetterbaum, "Self and Political Order," *Interpretation* 1 (Winter 1970). See also his "Self and Subjectivity in Political Theory," *Review of Politics* 44 (January 1982), 59–64.

21. On the problem of maintaining authority in a liberal democracy, see Robert Heineman, *Authority and the Liberal Tradition* (Durham, N.C.: Carolina Academic Press, 1984), pp. 13–32.

22. CS III.13.5.

23. Rousseau presents himself in the preface to the *Social Contract* as the citizen of a free state and a member of the sovereign. He pretends that his status as citizen is his warrant for thinking about questions of political right. However, he corrects himself, so to speak, in the *Confessions*, where he refers to the "right to think which I had by birth." O.C. I, 405. In the dedication to the *Second Discourse*, Rousseau gently indicates the philosophic distance that separates him from his fellow Genevans. While he acknowledges his good fortune at being "born among you," "born within your walls," he engages nonetheless in a reflective choice of birthplace and concludes that *Rome* is the model of all free peoples. DI 111–13/79–80.

24. O.C. III, 807. Regarding the basis of political obligation, Rousseau writes: "What more reliable basis could obligation among men have than the free engagement of the one who is obligated? One can dispute every other principle; one cannot dispute that one." Ibid., 806–07. Cf. CS I, preface.

25. Hannah Arendt, "What Is Freedom?" in *Between Past and Future: Six Exercises in Political Thought* (Cleveland: Meridian Books, 1963).

Arendt argues that the Western philosophical tradition has perpetuated a misunderstanding of the nature of freedom by locating it at the point where politics leaves off. I will argue that Rousseau is exempt from this criticism. While he engages contemporary metaphysical arguments involving freedom, his conception of freedom as independence maintains a consistent political focus.

26. Two writers in particular have noticed the significance of the notion of solitude for Rousseau's political thought: Polin, *La Politique de la solitude;* and Bronislaw Baczko, *Solitude et communauté* (Paris: Mouton, 1974).

27. CS IV.2.6. Cf. DI 144/117, 160/137, 162/140 on the "constancy" of the pure state of nature.

28. The speech of the Savoyard Vicar does, on the other hand, refer to two substances in the constitution of man, but that argument does not fit with the rest of the *Émile*, and it is an argument that Rousseau disowns. See E 229ff.; cf. Peter Emberley, "Rousseau Versus the Savoyard Vicar," *Interpretation* 14 (1986).

29. DI 143/115.

30. The contrast between natural man and civilized man is introduced in the frontispiece of the *Second Discourse* and emphasized at its conclusion. DI note P and 192/178–79. On the metaphysical-moral divide, see DI 142/114.

31. CS I.6.2, 9; CS II.1.1, II.3.2, II.4.7.

32. CS II.4.8.

33. CS III.1.2. Cf. CS III.1.8: "The government receives from the sovereign the orders that it gives to the people; and in order for the State to be in good equilibrium, all things considered, the product or power of the government must be equal to the product or power of the citizens, who are sovereigns on the one hand and subjects on the other." Mathematical metaphors aside, Rousseau's essential point is that the government must have sufficient power to carry out the will of the sovereign people.

34. CS IV.2.5.

35. F. M. Barnard likens these to "two models of public willing." "Patriotism and Citizenship in Rousseau: A Dual Theory of Public Willing." *Review of Politics* 46 (1984).

36. See MG I.1.1. On Rousseau's use of mechanical and other metaphors, see Michel Launay, "L'Art de l'écrivain dans le *Contrat social*," in *Études sur le Contrat social* de Jean-Jacques Rousseau (Paris: Société Belles Lettres, 1964).

37. Cf. Robert N. Bellah, Richard Madsen, William M. Sullivan, Ann Swidler, and Steven M. Tipton, *Habits of the Heart* (New York: Basic Books, 1984). Bellah derives his title from a remark of Tocqueville's that

was likely inspired by Rousseau.

38. Consider the example of the Spartan mother in E 249/40.

39. *Letter to d'Alembert*, in *Politics and the Arts*, Allan Bloom, ed. and trans. (Ithaca, N.Y.: Cornell University Press, 1960), p. 135. The translation and emphasis are my own.

40. Jouvenel, "Essai sur la politique de Rousseau," p. 100.

41. See, most significantly, Alasdair MacIntyre, *After Virtue*, 2nd ed. (Notre Dame, Ind.: Notre Dame University Press, 1984); and Michael Sandel, *Liberalism and the Limits of Justice* (Cambridge: Cambridge University Press, 1982).

42. See Mary Ann Glendon, *Rights Talk: The Impoverishment of Political Discourse* (New York: Free Press, 1991), which relies on a Rousseauian perspective to an even greater extent than the explicit references suggest.

43. I borrow the phrase from Hiram Caton, *The Politics of Progress: The Origins and Development of the Commercial Republic, 1600–1835* (Gainesville: University of Florida Press, 1988).

44. See Benjamin Barber, *The Conquest of Politics: Liberal Philosophy in Democratic Times* (Princeton: Princeton University Press, 1988), pp. 12–13.

45. Rousseau's complaint anticipates the grave injunction of Patrick Henry to the Virginia Ratifying Convention:

> You are not to inquire how your trade may be increased, nor how you are to become a great and powerful people, but how your liberties can be secured; for liberty ought to be the direct end of your government. Shall we imitate the example of those nations who have gone from a simple to a splendid Government? Are those nations more worthy of our imitation? What can make an adequate satisfaction to them for the loss they have suffered in attaining such a Government—for the loss of their liberty? Herbert Storing, ed., *The Complete Anti-Federalist* (Chicago: University of Chicago Press, 1981), V. 16.2.

Cf. Fabricius's rebuke of a corrupted Rome, and Rousseau's denunciation of "the political masterpiece of our century." DSA 14–15/45–46; preface to *Narcissus*, pp. 104–05.

46. O.C. III, 609.

47. *Leviathan*, ch. 17.

48. Ibid.

49. See E 347/252, "Let us extend *amour-propre* to other beings. . . ."

50. *Leviathan*, ch. 15.

51. Ibid., ch. 26.

52. Ibid., ch. 21.

53. Ibid., ch. 6.

54. DI 178/160.

55. DI note L 218/219–20.

56. DI 132/102.

57. DI note L 218/219–20. The crucial mistake of Hobbes and Locke is that they miss the ramifications of the isolated condition of men in the state of nature: having no dealings among themselves, they are disposed neither to fear nor to attack each other. On the other hand, Rousseau claims that dissociated individuals would be disposed toward pity if they encountered someone suffering. DI 156/133. All of the assumptions of Hobbes and Locke are predicated on the prior existence of social institutions.

58. See Maurice Cranston's introduction to his translation of the *Social Contract* (Hammondsworth, U.K.: Penguin Books, 1968), p. 42: "Is this a philosopher's concept of freedom? Perhaps; but is it not also like that of a footman?"

59. William T. Bluhm, *Force or Freedom? The Paradox in Modern Political Thought* (New Haven: Yale University Press, 1986), p. 83.

60. CS I.6.4.

61. Benjamin Constant, "De la Liberté des anciens comparée à celle des modernes."

62. DI 181/163.

63. See, inter alia, CS I.7.5, II.4 passim, IV.8.31 and note.

64. I will argue later that, upon examination, Rousseau's "political education" lacks the Spartan confidence in training the passions, in burning out of the soul its natural egoistic concern.

65. DSA 7/36.

66. DI 177–78/159–60 suggests that the crucial moment is the "official" founding of society. However, DI 171/151 reveals that once "commerce indépendant" is superseded, the fall into unfreedom is complete. It is apparent that the free man is the one who remains "sans liaisons." DI 160/137.

67. Preface to *Narcissus*; CS II.10.5; cf. O.C. I, 935.

68. Lester Crocker, *Rousseau's 'Social Contract': An Interpretive Essay* (Cleveland: Case Western Reserve University Press, 1968); cf. Jean Starobinski's review of Crocker's two-volume biography of Rousseau, *Jean-Jacques Rousseau: A New Interpretive Analysis of His Life and Work*, in which the thesis of Rousseau's totalitarian personality is advanced in painstaking detail. "Rousseau and Modern Tyranny," *New York Review of Books*, November 29, 1973, pp. 20–25.

69. See Patrick Riley, *The General Will Before Rousseau: The Transformation of the Divine into the Civic* (Princeton: Princeton University Press, 1986), p. 182 and ch. 5 passim. Cf. James Miller, *Rousseau: Dreamer of*

Democracy (New Haven: Yale University Press, 1984), pp. 196–97.

70. C. B. Macpherson, *The Real World of Democracy* (Toronto: CBC Publications, 1965), p. 29. Here and in the next few pages I am indebted to Joseph Masciulli's effort (in an unpublished paper) to categorize some of the critical responses to Rousseau.

71. Cf. Asher Horowitz, "Will, Community and Alienation in Rousseau's *Social Contract*," *Canadian Journal of Social and Political Theory* 10, no. 3 (Fall 1986).

72. The most prominent is surely Alexis de Tocqueville, *Democracy in America*, Phillips Bradley, ed. (New York: Vintage Books, 1945), vol. 2, pt. 2, pp. 333–39. Tocqueville argues that the insistence on equality menaces freedom; but he also suggests that it is the lure of wealth and luxury which first undermines it. While Rousseau did not formulate the problem precisely as Tocqueville did, he would certainly have recognized it.

73. Consider James Madison's discussion of the social effects of differences in the natural faculties of men, especially that of acquiring property. *The Federalist*, Edward Mead Earle, ed. (New York: Modern Library), no. 10.

74. Preface to *Narcissus*, p. 105.

75. See especially *The Spirit of the Laws*, Thomas Nugent, trans. (New York: Hafner Press, 1949), bks. 19–20.

76. DI 192/179.

77. Karl Marx, "On the Jewish Question," in *The Marx-Engels Reader*, Robert C. Tucker, ed. (New York: W. W. Norton, 1972), pp. 31–32.

78. See Bertrand de Jouvenel, "Rousseau the Pessimistic Evolutionist," *Yale French Studies* 28 (1961–62). Cf. Jouvenel's "Rousseau's Theory of the Forms of Government," in *Hobbes and Rousseau*, Maurice Cranston and R. S. Peters, eds. (Garden City, N.Y.: Anchor Books, 1972), pp. 495–96: "It is very significant that Rousseau declares so very forcefully as what 'is going to happen' the very reverse of what, at the doctrinal level, he has proclaimed 'ought to happen.'" See also Judith Shklar, *Men and Citizens*, 2nd ed. (Cambridge: Cambridge University Press, 1985), p. 1: "Rousseau was the last of the classical utopists. He was the last great political theorist to be utterly uninterested in history, past or future, the last also to judge and condemn without giving any thought to programs of action."

79. Riley, *The General Will Before Rousseau*, p. 248 (italics in original). The second quotation is from Norberto Bobbio, *The Future of Democracy*, Roger Griffin, trans. (Minneapolis: University of Minnesota Press, 1987), p. 43 (emphasis added).

80. "The world as it is demands resignation and prudence, and a

careful attention to a conscience that keeps us from causing harm to those around us. It offers no occasion for happiness and civic virtue." Shklar, *Men and Citizens*, p. 214.

81. Ibid., p. 183.

82. CS III.12.2, I.7.7.

83. Shklar, *Men and Citizens*, p. 184. Cf. Hilail Gildin, *Rousseau's Social Contract* (Chicago and London: University of Chicago Press, 1983), pp. 144–45.

84. Cf. Roger Masters, *The Political Philosophy of Rousseau* (Princeton: Princeton University Press, 1986), pp. 257–58.

85. "[T]he general will is not directed at political action which may involve prudential calculations. It is not concerned with government and policy. The general will is like the personal will, a state of mind, not a specific motive for action. The will creates, sets and strengthens character and standards of conduct. Specific courses of action are left to the determination of magistrates, even when war and peace are at stake." Shklar, *Men and Citizens*, p. 188.

86. Ibid., pp. 180ff.

87. Ibid., pp. 165–84.

88. Ibid., p. 18.

89. Jean Starobinski, *Jean-Jacques Rousseau: La Transparence et l'obstacle* (Paris: Presses Universitaires de France, 1957); "The Accuser and the Accused," *Daedalus* (Summer 1978), 41–58; "La Prosopopée de Fabricius," *Revue des sciences humaines* 161 (1976).

90. Jurgen Habermas, *Communication and the Evolution of Society*, Thomas McCarthy, trans. (Boston: Beacon Press, 1979).

91. See Russell L. Hanson, *The Democratic Imagination in America* (Princeton: Princeton University Press, 1985), p. 415.

92. For the most sustained critique of liberalism that is explicitly inspired by Rousseau, see Benjamin Barber, *Superman and Common Man* (New York: Praeger, 1971), ch. 2; *Strong Democracy: Participatory Politics for a New Age* (Berkeley: University of California Press, 1984), ch. 9; and, most recently, *The Conquest of Politics: Liberal Philosophy in Democratic Times* (Princeton: Princeton University Press, 1988), chs. 1, 8.

93. Barber, *Superman and Common Man*, p. 42. Barber quotes Lenin's statement that "While the state exists there is no freedom. When there is freedom, there will be no state." *State and Revolution* (New York, 1932), p. 79. Barber traces the "mechanistic" model of freedom, in which freedom is understood as unimpeded motion, to Hobbes's *Leviathan*, ch. 21. He expands on that discussion in *Strong Democracy*, pp. 26–45.

94. Madison, *The Federalist*, no. 10.

95. Commenting on the vision of the Port Huron Statement, Arnold

Kaufman observed: ". . . some have come to view participatory democracy as the single most important remedy for the accumulated ills of poverty, apathy, slavishness, inauthenticity, incompetence, manipulation, and, above all, powerlessness. These evils are the byproducts of a system that has, quite superbly, devoted an enormous amount of attention and energy to the task of mastering the problem of acute economic scarcity without destroying social order. But those who operated that system have tended to ignore what should have been the overarching purpose of all the furious activity; the promotion of a truly human existence for each and every human being. In demanding something radically different, advocates of participatory democracy have tried to replace Madison's pessimistic assumptions (on which he reared his constitutional proposals) with an affirmation of man's potentialities for creative, moral existence." "Participatory Democracy: Ten Years Later," in *The Bias of Pluralism*, William Connolly, ed. (New York: Atherton Press, 1969), p. 203. Cf. James Miller, *Democracy Is in the Streets* (New York: Simon and Schuster, 1987), pp. 96–97.

96. See John P. Diggins, *The Lost Soul of American Politics* (New York: Basic Books, 1984); Harvey C. Mansfield, Jr., "Constitutional Government: The Soul of Modern Democracy," *The Public Interest* 74 (1987).

97. See Marshall Berman, *The Politics of Authenticity* (New York: Athenaeum, 1972).

98. Cf. Miller, *Rousseau: Dreamer of Democracy*, p. 189 and ch. 7 passim.

99. Allan Bloom, "Introduction," in *Émile*, Allan Bloom, trans. (New York: Basic Books, 1979), p. 5. See also Bloom's "Jean-Jacques Rousseau," in *History of Political Philosophy*, Leo Strauss and Joseph Cropsey, eds., 2nd ed. (Chicago: Rand McNally, 1972).

100. Quoted in Miller, *Democracy Is in the Streets*, p. 97.

101. Sheldon Wolin, *The Presence of the Past: Essays on the State and the Constitution* (Baltimore and London: Johns Hopkins University Press, 1989), pp. 189–91.

102. See William Connolly, *Political Theory and Modernity* (Oxford: Basil Blackwell, 1988), ch. 3, "Rousseau: Docility Through Citizenship."

103. Wolin, *The Presence of the Past*, p. 191. The term "pluralistic dissensus" is taken from Giovanni Sartori, *The Theory of Democracy Revisited* (Chatham, N.J.: Chatham House, 1987), vol. I, p. 92.

104. CS I, preface.

105. Cf. *Lettre à M. de Franquières*, O.C. IV, 1146.

106. MG I.2.14–15.

107. EP 251/216; CS II.7.7–8.

108. Bloom, "Introduction" to *Émile*, p. 6.

109. CS III.15.3.

110. Ibid. On this score, Rousseau's attitude is remarkably similar to the perspective of the contemporary "rational choice" theorist of politics. The latter's principal assumption is that self-interest is a given and that politics therefore consists in the counting of preferences. Rousseau seems to agree that the passions and opinions associated with self-interest are not amenable to a process of refinement and enlargement, and certainly not through the medium of representation. Deliberation among competing concerns would only hold up a mirror to an incorrigible pluralism. See William H. Riker, *Liberalism Against Populism* (San Francisco: W. H. Freeman, 1982).

111. CS III.11.5.

112. O.C. I, 828. See Melzer, *The Natural Goodness of Man*, pp. 54–85.

113. CS II.6.10.

114. See Robert Wokler, "Rousseau's Two Concepts of Liberty," in *Lives, Liberties and the Public Good: New Essays in Political Theory for Maurice Cranston*, George Feaver and Frederick Rosen, eds. (New York: St. Martin's Press, 1989), pp. 84–85. While CS IV.2.2 distinguishes deliberation from mere acclamation, the sequel shows quite convincingly that Rousseau envisions an exercise in morality rather than in politics. A vote is a register of who allowed their private wills to prevail and who succeeded in subordinating them. CS IV.2.8.

115. Cf. James Q. Wilson, "Interests and Deliberation in the American Republic," *Political Science and Politics* 23, no. 4 (December 1990), 559.

Chapter 2: The Natural Paradigm

1. DSA 7/36.

2. CS I.6.4.

3. DI 178/160. Cf. DI 177/159, "All ran to meet their chains thinking they secured their freedom."

4. DI 123/93.

5. DI 135/105.

6. DI 135/106. Notice that Nature is portrayed, by turns, as hospitable and inhospitable to man. On the one hand, his needs are readily satisfied; on the other hand, Nature subjects man to the law of the survival of the fittest. However, both views of Nature establish the same point: natural man has the wherewithal of an independent existence.

7. DI 139/111.

8. DI 152/128.

9. "Although it may behoove Socrates and minds of his stamp to

acquire virtue through reason, the human race would have perished long ago if its preservation had depended only on the reasonings of its members." DI 157/133–34. Although the immediate context of this passage is an argument on behalf of man's natural sentiment of pity, the sequel shows that mutual indifference is far more instrumental in keeping the peace.

10. See DI 219/222, note O: "I say that in our primitive state, in the true state of nature, *amour-propre* does not exist; for each particular man regarding himself as the sole spectator to observe him, as the sole being in the universe to take an interest in him, and as the sole judge of his own merit, it is not possible that a sentiment having its source in comparisons he is not capable of making could spring up in his soul."

11. Allan Bloom, "Introduction," in *Émile*, Allan Bloom, trans. (New York: Basic Books, 1979), p. 14.

12. DI 142/114–15.

13. DI 162/140.

14. DI 219/221–22.

15. "L'homme vraiement libre ne veut ce qu'il peut, et fait ce qu'il lui plait. Voilà ma maxime fondamentale." E 309/84. Cf. R 1059/83; and *Lettres écrits de la montagne*, O.C. III, 841–42. In this section I make use of arguments from *Émile*, especially book II, which recapitulates much of the *Second Discourse*.

16. "His modest needs are so easily found at hand." DI 144/117.

17. DI 144/117.

18. DI 141/113.

19. Ibid.

20. DI 126/96; 160/137.

21. DI 161–62/139–40.

22. In an editoral note, Starobinski refers us to a similar conclusion in *Émile* IV: "Every attachment is a sign of insufficiency: if each of us would have no need of others, he would scarcely dream of uniting with them." O.C. III, 1337.

23. Edna Kryger argues for a different view of the relation of needs and freedom. She suggests the experience of need triggers the power of choice and thereby constitutes "the first moment of freedom." Desire is the second moment. For Kryger, there is no *external* cause of these experiences. Rather, it is man's own indeterminacy that constitutes the "void" which must be filled. In this view, the experience of need derives from man's very constitution; desire is the stimulus to invent ways to satisfy needs. Man can be regarded as his own creator since he determines his mode of being free. According to Kryger, man is the author of "true freedom and intelligence." *La Notion de la liberté chez Rousseau*

et ses repercussions sur Kant (Paris: Librairie A. G. Nizet, 1978), pp. 19–20.

But this account of freedom foists on Rousseau a distinction between "true freedom" and an ersatz freedom that he did not feel compelled to make in the *Discourse*. Moreover, it ignores the distinction that Rousseau does emphasize, between true and false *needs*. One might expect to find a coincidence of "true freedom" and true needs; but such a conjunction would occur in the state of nature. Furthermore, Kryger's emphasis on the internal cause of the activation of freedom overlooks Rousseau's explicit statement: "Everything seems to remove savage man from the temptation and means of ceasing to be savage. His imagination suggests nothing to him; his heart asks nothing of him. His modest needs are so easily found at hand, and he is so far from the degree of knowledge necessary for desiring to acquire greater knowledge, that he can have neither foresight nor curiosity." DI 144/117. In the sequel Rousseau alludes for the first time to the sentiment of existence. The latter, we saw, is prior to care and the true experience of need. It is a privileged moment that belies any natural restlessness of the human faculties.

24. E 303–04/80, quoted in O.C. III, 1320.

25. Rousseau repeatedly affirmed the importance of independence for goodness and happiness. See E 309-10/85: "Before prejudices and human institutions have corrupted our natural inclinations, the happiness of children, like that of men, consists in the use of their freedom. . . . Whoever does what he wants is happy if he is self-sufficient; this is the case of man living in the state of nature." R 1059/83: "As long as I act freely, I am good and do only good." *Lettres à Malsherbes*, O.C. I, 1137: "The condition in which I am placed is the only one where man can live good and happy, since it is the most independent of others, and the only one where one never finds one's own advantage in the necessity of denying another's." Cf. *Confessions*, O.C. I, 56, where Rousseau describes the "great maxim of morality" as "to avoid situations which put our duties in opposition to our interests," with CS I. preface, which expresses the intention to reconcile "justice" and "utility."

26. E 309/84; 311/85.

27. Cf. "L'Influence des climats sur la civilisation," O.C. III, 529: "Man cannot be self-sufficient; his needs, which are always being reborn, place on him the necessity of finding means outside himself to provide for them. He depends always on things and often on his fellow men. We feel this dependence more or less according to the extent and nature of our needs, and it is in these same needs, the more or less

great, the more or less felt, that we must seek the principle of all human action." In this fragment Rousseau seems to deny the possibility of self-sufficiency altogether. But in *Émile* he would draw the crucial distinction between dependence on men and dependence on things. O.C. IV 311/85. The fragment quoted here does nonetheless underscore the point that dependence is aggravated by needs which are great and strongly felt. The *Discourse* shows that these are the "moral needs" rather than the "physical needs," which is to say, the needs that are born of *amour-propre*.

28. Rousseau consistently defended the goodness of this affirmation. If man is only left free, "he will never do wrong." *Lettre à Christophe de Beaumont*, O.C. IV, 943.

29. Recall that Émile is to be a savage bred for the city. E 662/333.

30. William Galston has drawn attention to the ambiguity of "freedom" in Rousseau's reflections in his *Kant and the Problem of History* (Chicago and London: University of Chicago Press, 1975), pp. 123–27. At first glance freedom appears to separate man and animal; but it turns out that freedom separates man and man, that is, natural man and civil man, or original man and contemporary man. The crucial thesis of the *Second Discourse* is that the uniquely human quality adds nothing significant to the constitution of "l'homme physique," which is Rousseau's term for man purged of metaphysical and moral attributes.

31. DI 141–42/114.

32. In the *Social Contract* Rousseau does take such internal constraints more seriously, dubbing the impulsions of appetite as "slavery." CS I.8.3. See Robert Wokler, "Rousseau's Perfectibilian Libertarianism," in *The Idea of Freedom*, Alan Ryan, ed. (Oxford: Oxford University Press, 1979), p. 237. However, in the *Second Discourse*, when Rousseau extols the soul of natural man, he values not its "spirituality" but its simplicity, order, and health—in a word, its naturalness. In the pure state of nature, the "impulse of appetite alone" is the operative principle of *amour de soi*. As long as the natural equilibrium of power and desire obtains, man has no longing for anything that would require an enduring relation with another. Thus the soul of natural man is well ordered because natural men are free *of one another*. As the tutor remarks of Émile at the end of his first education, "He considers himself without regard to others and finds it good that others do not think of him. He demands nothing of anyone and believes he owes nothing to anyone. He is alone in human society; he counts on himself alone. . . . He has a healthy body, agile limbs, a precise and unprejudiced mind, a heart that is free and without passions." E 488/208. On the "first education" see the end of bk. II.

33. Wokler, "Rousseau's Perfectibilian Libertarianism," p. 236. Wokler also observes that "Rousseau's conception of liberty . . . introduces no substantive aim or purpose to which freedom is or ought to be directed and neither entails nor implies any moral claim about the manner in which it should be exercised." Ibid., p. 237. I will return to this latter point.

34. Particularly in "Des Cannibales," in *Essais* (Paris: Pléiade, 1962), I.31.

35. See Jean Starobinski's commentary at O.C. III, 144 n. 3.

36. Indeed, note J puts the whole question of the human nature in a new light. Rousseau informs us that mankind has undergone a physical as well as a moral evolution: "And without accepting in blind faith the reports of Herodotus and Ctesias, one can at least draw from them this very likely opinion: if one had been able to make good observations in those ancient times when various peoples followed ways of life with greater differences between them than peoples do today, one would have noted in the shape and habits of the body, much more striking varieties." DI 208/203. He suggests that the travelers who encountered orangutans might have been in the presence of natural men who remained in "the primitive state of nature," and ". . . had not acquired any degree of perfection." DI/208/204.

> [I]n the description of these supposed monsters are found striking conformities with the human species and lesser differences than those which could be assigned between one man and another. In these passages one does not see the reasons the authors have for refusing to give the animals in question the name of savage men; but it is easy to guess that it is due to their stupidity and also because they did not talk: weak reasons for those who know that although the organ of speech is natural to man, speech itself is nonetheless not natural to him, and who know to what point his perfectibility can have raised civil man above his original state. DI 210/207.

37. "[I]t is well demonstrated that the monkey is not a variety of man, not only because he is deprived of the faculty of speech, but especially because it is certain that his species does not have the faculty of perfecting itself, which is the specific characteristic of the human species." DI 211/208.

38. "But if the difficulties surrounding all these questions should leave some room for dispute on this difference between man and animal, there is another very specific quality that distinguishes them and about which there can be no dispute: the faculty of self-perfection, a faculty which, with the aid of circumstances, successively develops all the

others, and resides among us as much in the species as in the individual." DI 142/114.

39. DI 142/115.

40. Its cursory treatment notwithstanding, the same can be said of freedom of the will: "Thus dissolute men abandon themselves to excesses which cause them fever and death, because the mind depraves the senses and because the will still speaks when nature is silent." DI 141/114.

41. See Leo Strauss, *Natural Right and History* (Chicago and London: University of Chicago Press, 1953), pp. 265–66; cf. pp. 171–74, 280–81.

42. Victor Goldschmidt, *Anthropologie et politique: Les Principes du système de Rousseau* (Paris: Vrin, 1974), pp. 273–94, esp. pp. 292–94. Cf. Strauss, *Natural Right and History*, pp. 265–66:

> Rousseau questions . . . the traditional definition of man. Accepting the view that brutes are machines, he suggests that there is only a difference of degree between men and the brutes in regard to understanding or that the laws of mechanics explain the formation of ideas. It is man's power to choose and his consciousness of his freedom which cannot be explained physically and which proves [*sic*] the spirituality of his soul. . . . Yet, whatever Rousseau might have believed concerning this subject, the argument of the *Second Discourse* is not based on the assumption that freedom of the will is the essence of man, or, more generally expressed, the argument is not based on dualistic metaphysics. Rousseau goes on to say that the cited definition of man is subject to dispute, and he therefore replaces "freedom" by "perfectibility"; no one can deny the fact that man is distinguished from the brutes by perfectibility. Rousseau means to put his doctrine on the most solid ground; he does not want to make it dependent on dualistic metaphysics, which is exposed to "insoluble objections," to "powerful objections," or to "insurmountable difficulties." The argument of the *Second Discourse* is meant to be acceptable to materialists as well as to others. It is meant to be neutral with regard to the conflicts between materialism and antimaterialism, or to be "scientific" in the present-day sense of the term.

43. "*Perfectibility*, social virtues, and the other faculties that natural man had received in potentiality could never develop by themselves; in order to develop they needed the chance combination of several foreign causes which might never have arisen and without which he would have remained eternally in his primitive condition." DI 162/140.

44. DI 211/209. Masters's note refers to Aristotle's *Politics* 1253a3–5.

45. DI 212–13/211.

46. DI 133/103–4.

47. Cf. Lionel Gossman, "Time and History in Rousseau," *Studies on Voltaire and the Eighteenth Century* 30 (1964).

48. Note J, DI 208/203. Cf. Preface to *Narcissus*, p. 106, note:

I have noticed that at present a great many petty maxims hold sway in the world which seduce simple minds with a sham semblance of philosophy and are, besides, very handy for cutting off discussions in an authoritative and peremptory tone without having to consider the issue. One of them is "Men are everywhere subject to the same passions; everywhere *amour-propre* and interest guide them; hence they are everywhere the same." When Geometricians make an assumption which, argument by argument, leads them to an absurd conclusion, they retrace their steps, and so prove the assumption false. The same method, applied to the maxim in question, would readily show its absurdity.

In the *Réponse au roi de Pologne,* O.C. III, 42–43, Rousseau alludes to some considerations raised by D'Alembert apropos the thesis of the *First Discourse*: "I ought not to pass over here in silence a considerable objection that has already been made to me by a philosopher: Is it not, he tells me, to climate, to temperament, to the want of something, to the economy of the government, to Customs, to Laws, to any cause other than the Sciences that one must attribute this difference that is often observed in the *moeurs* of different countries and at different times?" Rousseau indicated that D'Alembert's question raised significant issues which required more extensive study. He fulfills the mandate in the *Second Discourse.* See also "L'Influence des climats sur la civilisation," *Fragments politiques,* O.C. III, 529–33.

49. Preface to *Narcissus*, p. 106, note.

50. DI 142–43/115; my emphasis.

51. DI 142/114.

52. DI 144/117.

53. "He had, in instinct alone, everything necessary for him to live in the state of nature." DI 152/127–28.

54. DI 125–26/95.

55. Cf. John Charvet, who makes this feature of natural man the key to his interpretation of Rousseau's thought. *The Social Problem in the Philosophy of Rousseau* (Cambridge: Cambridge University Press, 1974).

56. DI 152/128. In *Émile* Rousseau reinforces the point that natural

man and the child who resembles him are premoral. See the citations in O.C. III, 152, n. 2.

57. DI 152–53/128.

58. DI 152/127; cf. O.C. III, 152, n. 1.

59. DI 154/130, 157/133.

60. DI 157/133; cf. note O.

61. DI 157/133–34.

62. DI 157–62/134–40.

63. DI 143/116.

64. E 304/81. But natural man's imagination is dormant. DI 144/117.

65. E 304/80. "Only in this original state are power and desire in equilibrium and man is not unhappy." Notice that Rousseau's critique of reason reprises the argument against enlightenment that he launched in the *First Discourse* and defended in a series of replies to critics. Cf. *Réponse au roi de Pologne*, O.C. III, 36: "Science, however beautiful, however sublime, is not made for man; . . . his mind is too limited to make much progress in it, and his heart too full of passions to keep him from putting it to bad use." Cf. also ibid., 54: "There is another, reasonable sort of ignorance which consists in restricting one's curiosity to the scope of the faculties one has received."

66. E 305/81. Cf. 308–09/83–84.

67. DI 158/135.

68. Rousseau again dramatizes his point by assimilating the human to the animal condition and extends Buffonian arguments to natural man himself. On the use of Buffon's "Discourse on the Nature of Animals," see O.C. III, 158, n. 2. Starobinski remarks, "Rousseau follows very closely the famous pages of the 'Discourse on the Nature of Animals,' but he attributes to savage man the elementary happiness that Buffon reserved to animals alone."

69. DI 192/179, 152/127.

70. DI 136/107.

71. DI 138/110.

72. DI 157/134; 152–59/128–37.

73. DI 159–60/137.

74. DI 142/114–15.

75. DI 161/138.

76. Yves Simon has appreciated that Rousseau's idea of nature is "all invading" and "refractory to any inner differentiation, and in its passionate unity it confounds the picture of a state which is simply native. Thus primitive life acquires all the privileges of the perfect life, an initial condition is treated as a terminal condition, and the existence of the

blessed is confounded with the existence of savages. Finally, this exaltation of primitive life goes hand in hand with an exaltation of the irrational. In a certain sense, nature is opposed to reason, and it is from nature understood in this sense that Rousseau's idea of natural goodness stems. Rousseau's naturalism comprises a theory of the primacy of those emotions and instincts which man shares with the animals." *Freedom and Community* (New York: Fordham University Press, 1968), p. 151.

77. DI 161–62/139–40.

78. In this way Rousseau overthrows the traditional Christian view of freedom as a presupposition of morality. As Aram Vatarian explains, "The main role of such freedom was to render a culpable humanity responsible for its faults, thereby dissociating God from the presence of evil in the world." "Necessity or Freedom? The Politics of an Eighteenth Century Metaphysical Debate," *Studies in Eighteenth Century Culture* 7 (1978). According to Rousseau, since reason and morality come to light as manifestations of disorder, far from being the solution, they are part of the human problem. The traditional teaching allowed man a metaphysical and moral freedom while subjecting him everywhere in the world to a punishing discipline. Rousseau will offer a new paradigm of freedom that cannot be exploited to prop up the tyranny of church or state. As we shall subsequently see, natural freedom will point toward a democratic freedom that allows men to recoup their liberty from oppressors, whether spiritual or temporal.

79. CS I.6.1.

80. DI 176/158.

81. DI 177/159–60.

82. DI 178/160.

83. DI 179/162.

84. DI 180–81/162.

85. DI 181/163.

86. Rousseau quotes an ancient source to underscore his point that politics is a means to the end of freedom: "'If we have a prince', said Pliny to Trajan, 'it is so that he may preserve us from having a master.'" DI 181/164 and Masters's n. 44. We must keep this maxim in mind when we turn to the *Social Contract*, for it states two significant political rules: peoples must in fact have government or "chiefs," but never masters; and government is justified only as a means to freedom.

87. DI 193/178–79. Cf. CS I, preface.

88. DI 181/164.

89. William Galston argues in favor of Aristotle's agreement (*Politics* VII, 1327b25–31) with Rousseau on this score, in that the former "appears to redefine natural slavery as the lack of desire to preserve

one's independence." *Kant and the Problem of History*, pp. 106–07.

90. DI 181/164–65.

91. DI 184/168.

92. CS I.5.1.

93. DI 193/179, and 144/117.

94. DI 123/93.

95. Quoted in O.C. III, 1295.

96. Charvet, *The Social Problem*, p. 36.

97. Ibid., pp. 91–93.

98. Ibid., p. 107.

99. DI 171/151.

100. DI 162/140.

101. I am persuaded by the arguments of Heinrich Meier, "*The Discourse on the Origin and Foundations of Inequality among Men:* On the Intention of Rousseau's Most Philosophical Work," *Interpretation* 16, no. 2 (Winter 1988–89), 213–16.

102. DI 171/151.

103. DI note P, 220/224.

104. DI 220/223.

105. See the critique of Philopolis (Charles Bonnet), reprinted in O.C. III, 1383–86.

106. Cf. DSA 8/37; DI 169/148.

107. See the discussion of the golden age in the context of the *Essay on Language*, ch. 4, below.

108. See the discussion of the great soul of the Legislator, ch. 3, below.

109. E 304/81.

110. See Jean-Marie Salien, "Dialectique de la raison et des passions dans la pensée de Jean-Jacques Rousseau," *International Studies in Philosophy* 5, no. 12, (1980).

111. DI 152/127–28; cf. *Letter to Beaumont*, O.C. IV, 936.

112. *Réponse au roi de Pologne*, O.C. III, 34.

113. DI preface 125–26/95–96.

114. E 310–11/85.

115. CS I.8.3.

116. See Patrick Gardiner's argument that Rousseau conceived a type of freedom "radically different from that available to men living in a pre-social condition which . . . consisted not in being able simply to gratify spontaneous natural impulses as and when they arose, but rather in a power to order and restrain particular passions or desires in accordance with ethical values which the individual inwardly accepted and sought to realize in his life. Freedom so understood is termed

'moral liberty.'" "Rousseau on Liberty," in *Conceptions of Liberty in Political Theory*, J. N. Gray and Z. Pelcynski, eds. (London: Athlone Press, 1984), p. 91.

117. See DI 142/113–14; CS I.8.3; and Patrick Riley, *The General Will Before Rousseau* (Princeton: Princeton University Press, 1986), pp. 241–50, which offers a brief but decisive treatment of the question of will qua moral causality in Rousseau.

118. Ernst Cassirer, *The Question of Jean-Jacques Rousseau*, Peter Gay, trans. (Bloomington: Indiana University Press, 1954), p. 96.

119. MG I.2.2.

120. MG I.2.7. Cf. O.C. III, 841–42, where Rousseau contrasts independence and freedom and asserts that "there is no freedom without Laws."

121. Immanuel Kant, "Idea for a Universal History," in *Kant: On History*, L. W. Beck, ed. (Indianapolis: Bobbs-Merrill, 1974), p. 16. See Richard Velkley, *Freedom and the End of Reason: On the Moral Foundations of Kant's Critical Philosophy* (Chicago and London: University of Chicago Press, 1989), p. 11.

122. Cassirer, *The Question of Jean-Jacques Rousseau*, p. 54.

123. Ibid., pp. 55–56.

124. See E 652/325.

125. O.C. III, 842.

126. R 1059–60/83–84; cf. the the same thought expressed in a different context at O.C. III, 841–42. Independence remains the criterion for all "true freedom."

127. E 604/293.

128. DI 144/117.

129. MG I.2.7.

130. As argued by André Ravier, *L'Éducation de l'homme nouveau* (Paris: Issoudon, 1941), ch. 9.

131. E 455/184–85.

132. E 586/280.

133. O.C. III, 475, emphasis added.

134. CS IV.8.17.

135. See Immanuel Kant, "Conjectural Beginning of Human History," in Beck, *Kant,* pp. 63–68.

136. DI 144/117.

137. R 1046/68–69.

138. Allan Bloom, "Jean-Jacques Rousseau," in *History of Political Philosophy*, Leo Strauss and Joseph Cropsey, eds., 2nd ed. (Chicago: Rand McNally, 1972), p. 532.

139. Marc Plattner, *Rousseau's State of Nature* (DeKalb: Northern

Illinois University Press, 1979), p. 112. See also n. 25, this chapter.

140. See Immanuel Kant, *Groundwork of the Metaphysic of Morals*, H. J. Paton, trans. (New York: Harper & Row, 1964), pp. 72–83, 84–86.

141. Cassirer, *The Question of Jean-Jacques Rousseau*, p. 105.

142. DI 184/168: "Freedom is a gift they receive from nature by being men."

143. DI 162/140.

144. On Kant's view of nature, see Susan Meld Shell, *The Rights of Reason* (Toronto: University of Toronto Press, 1980), pp. 11–32, especially p. 15. Shell observes that "Rousseau presents human liberty and natural necessity as perfectly compatible" (p. 26).

145. DI 159–60/137.

146. DI 152 161/127, 139.

147. Jean Starobinski has suggested that Rousseau's first stage of the state of nature is itself an atemporal, metaphysical notion. *Études sur le Contrat social*, cited in Kryger, *La Notion de la liberté*, p. 26. I would amend the point to state that Rousseau eschews metaphysics in favor of a genealogy of man, and in so doing he says something novel about freedom. Its real significance is political rather than metaphysical.

148. DI 136/107; cf. 193/179: "The savage lives within himself; the sociable man, always outside himself, knows how to live only in the opinions of others." After a discipline of his sentiments, Émile achieves the same result and is "always entirely self-possessed." E 667/336.

In his note accompanying the passage cited above from the *Discourse*, Rousseau recounts the story of a savage in captivity who risked his life in an extraordinary bargain to regain his freedom. DI note F, end. The point appears to be that freedom is a higher good than life itself. Cf. DI 181 ff./164 ff. and Strauss, *Natural Right and History*, p. 278.

149. DI 133/104.

150. The solitary walker returns to the passive freedom that Rousseau derives from the natural condition. R 1059/83–84. Apparently one can return to the condition of freedom by a *rentrer en soi*, not a going back in time but a turning within. The natural mode *is* independence, and it can be regained without returning to the forest, by a *rentrer en soi*, a rediscovery of the laws of the heart, the *réalité intérieure* or the sentiment of existence. Bernard Groethuysen has shown that, for Rousseau, "Nature and freedom are two aspects of the same idea. To return to nature is to return to freedom." *Jean-Jacques Rousseau* (Paris: Gallimard, 1949), p. 53.

151. Pierre Manent, *Naissances de la politique moderne* (Paris: Payot, 1977), p. 11.

152. Arthur Melzer has argued that what leads Rousseau to absolutize either the natural or the conventional existence is the conclusion

that unity of soul is the essential ingredient of happiness. Arthur Melzer, "Rousseau and the Problem of Bourgeois Society," *American Political Science Review* 74, no. 4 (December 1980). I have shown above that Rousseau tends to identify freedom and happiness. Let us say that freedom is the sine qua non of happiness. If unity alone were sufficient, how could we explain Rousseau's tortuous efforts at conceiving civil unity in freedom? While unity of soul is indeed of cardinal importance to Rousseau, the *qualité d'homme* is said to be freedom. I read Rousseau as maintaining that real unity cannot exist without it. Melzer seems to adopt this view in a subsequent essay: "Men's ever-shifting relations of domination and servitude destroy their inner unity and strength and make them cowardly, spiteful, vain, and deceitful. Thus freedom from dependence on others is needed to maintain man's natural health of soul . . . ." "Rousseau's Moral Realism," *American Political Science Review* 77 (September 1983), 634. Cf. Melzer's *The Natural Goodness of Man*, pp. 102–04.

153. Arthur Lovejoy, "The Supposed Primitivism of Rousseau's Discourse on Inequality," in *Essays in the History of Ideas* (New York: Capricorn Books, 1960); Cassirer, *The Question of Jean-Jacques Rousseau.*

154. On the latter concept see Isaiah Berlin, "Two Concepts of Liberty," in *Four Essays on Liberty* (London and New York: Oxford University Press, 1969).

155. "I call positive education that which tends to form the spirit prematurely and to give the child understanding of the duties of an adult. I call negative education that which tends to perfect the organs, instruments of our understanding, before giving us these understandings and which prepares for reason by the exercise of the senses. Negative education is not idle, far from it. It does not produce the virtues, but it prevents vices; it does not teach the truth, but it prevents error." *Lettre à Beaumont*, O.C. IV, 945.

156. DI 170–73/150–53.

157. John Plamenatz, *Man and Society*, 2 vols. (London: Longman, 1963), vol. 1, 381–82.

158. Ibid., pp. 382–83.

159. DI 143/116 and note K.

Chapter 3: The Achievement of Democratic Freedom

1. E 311/85; cf. 362–63/119–20, "There is no subjection so perfect as that which keeps the appearance of freedom," and CS II.7.10, ". . . so that the peoples, subjected to the laws of the state as they are subjected to those of nature, and recognizing the same power in the formation of man and in that of the city, obey freely and wear docilely

the yoke of public happiness."

2. CGP 955.

3. MG I.2.2. The most accessible meaning of the term "men as they are" appears in the second chapter of the first version of the *Social Contract*, "On the General Society of the Human Race." Intended as a reply to Diderot's article "Natural Right" in the *Encyclopedia*, Rousseau rejects Diderot's version of the "general will of the human race" and clarifies his own. He here unites the topics of laws as they can be and men as they are. In the final text, Rousseau does not attend to this question until the second book, where he devotes chapters to the Legislator and the people. The Legislator's activity is the bridge between men as they are and laws as they can be. In the *Social Contract* Rousseau takes up the latter issue first, outlining the community of right before asking, "What people then is suited for legislation?" CS II.8.5.

4. MG I.2.3.

5. MG I.2.4.

6. CS I.4.1: "No man has natural authority over his fellow man." See also Rousseau's statement that civil men lose their natural freedom, which was limited only by their power. CS I.8.2.

7. Cf. CS I.1.1. Rousseau routinely uses these loaded terms to emphasize the calamity of social dependence.

8. Note that Rousseau denied that this antagonism existed in the pristine natural condition. See DI 193/180: ". . . this is not the original condition of man . . . it is the spirit of society alone."

9. CS I.6.1–2.

10. CS I.6.3–8. These six paragraphs were added in the final version of the *Social Contract*.

11. "It is false that in the state of independence, reason leads us to cooperate for the common good out of a perception of our own interest. Far from there being an alliance between private interest and the general good, they are mutually exclusive in the natural order of things, and social laws are a yoke that each wants to impose on the other without having to bear himself." MG I.2.10.

12. Preface to *Narcissus*, pp. 104–05.

13. DI note I, 202/194.

14. MG I.2.3.

15. MG I.5.1.

16. CS I.5.1. Rousseau employs the organic metaphor "body politic" only to emphasize the distinction between an aggregation and an association. He knows very well that it is imprecise. Indeed, a true association is best described as an artificial being rather than an organism, for its foundation cannot be simply natural.

If the general society did exist somewhere other than in the systems of philosophers, it would be . . . a moral being with qualities separate and distinct from those of the particular beings constituting it, somewhat like chemical compounds which have properties that do not belong to any of the elements composing them. . . . The public good or ill would not merely be the sum of private goods and ills as in a simple aggregation, but would lie in the liaison uniting them. It would be greater than this sum, and public felicity, far from being based on the happiness of private individuals, would itself be the source of this happiness. MG I.2.9.

Michel Launay has noted that Rousseau uses three metaphors for political association in the *Social Contract*: the first is organic, the second mechanical (political machine), the third architectural (political edifice). "L'Art de l'écrivain dans le *Contrat social*," in *Études sur le contrat social* (Paris: Société Belles Lettres, 1964).

17. Cf. David Braybrooke, "The Insoluble Problem of the Social Contract," which adopts a "rational choice" perspective and outlines in a sophisticated manner the dilemma on which Rousseau meditated in the *Geneva Manuscript*. *Dialogue* 15 (March 1976).

18. CS I.7.7.

19. "Renonçant à la qualité d'homme, doit être traité comme un être dénaturé." Denis Diderot, "Droit naturel," in *Political Writings of Rousseau*, C. E. Vaughan, ed. (New York: John Wiley and Sons, 1962 rpt.; 1915) vol. 1, pp. 430–31. Rousseau would later invest Diderot's categories—general will, *qualité d'homme, être dénaturé*—with his own meanings. See Edna Kryger, *La notion de la liberté chez Rousseau* (Paris: Librairie A. G. Nizet, 1978), p. 173.

20. MG I.2.14. See Terence Marshall, "Rousseau and Enlightenment," *Political Theory* 6 (November 1978), 429–30.

21. See Patrick Riley, *The General Will before Rousseau*, (Princeton: Princeton University Press, 1986), pp. 202–11, and Roger Masters, *The Political Philosophy of Rousseau*, (Princeton: Princeton University Press, 1986), pp. 257–76.

22. Hence Rousseau's rejection of natural law in favor of the particularity of the conventions of this or that community. See DI, preface, for his critique of natural law. Rousseau could not subscribe to Diderot's universalism for two related reasons. Will had to be distinguished from reason or understanding. Will can be predicated only of a "moral being," and Diderot's alleged "general society of the human race" does not qualify, since universal humanity remains an abstraction rather than a covenanted body. Second, a "law of reason" is an incoherent concept since the development of reason is preceded by the emergence of passions that neutralize it. "Concepts of the natural law, which should

rather be called the law of reason, begin to develop only when the prior development of the passions renders all its precepts impotent." MG I.2.8.

23. MG I.2.15.

24. Thomas H. D. Mahoney, ed. Quoted in Charles Murray, *In Pursuit of Happiness and Good Government* (New York: Simon and Schuster, 1988), p. 260. Murray avers that

> Strongly bound communities, fulfilling complex public functions, are not creations of the state. They form because they must. Human beings have needs as individuals (never mind the "moral sense" or lack of it) that cannot be met except by cooperation with other human beings. To this degree, the oft-lamented conflict between "individualism" and "community" is misleading. The pursuit of individual happiness cannot be an atomistic process; it will naturally and always occur in the context of communities. The state's role in enabling the pursuit of happiness depends ultimately on nurturing *not* individuals, but the associations they form. (italics in the original)

From a Rousseauian perspective, Murray's political conclusion is generally correct, but his crucial assumption is wrong. One ought indeed to forgo appeals to the moral sense and concentrate on the pull of mutual needs in conceiving civil association; and, second, that association must be "nurtured." But according to Rousseau, *strongly* bound communities *are* political constructs precisely because "the pursuit of individual happiness" is no longer natural and does not naturally point to community. Furthermore, it is the very unnaturalness of human needs that will require "strong community," not in order to satisfy those needs so much as to keep them in check. Cf. Michael Ignatieff, *The Needs of Strangers* (Hammondsworth, U.K.: Penguin Books, 1984), pp. 110, 114: "For Rousseau, the spiral of needs is a tragedy of alienation. . . . For what Rousseau saw so clearly was that the very processes which freed men from their enslavement to natural scarcity in turn enslaved them to social scarcity."

25. CS II.4.5.

26. OC I, 56.

27. One meaning of the phrase "man is born free" is that man acknowledges no duty from a source outside himself.

28. In the first version of the passage quoted above, Rousseau explained that the general will is always right, and all constantly want the happiness of each because "there is no one who does not *secretly* apply this word 'each' to himself." MG I.6.6; my emphasis.

29. Cf. OC III, 510; E 249/40.

30. CS II.4.10.

31. CS I.1.2. I.7.3 refers to the "sanctity of the contract," and IV.8 describes the "sacred dogmas" of civil association. Cf. DI 186/170: "Human governments" need "a base more solid than reason alone." "Divine will" must "give sovereign authority a sacred and inviolable character." It is the need for an *inviolable* commitment from a free will that generates a political conundrum.

32. MG I.2.8.

33. CS I.6.10.

34. See Derathé's useful discussion of the concept of "des êtres moraux" in his *Jean-Jacques Rousseau et la science politique de son temps* (Paris: Presses Universitaires de France, 1950), appendix.

35. CS II.4.5.

36. In the first version Rousseau wrote, "judging what is not us," thereby emphasizing even more the idea of a new "personality." What is individual is no longer part of the collective identity. MG I.6.6.

37. CS I.7.1.

38. CS I.6.4.

39. In Rousseauian democracy, the "encounter with difference" is the one thing to be avoided. Cf. Sheldon Wolin, *The Presence of the Past* (Baltimore: Johns Hopkins University Press, 1989), p. 191.

40. CS I. pref. 1.

41. CS I.7.5.

42. CS I.6.4.

43. DI 181/164.

44. On the Smithian vision of achieving independence *through* market transactions, see Ignatieff, *The Needs of Strangers*, p. 121.

45. Rousseau explained, in his more practical works, how *amour-propre* might be redirected away from discrete individuals toward the civic whole, so that the "fureur de se distinguer" (the furious desire to distinguish oneself) would play itself out in heroic service to the polity. This patriotic strategy is developed very clearly in both *Corsica* and *Poland*; the theoretical foundation for the rechanneling of *amour-propre* is expressed in *Émile* IV: "Let us extend *amour-propre* toward others, we will transform it into a virtue." E 547/252.

46. Compare CS I.7.7 with I.6.10.

47. CS I.8.1. One might say that with the passage of the individual into the *moi commun*, Rousseau's primary focus shifts accordingly from the psychology of the individual contractor to "the people," although his attention does oscillate back and forth between them.

48. See chapter 4 below.

49. DI 122/91. Rousseau identified those principles as *amour de soi*

and pity, both of which are anterior to reason; however, pity turns out to be only a variation of *amour de soi*, an application of it, so to speak. Pity involves the identification of *oneself* with the suffering of another being. DI 126/95, 155–56/131–32.

50. CS II.3.1.

51. CS II.1.1.

52. MG I.4.4.

53. CS II.3.1; EP 246/213.

54. Bertrand de Jouvenel, "Essai sur la politique de Rousseau," in *Du Contrat social* (Genève: Éditions Cheval-Ailé, 1947), p. 98.

55. CS IV.1.6.

56. DI 122/91. Apropos the general will, Rousseau states flatly: "Either the will is general or it is not." CS II.2.1.

57. Turning to the metamorphosis associated with citizenship, Rousseau writes: "This passage from the state of nature to the civil state produces a remarkable change in man, by substituting justice for instinct in his behavior and giving his actions the morality they previously lacked. Only then, when the voice of duty replaces physical impulse and right replaces appetite, does man, who until that time only considered himself, find himself forced to act upon other principles and to consult his reason before heeding his inclinations." CS I.8.1.

By "civil state" Rousseau means the community of right established by the social contract rather than the general condition wrought by mankind's historical evolution. A sense of justice must forestall any citizen's attempt to use the laws to private advantage. Similarly, being "forced to act upon other principles" is but an elaboration of the meaning of being forced to be free; "right" and "duty" are characteristic of man's new juridical personality. Whereas in the natural order of things men experienced "a multitude of relationships lacking order, regulation and stability," their passage into the community of right endows them with moral relationships that they did not have before.

58. CS I.8.1.

59. Eric Weil, "Rousseau et sa politique," in *Pensée de Rousseau*, Gerard Genette and Tzvetan Todorov, eds. (Paris: Éditions du Seuil, 1984), p. 16.

60. CS I.6.9.

61. CS I.7.5.

62. Patrick Riley, "A Possible Explanation of Rousseau's General Will," *American Political Science Review* 64 (March 1970), 86.

63. CS II.2.1; cf. I.6.10.

64. CS II.3.4.

65. CS II.4.5.

66. See CS I.6.9.
67. CS II.4.5.
68. Riley, "A Possible Explanation," p. 95.
69. CS II.1.3: "car la volonté particulière tend par sa nature aux préférences, et la volonté générale à l'égalité."
70. CS I.7.7.
71. CS II.7.3.
72. CS III.2.5–6.
73. EP 246/212.
74. CS IV.1.1.
75. CS II.4.5; II.6.6. Judith Shklar, *Men and Citizens*, 2nd ed. (Cambridge: Cambridge University Press, 1985), pp. 165–84. In his critique of populist or "Rousseauist" democracy, William H. Riker fails to notice that the general will is intended to express a negative freedom, the value promoted by contemporary "libertarians." *Liberalism against Populism: A Confrontation Between the Theory of Democracy and the Theory of Social Choice* (San Francisco: W. H. Freeman, 1982). For Riker, "The theory of social choice is a theory about the way the tastes, preferences, or values of individual persons are amalgamated and summarized in the choice of a collective group or society." Ibid., p. 1. But the issue between "Rousseauist democracy" and the "liberal" (Madisonian) system advocated by Riker is precisely the assumption that preferences be understood as given, that is, as intractable to political leadership and considerations of justice or "right." Rousseau's goal is to reconcile what right permits with what interest prescribes (CS, preface), which foreshadows his argument that while particular wills must be acknowledged, they are not to be regarded as sacrosanct. Rousseau's teaching is that on the latter premise, freedom cannot be established at all. I am indebted to William T. Bluhm for this point. See his "Liberalism and the Aggregation of Individual Preferences: Problems of Coherence and Rationality in Social Choice," in *The Crisis of Liberal Democracy*, Kenneth Deutsch and Walter Soffer, eds. (Albany: State University of New York Press, 1987), pp. 280–90.
76. Weil, "Rousseau et sa politique," p. 29.
77. CS III.15.5; cf. II.1.
78. CS II.4.8.
79. EP 248/214.
80. Shklar, *Men and Citizens*, p. 168.
81. CS II.4.6.
82. CS II.5.5.
83. CS II.12.3.
84. To prevent men from harming one another, each must live as a

"moral person" rather than as a "man." CS II.5.4.

85. CS II.12.1.

86. CS I.7.8. For twentieth-century thematic discussions of membership, see Joseph Tussman, *Obligation and the Body Politic* (New York: Oxford University Press, 1960), pp. 23–57; and Michael Walzer, *Spheres of Justice* (New York: Basic Books, 1983), pp. 31–63.

87. CS I.8.3.

88. CS I.4.6.

89. CS I.4.1. The original version of this discussion should be consulted. MG I.5.10.

90. CS I.8.1.

91. EP 259/222. Rousseau's conception would seem to differ from "the self-forgetting of the modern idealist," whose cause, according to Harvey C. Mansfield, Jr., is "not the public good but always someone else's good." "Thomas Jefferson," in *American Political Thought: The Philosophic Dimension of American Statesmanship*, Morton J. Frisch and Richard G. Stevens, eds. (Dubuque, Iowa: Kendall/Hunt, 1971), p. 50. The citizen's cause is the public good, but for reasons linked to his own good. The general will remains in service to the individual's own good by guaranteeing him against personal dependence. Once again, the fact that Rousseau maintains a connection between happiness and independence would seem to mark a decisive break between his project and that of Kant and post-Kantian idealism.

92. See Hilail Gildin, *Rousseau's Social Contract* (Chicago and London: University of Chicago Press, 1983), pp. 53–57.

93. CS II.1.3.

94. CS I.8.1.

95. On Rousseau's view of ethics as a branch of politics, see Kryger, *La Notion de la liberté*, pp. 162–63.

96. CS II.3.4.

97. CS II.1.3.

98. CS IV.2.8.

99. Ibid.

100. CS II.1.1. Rousseau expressed his point more clearly in the first draft, when he added, "Now since the will always tends toward the good of the being who wills, since the private will always has as its object private interest and the general will common interest, it follows that this last alone is or ought to be the true motivation of the social body." MG I.4.2.

101. CS II.4.8.

102. "A general will cannot pass judgement on a man or a fact." CS II.4.6.

103. CS II.4.7.

104. Cf. Aristotle, *Politics*, bk. VI, and Niccolo Machiavelli, *Discourses on Livy*, bk. I, ch. 5.

105. MG I.4.6.

106. CS II.3.1.

107. CS II.4.2. In the first draft, Rousseau said, less confusingly, "life and existence." MG I.6.3.

108. CS II.4.10.

109. O.C. III, 841–42; my emphasis.

110. CS II.12.3.

111. CS IV.2.8. Once again, the Rousseauian case against Rikerian social choice theory would emphasize the folly of granting an unlimited domain to preference. For if we understand freedom (as libertarianism seems to) as an infinitely variable preference, we can never establish it in a political regime. The latter requires that freedom or independence be construed as a constant preference to which variable preferences must accede.

112. CS II.1.1. Rousseau concedes that sometimes the general will need not be positively expressed by the people themselves: "This is not to say that the commands of leaders cannot pass for expressions of the general will, as long as the sovereign, being free to oppose them, does not do so. In such a case one ought to presume the consent of the people from universal silence." CS II.1.4. This concession opens the door to the possibility that the people might legitimately be confined to a passive, or at least reactive, legislative role.

113. CS II.1.3.

114. CS II.7.3.

115. MG I.4.1; my emphasis. See also *Lettres écrites de la montagne*, O.C. III, 807. I have profited from Robert Derathé's illuminating "La Notion de personnalité morale et la théorie des êtres moraux," which traces Rousseau's formulations to Samuel Pufendorf and the early modern school of natural right. *Jean-Jacques Rousseau et la science politique de son temps*, pp. 397–413.

116. CS II.7.4.

117. CS II.7.1.

118. Cf. E 546–48/252–53, where the same theme is introduced from a different perspective.

119. MG I.5.7.

120. Rousseau occasionally equates these terms. Cf. MG I.2.14.

121. MG I.5.7.

122. CS II.7.7. Eventually, the "free vote of the people" will (as we saw above) be interpreted in such a way as to reflect a constant preference for the general on the part of all, thereby calling into question Rousseau's commitment to freedom qua agency. In the passage under

consideration, Rousseau cleaves to the requirements of legitimacy and resists the conclusion that sovereignty be in any way represented. As we shall see, the tension between what is legitimate and what will make the good reliable will become irrepressible in Rousseau's theory.

123. While he admits that "a people is always the master to change its laws—even the best laws," Rousseau concedes that the best laws will be the gift of the Legislator. CS II.12.2; II.7.1.

124. Cf. Shklar, *Men and Citizens*, ch. 4.

125. Order, in Rousseau's mind, is associated with an "artful" fidelity to the natural. In its perfect expression such an order confounds the distinction between nature and artifice. As Julie teaches Saint-Preux, who is awed by her garden: "Nature has done everything, but under my direction, and there is nothing there that I have not ordered." *La Nouvelle Héloïse*, O.C. II, 472.

126. MG I.7.2.

127. CS IV.1.1.

128. E 249/40.

129. Biographers and psychologists have little difficulty presenting evidence that Rousseau himself experienced the evils he condemns, but one cannot conclude that he merely rationalized his personal resentment in his social criticism. Rousseau's historical and autobiographical portraits are indeed evidentiary. They point, however, to what Baczko has called "general anthropological questions: the relation of man to nature and his own history; human freedom and man's alienation from his products and activities." Bronislaw Baczko, *Solitude et communauté* (Paris: Mouton, 1974), p. 290.

130. *Confessions* IX, O.C. 1, 404.

131. CS IV.8.17.

132. As Derathé observes in his annotation of this passage, Rousseau develops the theme of avoiding contradiction with oneself at length in *Émile*. O.C. III, 1503. Arthur Melzer has made the theme of unity of soul the centerpiece of his interpretation of Rousseau's thought and the key to his explanation of the natural goodness of man. See "Rousseau and the Problem of Bourgeois Society," *American Political Science Review* 74, no. 4 (December 1980); and *The Natural Goodness of Man*, (Chicago: University of Chicago Press, 1990), pp. 20–23.

133. CS II.7.3.

134. MG II.2.13.

135. EP 259–60/222–23, 314, 381; E 248–49/39–40 (but cf. 600–01/290–91).

136. Montesquieu's paradigmatic community of virtue was the ascetic monastery. "Why do monks love their order so much? It is precisely due to what makes it unbearable for them. Their rule deprives

them of all the things the ordinary passions press after: there remains therefore this passion for the very rule which afflicts them. The more austere it is, that is to say, the more it cuts off their inclinations, the more force it gives to the only one left to them." *Spirit of the Laws* IV.12. Cf. Thomas Pangle, *Montesquieu's Philosophy of Liberalism* (Chicago and London: University of Chicago Press, 1973), pp. 81–83.

137. CS II.4.10.

138. CS I.8.1, I.8.3,

139. CS II.7.3.

140. CS II.7.4.

141. CS II.12.5.

142. EP 251/216.

143. E 654/327.

144. EP 255/219.

145. As an artificial passion, *amour-propre* is malleable; it can express itself as civic pride as well as vanity. O.C. III, 937–38.

146. EP 251–52/16–17.

147. See Richard Kennington, "René Descartes," in *History of Political Philosophy*, Leo Strauss and Joseph Cropsey, eds., 2nd ed. (Chicago: Rand McNally, 1972).

148. Leo Strauss described this aspect of Rousseau's vision as the "totalitarianism of a free society." *What Is Political Philosophy? and Other Essays* (Glencoe, Ill.: The Free Press, 1953), p. 51.

149. EP 252/217.

150. Michel Foucault coined the term "governmentality" to characterize Rousseau's political economy. See his essay by that title in *Ideology and Consciousness* 6 (1979). Cf. James Miller, *Rousseau: Dreamer of Democracy* (New Haven: Yale University Press, 1984), pp. 196–98.

151. Cf. Reinhart Kosselleck, *Critique and Crisis: Enlightenment and the Pathogenesis of Modern Society* (Cambridge, Mass.: MIT Press, 1988), p. 164: "The citizen gains his freedom only when he participates in the general will, but as an individual this same citizen cannot know when and how his inner self is absorbed by the general will. Individuals might err, but the *volonté générale* never does."

152. Cf. F. M. Barnard and Jene Porter, "Will and Political Rationality in Rousseau," paper presented at the 1983 annual meeting of the Canadian Political Science Association, Vancouver, Canada.

153. Letter to Mirabeau, 26 July 1767, in *Political Writings*, Vaughan, ed. vol. 2, pp. 159–62.

154. CS I.7.8.

155. Cf. Riley, *The General Will Before Rousseau*, pp. 182, 205, 208–10, 245, 247.

156. Roger Masters has stressed Rousseau's distinction between

"maxims of politics" and "rules of right." *The Political Philosophy of Rousseau*, pp. 291–93, 369–409.

157. Miller, *Rousseau: Dreamer of Democracy*, p. 203; Riley, *The General Will Before Rousseau*, p. 245: "Do Rousseau's notions of education—private and civic—leave will as the autonomous producer of moral effects that he originally defines it as?"

158. On the relation of educative authority to will, see Riley, *The General Will Before Rousseau*, pp. 245–48; cf. Miller, *Rousseau: Dreamer of Democracy*, pp. 196–98.

159. EP 259/222.

160. CS I.6.10.

161. Ibid.

162. Samuel Baud-Bovy, ed., *Jean-Jacques Rousseau* (Neuchâtel: Éditions de la Baconnière, 1962), p. 96.

163. The latter topic is treated in detail in chapter 4.

164. See Bernard Groethuysen, *Jean-Jacques Rousseau* (Paris: Gallimard, 1949), p. 109.

165. Sovereignty is created out of the wills of dissociated, precivil men; its being derives solely from contract. CS I.7.3.

166. DI 127/97.

167. Preface to *Narcissus*, p. 106.

168. *Confessions*, O.C. I, 404–05.

169. MG I.7.3.

170. CS I.6.4.

171. Cf. Richard Flathman, *The Practice of Political Authority* (Chicago and London: University of Chicago Press, 1980), pp. 197–201.

172. CS I.6.10.

173. CS II.8.

174. CS II.10.3.

175. CS II.10.5.

176. Since "civilization" must await the preparation of a common identity, only in rare circumstances will a people be ripe for subjection to laws. Rousseau points out the mistake by Peter the Great, who attempted to civilize his people prematurely. "He wanted first to make Germans and Englishmen, whereas it was necessary to begin by making Russians." CS II.8.5.

177. CS III.16.4.

178. CS I.7.1.

179. CS IV.6.6.

180. For a careful treatment of Rousseau's political geometry, see Masters, *The Political Philosophy of Rousseau*, pp. 340–48; and Richard Carter, "Rousseau's Newtonian Body Politic," *Philosophy and Social Criticism*, 7 (1980), 143–67.

181. Notice that the Legislator must pretend to intercede with the divine to effectively communicate with the people. CS II.7.10.

182. Ibid.

183. CGP, ch. 2. Cf. Machiavelli, who was prepared to disguise inequality by manipulating titles while preserving actual power. *Discourses on Livy* I.2.

184. CS IV.6.1.

185. The Tribunate resembles the Legislator himself. It is not a constituent part of the city, and it has no portion of the legislative or executive power. Yet in its role as defender of the laws it is, according to Rousseau's description, more sacred and revered than either the sovereign or the prince. CS IV.5.3.

186. Cf. CS IV.6.10 on Cicero's "error."

187. O.C. III, 948; my emphasis.

188. EP 254/218.

189. EP 261/223.

190. EP 262/224.

191. EP 248/214.

192. EP 250/215.

193. EP 251/216.

Chapter 4: Citizenship, Community, and the Politics of Identity

1. See *Letter to D'Alembert*, p. 135 note, concerning the "general emotion" communal identity.

2. Stephen Salkever, "Virtue, Obligation and Politics," *American Political Science Review* 68 (March 1974), 78–92.

3. CS IV.1.1.

4. CS II.7.9.

5. CS I.6.10.

6. Presumably, there are numerous private matters that would fall under the purview of the sovereign. Rousseau does refer to a sphere that is of no concern to the state. However, he refuses to draw the boundary between private and public once and for all, and leaves the authority to do so in the hands of the sovereign. If this is a sinister concession, it is one characteristic of liberal states, too. Normally, a blood test is irrelevant to employment or accommodation. But should an alarmingly infectious disease appear, the people may demand intrusions upon hitherto private domains to protect the public. Rousseau merely acknowledges that one cannot define once and for all what is a public concern, and that is a reasonable concession to authority.

7. Cf. CGP ch. 2, "On the Spirit of Ancient Institutions."

8. CS IV.1.5.

9. CS II.12.5.

10. O.C. III, 556.

11. CS IV.4.35.

12. CS IV.7.

13. CS IV.8.15.

14. CS I.1.2.

15. CS IV.8.17.

16. CS IV.8.18. The sacred dogmas relate only to morality; they are better described as "sentiments of sociability," without which one cannot be a good citizen. CS IV.8.31–32.

17. CS II.7.10.

18. See Harvey C. Mansfield, Jr., "The Forms and Formalities of Liberty," *The Public Interest* 70 (Winter 1983).

19. See Burke's *Reflections on the Revolution in France*, Thomas H. D. Mahoney, ed. (Indianapolis: Bobbs-Merrill, 1955), pp. 70–71, 98–100, 110.

20. O.C. III, 555; George A. Kelly, *Idealism, Politics and History* (Cambridge: Cambridge University Press, 1969), p. 58, cites the influence of Montaigne on Rousseau's argument.

21. O.C. III, 950. Cf. CGP 955, wherein Rousseau speculates about the requirements of actually reaching the hearts of citizens. "But how does one reach the hearts? About this our founders, who never see anything other than force and punishments, have scarcely dreamed. On this matter material benefits work no better. The most worthy justice will not reach the heart, because justice is the sort of good one enjoys without feeling it. Thus it inspires no enthusiasm whatsoever, and it is a good whose value is experienced only after it is lost."

22. "When, among the happiest people in the world, groups of peasants are seen deciding the affairs of State under an oak tree, and always acting wisely, can one help scorning the refinements of other nations, which make themselves illustrious and miserable with so much art and mystery? A State governed in this way needs very few laws, and to the degree that it becomes necessary to promulgate new ones, this necessity is universally seen." CS IV.1.1–2.

23. O.C. III, 914–15.

24. "These rustic men who at first know only themselves, their mountains and their animals." O.C. III, 915. Rousseau refers to the Swiss and the Corsicans.

25. John Stuart Mill, *On Liberty*, Gertrude Himmelfarb, ed. (London: Penguin Books, 1974), p. 123.

26. See *Letter to Mirabeau* in *Political Writings*, Vaughan, ed., vol. 2,

pp. 159–62: "In a word, I see no viable middle ground between the most austere democracy and perfect hobbism."

27. Rousseau intuited that the immersion in a social context was not painful so long as it was complete, because it is exclusively the pain of division, the combat of duty and inclination, which rends the soul. O.C. III, 510.

28. O.C. II, 971.

29. *Letter to D'Alembert*, p. 17.

30. O.C. II, 971.

31. EOL 248.

32. CS II.7.9; see also *Émile* IV; O.C. IV, 630/310–11, on the persuasion that can work on young, "flexible souls" which are open to certitudes for a privileged moment. The founding moment is a fleeting opportunity.

33. We might remark that *persuasion* is the preferred tactic when confronting immaturity with the intention of control, whether this be in the individual (the adolescent who is "persuaded" by the Savoyard Vicar's speech) or in the community (the nascent society the Legislator must form).

34. EOL 294.

35. Jean Starobinski, "Eloquence and Liberty," *Journal of the History of Ideas* 38 (1977), 204.

36. EOL 249.

37. EOL 262.

38. EOL 266 and note.

39. EOL 267–69.

40. EOL 272.

41. EOL 271.

42. "Around a common hearth people gather, feast, dance; the sweet bonds of familiarity imperceptibly draw man to his kind, and on this rustic hearth burns the sacred fire that introduces the first sentiments of humanity into men's hearts." EOL 268–69.

43. "The *sweet* bonds of familiarity *imperceptibly* draw man to his kind." EOL 269, my emphasis.

44. Note the myriad allusions to force in the *Social Contract*.

45. EOL 274.

46. EOL 275.

47. EOL 283. Let us recall that Rousseau projected a comprehensive work titled *La Morale sensitive* to chart the production of morality through manipulation of the feelings. See *Confessions* IX; for an analysis of the project, see Denise Leduc-Fayette, "Le Materialisme du sage et l'art de jouir," *Revue philosophique* 3 (1978). *Moeurs* operate on the

feelings of patriotic citizens with the power of nature. Cf. EOL 282, 293.

48. "Divertissement" is a theme of Pascal's *Pensées*, introduced to characterize the life of men cut off from God. On the softening of human character intended by modern proponents of commercial republicanism, see Ralph Lerner, "Commerce and Character: The Anglo-American as New Model Man," *William and Mary Quarterly* 36 (1979), reprinted in his *The Thinking Revolutionary* (Chicago: University of Chicago Press, 1987); and Thomas Pangle, "The Federalist Papers' Vision of Civic Health and the Tradition out of Which That Vision Emerges," *Western Political Quarterly* 39 (December 1986).

49. Allan Bloom, "Introduction," *Émile*, pp. 4–5.

50. CS IV.1.1.

51. Kelly, *Idealism, Politics and History*, pp. 60–61.

52. CGP 955.

53. Kelly, *Idealism, Politics and History*, pp. 60–61.

54. Ibid., p. 67.

55. Jean Starobinski, *Jean-Jacques Rousseau: La transparence et l'obstacle* (Paris: Presses Universitaires de France, 1957), p. 121.

56. Robert Wokler concludes rightly that politics for Rousseau meant making a tradition out of nature by giving civic foundations to a once spontaneous enterprise. Robert Wokler, "Rousseau's Perfectibilitarian Libertarianism," in *The Ideal of Freedom*, Alan Ryan, ed. (Oxford: Oxford University Press, 1979), pp. 246–52.

57. Preface to *Narcissus*, pp. 107–08.

58. *Letter to D'Alembert*, p. 17.

59. Preface to *Narcissus*, p. 107.

60. DSA 17/48. Rousseau has been rightly called "the father of nationalism." Ann Cohler, *Rousseau and Nationalism* (New York: Basic Books, 1970).

61. Rousseau's consideration of the exclusive civic identity led him to the conclusion that civic education must be national education. Nothing separated Rousseau from his cosmopolitan colleagues so much as his defense of chauvinistic prejudice; but his dissent against the vision of "the party of humanity," his defense of irrational patriotism, was a reasoned choice. Rousseau never truly celebrated imperialistic, aggressive nationalism. His vision was of a defensive rather than an offensive nationalism. And while Rousseau was unsurpassed in teaching citizens the language of national pride, he himself always remained outside those particular caves. He could produce patriotic rhythms, but his music did not seem to genuinely move his own soul. Like the Legislator, and indeed like all his "images of authority," Rousseau

stands aloof from his creations. Breaking ranks with the party of humanity out of a concern for humanity more genuine than theirs, Rousseau's cosmopolitanism may ultimately be more authentic than that of the philosophes who so affected it. He belongs to the tribe of the "preceptors of the human race," a truly "cosmopolitan soul" who surmounts the imaginary boundaries that separate peoples. Nonetheless, as we shall see, the Rousseauian community of the heart became a model to conjure with.

62. It is a testament to his rhetorical power that Rousseau could generate images of "natural community" which captured the imagination of later thinkers. On Romantic expressivism, see Charles Taylor, *Hegel* (Cambridge: Cambridge University Press, 1974), ch. 1.

63. Still, it is not so much the artificiality of *moeurs* to which Rousseau objects, as their depravity in contemporary civilization. See generally DSA.

64. E 855ff./471ff.

65. E 855/471.

66. E 814–20/442–46.

67. E 855–56/471–72.

68. E 857/472.

69. E 858/473–74.

70. E 857/473.

71. This passage sheds light on the proper interpretation of CS I.8.1 and Rousseau's general evaluation of the moral life.

72. Bertrand de Jouvenel, "Essai sur la politique de Rousseau," in *Du Contrat social* (Genève: Editions Cheval-Ailé, 1947), p. 57.

73. Jouvenel convincingly demonstrates how Rousseau retreats systematically from a "morality of effort." He argues that Rousseau was always deflected from that path ("il nous arrête sur le chemin qui menait à Lacédémone"), tending instead toward passivity and inertia. See "Essai," p. 56.

74. See the incisive treatment of this issue in Leo Strauss, "On the Intention of Rousseau," in *Hobbes and Rousseau,* Maurice Cranston and R. S. Peters, eds. (Garden City, N.Y.: Anchor Books, 1972), pp. 280–87.

75. MG I.7.3; EP 248/214.

76. "Letter to Malsherbes," O.C. I, 1132.

77. See Starobinski's illuminating account of the significance of the festival in *Jean-Jacques Rousseau,* pp. 116–21.

78. Ibid., p. 120.

79. Ibid., p. 121.

80. See *Letter to D'Alembert,* pp. 135–36 note.

81. Cf. E 247/38.

82. R 1059/83.

83. "Justice is like health, a good which one enjoys without feeling it, which inspires no enthusiasm." CGP 955. Cf. O.C. III, 937, on fear and hope as the "instruments" of "governing men."

84. CGP 95.

85. O.C. I, 823.

86. "L'État de guerre," O.C. III, 606.

87. EP 251–52/216–17; CGP 955; *Letter to D'Alembert*, p. 87.

88. EP 254/218.

89. Immanuel Kant, "Conjectural Beginning of Human History," in *Kant*, Beck, pp. 67–68.

90. In the discussion that follows, I will speak of the "strong democratic" perspective both for economy of expression and because the case for participatory democracy has been argued most thoroughly and brilliantly by Benjamin Barber.

91. The threat of order and community to "politics" was outlined by Sheldon Wolin: "For Plato, . . . order was in the nature of a mould shaped after a divine model; a concept to be used for stamping society in a definite image. But what kind of an order could issue from a political science dedicated in large measure to the eradication of conflict; that is, to the elimination of politics? If order could only flourish in the absence of conflict and antagonism, then it followed that the order thus created had surrendered its distinctively political element; order it might be, but not a 'political' order." *Politics and Vision* (Boston: Little Brown, 1960), pp. 43–44. Wolin's discussion of Rousseau occurs in the chapter entitled "The Age of Organization and the Sublimation of Politics." In characterizing Rousseau's political conception, Wolin refers to "the high value of social solidarity, the necessary subordination of the individual to the group, the importance of impersonal dependence, the redemptive vocation of membership, and the benefits accruing from a close identification between individual and aggregate." Ibid., p. 375.

92. I follow the terms used by Charles Taylor in "Cross-Purposes: The Liberal-Communitarian Debate," in *Liberalism and the Moral Life*, Nancy Rosenblum, ed. (Cambridge, Mass.: Harvard University Press, 1989), p. 170. Cf. in the same volume the essay by Benjamin Barber, "Liberal Democracy and the Costs of Consent," p. 65.

93. As the subsequent pages will show, I take exception to Barber's interpretation of Rousseau. I do not mean to suggest that the case for democracy can be made only by reference to Rousseau—the very richness of Barber's work belies such a claim. However, it does seem to me

that the correct interpretation of Rousseau is a matter of large significance to Barber's theory of strong democracy, for some of its crucial assumptions plainly derive from Rousseau's writings. If my reading of Rousseau is correct, those assumptions are uprooted and consequently need to be rethought and grounded elsewhere, if not simply abandoned. While Barber is critical of the influence of philosophical "foundationalism" in political theory, he clearly intimates that Rousseau is the model for the "politically minded" philosopher. *The Conquest of Politics* (Princeton: Princeton University Press, 1990), pp. 6, 12–14.

According to Carole Pateman, "Rousseau might be called the theorist *par excellence* of participation, and an understanding of the nature of the political system that he describes in *The Social Contract* is vital for the theory of participatory democracy. . . . it is in his theory that the basic hypotheses about the function of participation in a democratic polity can be found. *Participation and Democratic Theory* (Cambridge: Cambridge University Press, 1970), p. 22. My quarrel with Pateman is that her enthusiasm for participation tends to obscure Rousseau's basic hypotheses. Confident that she has grasped the essentials of Rousseau's teaching, she translates them into her own jargon. Whereas Rousseau spoke about the elements of politics (passion, egoism, patriotism) with clarity and an unsettling power (denaturing, force, renunciation), Pateman refers to the familiar yet fuzzy concepts of "integrative effects" and "psychological orientations." Having blunted Rousseau's edge, she assures us that there is nothing frightening about his notorious proposals. *Participation*, pp. 26, 42–43. See also Pateman's *The Problem of Political Obligation* (New York: John Wiley and Sons, 1979), ch. 7.

94. Charles Taylor's writings are the significant exception. Taylor knows Rousseau's works intimately, and while his essay style occasionally precludes "naming names," he frequently uses Rousseau as a touchstone for elaborating a certain tradition of thought.

95. See Bruce Ackerman, *Social Justice in the Liberal State* (New Haven: Yale University Press, 1980); Ronald Dworkin, *Taking Rights Seriously* (Cambridge, Mass.: Harvard University Press, 1977); John Rawls, *A Theory of Justice* (Cambridge, Mass.: Harvard University Press, 1971). Cf. Charles Larmore, *Patterns of Moral Complexity* (Cambridge: Cambridge University Press, 1987), pp. 40–68. For a searching critique of liberal neutrality by a friend of liberalism, see William Galston, "Defending Liberalism," *American Political Science Review* 76 (September 1982), 621–29.

96. Raymond Plant, "Community: Concept and Ideology," *Politics and Society* 8 (1978), 99.

97. There is a conservative and a radical version of this critique, but

I shall not pursue the distinction between them here. See Samuel Huntington, *American Politics: The Promise of Disharmony* (Cambridge, Mass.: Harvard University Press, 1981); Jurgen Habermas, *Legitimation Crisis*, Thomas McCarthy, trans. (Boston: Beacon Press, 1975); and Claus Offe, *Contradictions of the Welfare State* (Boston: M.I.T. Press, 1984).

98. Alasdair MacIntyre, *After Virtue*, 2nd ed. (Notre Dame: Notre Dame University Press, 1984), p. 254.

99. William Connolly, *Appearance and Reality in Politics* (New York and London: Cambridge University Press, 1981), p. 94.

100. The phrase belongs to Mary Ann Glendon, *Rights Talk: The Impoverishment of Political Discourse* (New York: Free Press, 1991).

101. George Grant, *English-Speaking Justice* (Toronto: Anansi, 1974), p. 12.

102. Bertrand de Jouvenel, *Sovereignty*, J. F. Huntington, trans. (Chicago: University of Chicago Press, 1957), p. 138.

103. Michael Walzer, *Obligations* (Cambridge, Mass.: Harvard University Press, 1970), p. 204.

104. Wilson Carey McWilliams, "Parties as Civic Associations," in *Elections in America*, Gerald Pomper, ed. (New York: Praeger, 1980), p. 55. A similar point is made in Jean Elshtain, *Women and War* (New York: Basic Books, 1987).

105. In what follows, I draw generally from Michael Sandel, *Liberalism and the Limits of Justice* (Cambridge: Cambridge University Press, 1982); "The Procedural Republic and the Unencumbered Self," *Political Theory* 12 (1984); and "Morality and the Liberal Ideal," *The New Republic*, May 7, 1984.

106. Rawls, *A Theory of Justice*, p. 560.

107. Ibid., pp. 128–29.

108. Ibid., pp. 251ff.

109. Sandel, *Liberalism and the Limits of Justice*, p. 55; my emphasis.

110. Charles Taylor, "Atomism," in *Powers, Possessions and Freedoms*, Alkis Kontos, ed. (Toronto: University of Toronto Press, 1979), p. 58.

111. MG I.2.18.

112. Michael Sandel, "The Procedural Republic and the Unencumbered Self," *Political Theory* 12 (1984), p. 87.

113. Charles Taylor, "Why Do Nations Have to Become States?" in *Philosophers Look at Canadian Confederation*, Stanley French and Storrs McCall, eds. (Montreal: Canadian Philosophical Association, 1979), pp. 22–23. Roberto Unger also argues that the self is defined by the totality of its relations with others; putting it simply, "we are our relations," in *Knowledge and Politics* (New York: Free Press, 1975), p.

216. According to Unger, the manner in which a person is an individual also makes him social. Hence, selfhood and community are complementary. "Consciousness implies autonomous identity . . . but the medium through which consciousness expresses itself is made up of symbols of culture, and these . . . are irreducibly social" (p. 215).

114. Cf. MacIntyre, *After Virtue*, pp. 220ff.

115. DI 223/227 (note S). See Masters's commentary in his editorial note at pp. 247–48.

116. The argument of *Second Discourse*, note S, is strikingly similar to that of Mill, *On Liberty*, pp. 144–45. One suspects, however, that Rousseau was more genuine than Mill in acknowledging the legitimacy of moral judgments in social life.

117. Glendon, *Rights Talk*, p. 14. "Our rights talk, in its absoluteness, promotes unrealistic expectations, heightens social conflict, and inhibits dialogue that might lead toward consensus, accommodation, or at least the discovery of common ground. . . . In its neglect of civil society, it undermines the principal seedbeds of civic and personal virtue."

118. See the acerbic critique of communitarianism's alleged theoretical weaknesses by Stephen Holmes, "The Permanent Structure of Antiliberal Thought," in *Liberalism and the Moral Life*, Nancy Rosenblum, ed. (Cambridge, Mass.: Harvard University Press, 1989), esp. pp. 229–36.

119. See Michael Walzer, *Spheres of Justice* (New York: Basic Books, 1983), pp. 28–29. For Walzer, political communities ought to be "*communities of character*, historically stable, ongoing associations of men and women with some special commitment to one another and some special sense of their common life." Ibid., p. 62. Charles Taylor prefers the term "shared goods" to characterize genuine community:

> Shared goods are essentially of a community; their common appreciation is constitutive of them.
>
> The well-known example is the one central to the tradition of civic humanism, the citizen republic. This takes its character from its laws; so that the citizen's action takes on a crucial significance by its relation to the laws: whether it tends to preserve them, or undermine them, to defend them from external attack, or to weaken them before enemies, and so on. But the good is essentially shared. The laws are significant not *qua* mine, but *qua* ours; what gives them their importance for me is not that they are a rule *I* have adopted. . . . Rather the laws are important because they are *ours*." *Philosophy and the Human Sciences* (Cambridge: Cambridge University Press, 1985), vol. 2, p. 96.

120. George J. Graham, Jr., "Consensus," in *Social Science Concepts*, Giovanni Sartori, ed. (Beverly Hills, Calif.: Sage, 1984), pp. 93–94. Cf. Giovanni Sartori, *The Theory of Democracy Revisited* (Chatham, N.J.: Chatham House, 1987), vol. 1, pp. 90–92, where consensus on "value beliefs and value goals" is understood to be a facilitating (though not a necessary) condition of democracy.

121. Edmund Burke, *Works* (Rivington ed.), vol. 9, p. 178; vol. 10, p. 93. Cited in Francis P. Canavan, "The Levels of Consensus," *Modern Age* 5 (1961), 239.

122. Samuel Huntington, *American Politics: The Promise of Disharmony* (Cambridge: Harvard University Press, 1983), p. 12.

123. Walzer, *Spheres of Justice*, p. 313.

124. In a review of *Spheres of Justice*, Ronald Dworkin complains that at Walzer's hands, political theory threatens to become "only a mirror, uselessly reflecting a community's consensus and division back upon itself." *New York Review of Books*, July 12, 1983, p. 46.

125. A subsidiary question involves procedures. If a consensus exists, procedures merely facilitate its expression. If consensus does not exist, then procedures will discipline the efforts to establish a consensus, or perhaps agreement on procedures will emerge as the paramount consensus itself—which is the understanding underlying the "procedural republic."

126. Barber, *Strong Democracy*, p. 129.

127. MacIntyre, *After Virtue*, p. 263.

128. Barber, *The Conquest of Politics*, p. 190.

129. Barber, *Strong Democracy*, p. 148.

130. Ibid., p. 128; cf. p. 152, top.

131. CS IV.1.1.

132. CS IV.2.1.

133. CS IV.2.2.

134. CS IV.1.6.

135. CS IV.2.4, 7.

136. Cf. Carol Gould, *Rethinking Democracy* (Cambridge: Cambridge University Press, 1988), p. 290. If I am correct in arguing for the essential passivity of Rousseauian citizenship, the first character trait of Gould's "democratic personality" (rational initiative) is as subject to a Rousseauian critique as the second, the "disposition to reciprocity." Gould neither relies on Rousseau for her rethinking of democracy nor considers possible Rousseauian objections to her account of democratic personality in her discussion of possible objections at pp. 294–97. Although he does not use the term, Benjamin Barber also grounds his notion of a revitalized democracy in a disposition to reciprocity: "what is crucial is not consent pure and simple

but the active consent of participating citizens who have imaginatively recon-
structed their own values as public norms through the process of identifying
and empathizing with the values of others." *Strong Democracy*, p. 137. Unlike
Gould, Barber has Rousseau constantly before his eyes, as his frequent
references attest. I submit that Rousseau is indeed after consent pure and
simple, for his political scheme strains to the breaking point to fulfill the
criterion of legitimacy and seems to provide for the activity of willing in
only the most oblique fashion. Cf. James Miller, *Rousseau: Dreamer of
Democracy* (New Haven: Yale University Press, 1984), pp. 196–98.

137. In the words of Sheldon Wolin, the political paradigm is fulfilled
"when shared and common concerns are discovered through a process of
deliberation among civic equals and effected through cooperative action."
"The New Public Philosophy," *Democracy* 1, no. 4 (October 1981), 36.
Cf. Barber, *Strong Democracy*, pp. 151–52:

> Participatory politics deals with public disputes and conflicts of
> interest by subjecting them to a never-ending process of delibera-
> tion, decision, and action. . . . In place of the search for a prepolitical
> independent ground or for an immutable rational plan, strong de-
> mocracy relies on participation in an evolving problem-solving com-
> munity that creates public ends where there were none before by
> means of its own activity. . . . In such communities, public ends are
> neither extrapolated from absolutes nor "discovered" in a preexisting
> "hidden consensus."

138. Michael Walzer has observed that the *techné* of the Platonic
statesman displaces the activity of the citizen. *Spheres of Justice*, pp. 284–
87; see also Walzer's "Philosophy and Democracy," *Political Theory* 9
(August 1981), 384–85, where he senses that the role of the Legislator
"raises the most serious questions about Rousseau's fundamental argument, that political legitimacy rests on will (consent) and not on reason
(rightness)." Because democracy is a way of allocating and legitimating
power, citizens must enter the public forum, as Walzer suggests, "with
nothing but their arguments." *Spheres of Justice*, p. 304. Democracy intends
to diminish the advantages of force and wealth by privileging persuasive
speech. What should be most troubling to proponents of strong democracy, therefore, is Rousseau's depreciation of deliberation.

139. W. T. Jones, "Rousseau's General Will and the Problem of Consent," *Journal of the History of Philosophy* 25 (January 1987), 110.

140. Bernard Manin, "On Legitimacy and Political Deliberation," *Political Theory* 15 (August 1987), 343–48. "The citizens of Rousseau's
democracy do not deliberate, even within themselves, because Rousseau
regards politics to be essentially a simple matter. That is why the process
of the formation of the will, individual as well as collective, does not

concern him. He is thus able to identify deliberation with decision making, and decision making with self-evidence." Ibid., p. 347. The crucial passage is CS II.3.1: "If, when an adequately informed people deliberates, the citizens were to have no communication among themselves, the general will would result from the large number of small differences, and the deliberation would always be good." (I shall return to the interpretation of this passage below.) In his translation, G. D. H. Cole renders the second occurrence of *délibération* as "decision." *The Social Contract and Discourses* (London: J. M. Dent, 1973), p. 184. Other passages where *délibération* seems to refer to decision are CS I.7.2 and II.4.7.

141. See, however, Pierre Favre, "The Rationality of the Social Treaty," which argues that Rousseau regarded the principle of majority rule as deeply problematical, and indeed viewed the existence of a majority as "a symptom of social decay." *Democracy, Consensus and Social Contract* (Beverly Hills, Calif.: Sage, 1978), p. 117.

142. CS IV.2.9.

143. CS IV.1.1.

144. Aristotle, *Nicomachean Ethics*, Martin Ostwald, trans. (New York: Macmillan, 1962), pp. 17, 43, 151–54, and bk. VI passim.

145. However, Rousseau's conception of legitimacy is incompatible with "moralistic formalism" or the principle that the government of human beings can be equated with the government of rational beings. Legitimacy requires that the conditions of freedom must be the object of popular consent. Rousseau does not shrink from the difficulty of fulfilling the legitimacy criterion. In this regard he is more "politic" than twentieth-century contractarians, such as John Rawls, for whom principles of right are those to which contractors *would* agree in "the original position." Rousseau rejects such hypothetical consent and insists that the general will *actually* be expressed through formal procedures. On the distinction between mundane and idealist liberalism, and how the latter gives rise to a moralistic formalism, see Harvey C. Mansfield, Jr., *The Spirit of Liberalism* (Cambridge, Mass.: Harvard University Press, 1978), pp. 46–51. Cf. Rawls, *A Theory of Justice*, p. 507.

What matters, for Rawls, is whether a law could have been willed by free and equal persons. We have already seen the reasons why Rousseau would not follow Rawls in relying upon a calculative rationality among his hypothetical contractors. As Mansfield points out, one can *assume* the consent of a rational being. *The Spirit of Liberalism*, p. 48. Thus moralistic formalism threatens "majority tyranny without the majority." Rousseau insists that for law to be legitimate, it must actually be declared to be the general will by a majority vote. We have also seen that it would not suffice for the wisest or the most rational to declare the general will. The people must actually register their vote, because the will of the sovereign cannot be represented. CS II.1.2. "One can never be assured that a private will is in conformity with the general will until it has been submitted to the free vote of the people." CS II.7.7.

146. Bernard Grofman and Scott Feld defend Rousseau's claims on behalf of the general will against the public choice theory, which regards voting exclusively as a means of preference aggregation (and one subject to fatal liabilities). They note en passant that Rousseau "sees the 'deliberative process' as one taking place within individuals rather than in terms of a process of group debate. Thus each voter is seen as seeking to reach individual and independent judgement about alternatives." "Rousseau's General Will: A Condorcetian Perspective," *American Political Science Review* 82, no. 2 (June 1988), 568–69.

147. CS I.7.7.

148. See CGP, 959. Cf. Barber, *Strong Democracy*, pp. 136–37.

149. CS IV.2.8.

150. Cf. Carol Gould, *Rethinking Democracy*, p. 287: "The priority of activity to passivity and of self-development to the simple satisfaction of needs follows from the centrality of the value of self-development as the meaning of human freedom." Cf. pp. 40–42.

151. As Patrick Riley has cogently explained, "To retain the moral attributes of will while doing away with will's particularity and selfishness and 'willfulness'—to generalize this moral cause without destroying it—is one of the central problems of Rousseau's political and moral thought, and one that reflects the difficulty Rousseau found in making free will and rational educative authority coexist in his political and moral thinking." *The General Will Before Rousseau*, p. 245.

152. In his thematic discussion of representation, Rousseau underscores the people's interest in freedom. CS III.15. As is well known, the *Social Contract* excludes representation of the popular will. Representation is a symptom of "the waning of patriotism" and "the activity of private interest." The danger of representation is the substitution of the corporate will of a representative body for the general will; to prevent that, the people must keep their sense of community alive. The greatest function of the assembly is periodically to evoke that identification in a tangible way: the sovereign must *present* itself. CS III.13.3.

153. CS III.14.2; cf. O.C. III, 858. Hilail Gildin argues that Rousseau intended a more substantive legislative role for the people than I have suggested here. He also notes that Rousseau even included the people in the exercise of *governmental* functions. Noting that bk. IV, ch. 1, of the *Social Contract* appears to reserve the functions of initiating and deliberating to the government, Gildin suggests that Rousseau was referring to fact

rather than principle. The second part of bk. III discloses government's tendency to threaten sovereign right. *Rousseau's Social Contract* (Chicago and London: University of Chicago Press, 1983), pp. 158–60. Roger Masters describes Rousseau's statement as ironical. See his editorial note 112.

Gildin refers to Rousseau's criticism of the Genevan Petit Conseil, which did usurp certain sovereign prerogatives, as proof that Rousseau's principles comprehend a popular legislative role beyond ratification. On the other hand, as Robert Derathé points out in a note (which Gildin cites), Rousseau had affirmed the same limitation on the popular assembly in the dedication to the *Second Discourse*. Gildin, *Rousseau's Social Contract*, p. 203, n. 18: "I would have chosen that Republic where the individuals, being content to give sanction to the laws and to decide in a body and upon report of their chiefs the most important public affairs, would establish respected tribunals, distinguish with care their various departments, elect from year to year the most capable and most upright of their fellow citizens to administer justice and govern the State; and where, the virtue of the magistrates thus being evidence of the wisdom of the people, they would mutually honor each other." DI 114–15/82–83; for Derathé's note see O.C. III, 1492, n. 1.

It is worth noting that the preceding quotation occurs in the part of the dedication that addresses the sovereign people. I submit that Rousseau's "choice" is preserved unchanged in the *Social Contract*. Rousseau tells the Genevan people that once sovereignty is fully and universally *recognized*, what remains is to preserve it. [Cf. Abraham Lincoln's "Lyceum Speech" on the perpetuation of political institutions in *Collected Works of Abraham Lincoln*, Roy P. Basler, ed. (New Brunswick: Rutgers University Press, 1953), vol. I, pp. 108–15.] He then indicates the mode: "It is upon your perpetual unity, your obedience to the laws, your respect for their ministers that your preservation depends." DI 116/84–85. Derathé remarks that Rousseau had a "horror of innovations," and for that reason desired to exclude the "people assembled" from the legislative initiative. See *Lettres écrites de la montagne*, O.C. III, 846 and note: "For [Rousseau,] the legislative task is so to speak accomplished once and for all by the legislator and, thereafter the essential task of the legislative power is to control the executive." O.C. III, 1492. Thus, the portion of executive power exercised by the people, to which Gildin refers, is confined to the *election* of executive officials. Having unequivocally defended the people's rights, Rousseau goes on to prescribe how the exercise of those rights should be limited. Although the power of the people is great, its role is narrowed to the function of legitimation; the legitimate regime is not a direct democracy.

154. CS II.3.3.

155. Rousseau agrees with Madison that the causes of faction are sown in the nature of man. But Rousseau nevertheless opts for something very close to the remedy Madison excluded: to give citizens the same opinions, passions, and interests.

156. CS III.4.2.

157. "To see without feeling is not knowledge." Quoted in Jones, "Rousseau's General Will," p. 113.

158. Rousseau tries to evoke this feeling in his dedication to Geneva: "My dear fellow citizens, or rather my brothers, since the bonds of blood as well as the laws unite almost all of us." DI 115/83.

159. "The greatest wellspring of public authority lies in the hearts of citizens." EP 252/217.

160. In the transition from "each of us" to "we." CS I.6.9.

161. Cf. Thomas Hobbes, *Leviathan*, C. B. Macpherson, ed. (London: Penguin Books, 1968), ch. 21; and John Locke, *Second Treatise*, sec. 95.

162. CS I.6.8.

163. Preface to *Narcissus*, p. 105. I have altered the translation slightly.

164. Jones, "Rousseau's General Will and the Problem of Consent," pp. 107–08.

165. "Freedom does not express itself in political activity, in the art of formulating and enacting laws. Rather this art is the condition of liberty, and liberty itself is the fruit of living under laws, conforming one's will to them so that life is tranquil and stable. Liberty is not an activity but a habit." David Gauthier, "The Politics of Redemption," in *Trent Rousseau Papers*, James MacAdam, M. Neumann, and Guy LaFrance, eds. (Ottawa: University of Ottawa Press, 1980), pp. 93–94.

166. Rousseau concedes that the best form of government is aristocratic. CS III.5.7.

167. CS III.18.6.

168. CS IV.2.9. See Margaret Canovan, "Arendt, Rousseau and Human Plurality in Politics," *Journal of Politics* 45 (1983), 292.

169. Robert A. Dahl, *Dilemmas of Pluralist Democracy* (New Haven: Yale University Press, 1982), p. 1.

170. Barber acknowledges that Rousseau confronted the problem of "contriv[ing] institutions that facilitate democracy without supplanting it and that enhance participation without making it unnecessary." *Strong Democracy*, p. 233. But he is reluctant to conclude that Rousseau crossed the line. See below.

171. Barber, *Strong Democracy*, pp. 152–53. Cf. John Charvet, who argues that Rousseau's philosophy involves "the systematic abolition of the other." *The Social Problem in the Philosophy of Rousseau* (Cambridge:

Cambridge University Press, 1974), p. 145, quoted in Canovan, "Arendt, Rousseau and Human Plurality in Politics," p. 292.

172. CS IV.2.

173. Rousseau engages in some tortured reasoning to maintain the fiction that the people are never corrupted and always will the good. See CS IV.1.6.

174. See George J. Graham, Jr., "Rousseau's Concept of Consensus," *Political Science Quarterly* 85 (March 1970), 98: "Rousseau did not tell us what should be *the* consensual values, but he did tell us two perhaps more important things. He told us how and why these values should be maintained." According to Sartori, "Rousseau still postulated (indeed more than his contemporaries) a monolithic unity and unanimity." *The Theory of Democracy Revisited*, vol. 1, p. 92.

Rousseau figures prominently in other recent attempts to rethink liberalism from a perspective more hospitable to community and participatory politics. For a series of essays that give great prominence to the role of consensus in Rousseau's political model, see Pierre Birnbaum, Jack Lively, and Geraint Parry, eds., *Democracy, Consensus and Social Contract* (London and Beverly Hills, Calif.: Sage, 1978).

175. Barber, *The Conquest of Politics*, pp. 204, 208.

176. Barber, *Strong Democracy*, p. 128. The reference to Rousseau is to CS II.3.2, note.

177. Cf. Barber, *Strong Democracy*, pp. 151–52 with p. 128.

178. Barber, *The Conquest of Politics*, p. 90.

179. Ibid., pp. 203 bottom–205 top.

180. CS II.3.2; Barber, *The Conquest of Politics*, p. 204.

181. Connolly, *Appearance and Reality*, ch. 4.

182. See William Connolly, *Political Theory and Modernity* (Oxford: Basil Blackwell, 1988), pp. 53–61. "When they are all intact, assembled citizens, following their sense of the public good and ignoring those private interests that would give some a particular advantage, concur on a finding that expresses conditions, virtues and traditions already intact. The general will works when will is enclosed in a circle of prior determinations expressing Rousseau's prior sense of the good life; it unites subjective will and objective truth if and because its prior determinations do" (p. 60).

183. Hannah Arendt, *On Revolution* (New York: Viking, 1965), p. 71.

184. Ibid., pp. 72–73.

185. Ibid., p. 73.

186. Cf. Arthur Melzer, *The Natural Goodness of Man* (Chicago: University of Chicago Press, 1990), pp. 20–23. Once more, Arendt is instructive:

We are so used to ascribing the rebellion against reason to the early romanticism of the nineteenth century and to understanding, in contrast, the eighteenth century in terms of an "enlightened" rationalism, with the Temple of Reason as its somewhat grotesque symbol, that we are likely to overlook or to underestimate the strength of these earlier pleas for passion, for the heart, for the soul, and especially for the soul, torn into two, for Rousseau's *âme déchirée*. It is as though Rousseau, in his rebellion against reason, had put a soul, torn into two, into the place of the two-in-one that manifests itself in the silent dialogue of the mind with itself which we call thinking. And since the two-in-one of the soul is a conflict and not a dialogue, it engenders passion in its two-fold sense of intense suffering and of intense passionateness. *On Revolution*, p. 75.

187. DI 169/149.

188. DI 188–89/174. Cf. the withering critique of the "assemblies" of modern people where they "form secret relations, seek those pleasures which most separate and isolate them, and which most *unbind their hearts*." CGP 958–59; my emphasis.

189. CS II.3.2 note.

190. CS II.1.3.

191. CS II.3.1. "The people is never corrupted, but it is often fooled [*souvent on le trompe*], and only then does it appear to want what is bad." This was literally Rousseau's last word in the *Second Discourse*: "The magistrate is judge only of rigorous right; but the people are the true judges of morals [*moeurs*]: an upright and even enlightened judge on this point, sometimes deceived but never corrupted." DI 223/228 note S.

192. CS II.3.3.

193. CS II.3.4. In a valuable discussion of this vexing chapter of the *Social Contract*, Hilail Gildin pursues Rousseau's mathematical metaphor on its own terms and rescues it from the opprobrium of earlier critics. *Rousseau's Social Contract*, pp. 54–57. My reading interprets "the pluses and minuses that cancel each other" to refer to the "variety of difference," to the fact that differently situated individuals have unique reasons for resisting the general will. Gildin understands the phrase to pertain to the citizen's perception of the extent to which the common interest benefits him and to the stronger perception of his strictly individual good: "Each citizen will bring to the sovereign assembly both his desire for the common advantage and his desire to be spared the burden which he wishes others to shoulder in order for the common advantage to be achieved" (p. 54). Here Gildin draws on a passsage from CS IV.1.6 (which Rousseau used to bolster the notion of a constant will) and uses it to illuminate the

discussion in II.3.2. Gildin's interpretation emphasizes the extent to which the particular will and the general will mutually "acknowledge" one another because "The public or common interest is a part of the private interest" (p. 54; cf. pp. 33–34). Gildin's reading is guided by the effort to reconstruct how a general will might emerge, "taking men as they are"; consequently, he portrays the antagonism of the particular and the general as something less than total and fatal. But even as he carefully pursues this analysis, Gildin notes that the conclusion is only provisional and quickly becomes problematized (p. 53, bottom).

My own argument for the necessity of (first) moral freedom and (second) civic education is premised on a stark antagonism of the particular and the general that I see (contra Gildin) emerging very early in the *Social Contract*. I have assumed throughout that Rousseau never retreated from the argument he advanced against Diderot in the *Geneva Manuscript*, and that the assumptions he made there about the difficulty of achieving generality and the tendency of reason to mirror only partiality continued to inform the *Social Contract*.

194. Barber, *Strong Democracy*, pp. 242–43. The problem is that "The more effective such affective institutions are, the less need there will be for democratic politics, and the more likely it is that a community will take on the suffocating unitary character of totalistic states." Ibid., p. 243.

195. DI 193/179.

196. Barber, *Strong Democracy*, p. 36.

197. Ibid., p. 128

198. Barber, *The Conquest of Politics*, pp. 13–14.

199. CS III.13.1.

200. E 334–35/101; cf. Preface to *Narcissus*, p. 106, note: "In Europe, the government, the laws, the customs, self-interest, everything places individuals under the necessity of deceiving one another, and of doing so incessantly; everything conspires to make vice a duty for them; they have to be wicked if they are to be wise, since there is no greater folly than to provide for the happiness of scoundrels at the expense of one's own."

201. Melzer, *The Natural Goodness of Man*, p. 12. Cf. p. 4, n. 5.

202. Ibid., p. 287. On p. 16, Melzer notes that natural man's "goodness for others" is primarily negative.

203. Ibid., p. 287; cf. p. 285, bottom.

204. Rousseau expresses this point negatively in "Thus the same causes that make us bad also make us slaves." O.C. III, 479.

205. This problem is noticeable in Melzer's introductory chapter, where he argues that the radicalism of Rousseau's notion of natural goodness makes possible a new moral posture. But, given that "the ethic of goodness" can be predicated unqualifiedly only of those who are somehow "outside" society,

what sort of moral posture can derive from a nonsocial principle? If the true nature of man is "solitary, amoral, arational, subhuman," can this elemental nature supply "the basis of a more effectual morality"? Granted that Rousseau's critique of the moral tradition "*exculpates* man's *lower*, bodily nature," does it follow that its "unsuspected goodness" is something that might provide the foundation for something higher? *The Natural Goodness of Man*, pp. 22, 25–26; italics in the original.

206. Leo Strauss suggested that Rousseau replaces a hierarchical notion of good with a horizontal one. *What Is Political Philosophy?*, pp. 51–52. Because the operations of the sovereign will not distinguish among citizens, it keeps them free. But the sovereignty of the general is quite different from the sovereignty of the good. The latter seems to entail the rule of the wise. The former is compatible with democracy, as Rousseau understands it. The good of political society is *freedom*. It is a "horizontal" rather than a "vertical" good; which is to say, the political good is not congruent with moral good. Cf. Yves Simon, *Freedom and Community* (New York: Fordham University Press, 1968), pp. 140ff.

207. O.C. I, 1136.

208. "Quand on observe *la constitution naturelle des choses*, l'homme semble évidemment destiné à être la plus heureuse des créatures; quand on raisonne d'après l'état actuel, l'espèce humaine paraît de toutes la plus à plaindre. Il y a donc fort grande apparence que la plupart de ses maux sont son ouvrage, et l'on dirait qu'il a plus fait pour rendre sa condition mauvaise que la nature n'a put faire pour la rendre bonne. . . . Tous ces désordres tiennent plus à la constitution des sociétés qu'à celle de l'homme." O.C. III, 477–78; emphasis mine. Heinrich Meier provides an exact if somewhat awkward formulation of Rousseau's intention when he refers to Rousseau's attempt to "reconstruct the state of nature of man." "The *Discourse on the Origin and Foundations of Inequality Among Men*: On the Intention of Rousseau's most Philosophical Work," *Interpretation* 16 (Winter 1988–89), 218.

209. See Meier, "The *Discourse on the Origin and the Foundations of Inequality Among Men*," p. 219: "Rousseau examines the state of nature as the *natural* state of man. The state of nature becomes the *primitive* state only in the light of the historical development that has occurred." In explicating the case for the positive good of unity and existence, Melzer cites passages from several of Rousseau's works that describe a form of consciousness which seems to be more "forceful" than the listless experience of natural man per se. *The Natural Goodness of Man*, pp. 36–40, 65–68. He concludes that "Unified souls harness the total energy of their 'desire to exist' in a single direction. . . . Lacking 'alignment,' the social man's force of soul is both scattered and turned against itself." Ibid., pp.

67–68. It is not clear, however, what resources the self has to "impose any order on this inner chaos." It would seem that unity of soul either is present or it is not, and that Rousseau presents no account of human agency that might realign the soul. For what are the points of such a realignment, given that Rousseau rejects dualistic theories of the soul which point toward a hierarchical ordering of its parts (p. 21) and teleological doctrines which identify some natural end? (p. 45). Melzer concludes that for Rousseau, "The positive goal of human desire is existence, which is maintained or enhanced through *formal* unity," (p. 65; italics in the original), without suggesting *how* any self might reverse or forestall the process of its enervation or fragmentation. Once again, if unity is conditional and the sources of disorder are external to the self, what leverage can the latter acquire over its state? Put differently, if man's natural end is unity of soul, why should one expect the availability of *any* means to secure it in the social condition, given that Rousseau considers the natural and social conditions to be discontinuous?

210. Meier, "The *Discourse on . . . Inequality,*" p. 220.

211. Melzer, *The Natural Goodness of Man,* p. 34.

212. Ibid; cf. p. 44, where self-love is linked to "benign indifference" to others. R 1056–57/80–81; DI 156/132–33; cf. DI 126/95.

213. Melzer, *The Natural Goodness of Man,* p. 38; DI 196/183.

214. Melzer, *The Natural Goodness of Man,* p. 41.

215. Cf. Susan Shell's discussion of Kant's anthropological speculations on the origin of rights in *The Rights of Reason* (Toronto: University of Toronto Press, 1980), ch. 1.

216. "Moved by self-love, men are 'individuals,' who truly respond only to the inner and are utterly intractable from without." Melzer, *The Natural Goodness of Man,* p. 46.

217. See Charles Taylor, "Kant's Theory of Freedom," in his *Philosophy and the Human Sciences,* vol. 2; Henry E. Allison, *Kant's Theory of Freedom* (Cambridge: Cambridge University Press, 1990), pp. 184–98.

Bibliography

Ackerman, Bruce. *Social Justice in the Liberal State*. New Haven: Yale University Press, 1980.

Arendt, Hannah. "What Is Freedom?" In *Between Past and Future: Six Exercises in Political Thought*. Cleveland and New York: Meridian Books, 1963.

———. *On Revolution*. New York: Viking Press, 1965.

Baczko, Bronislaw. *Solitude et communauté*. Paris: Mouton, 1974.

Barber, Benjamin. *Superman and Common Man*. New York: Praeger, 1971.

———. "The Compromised Republic." In Robert Horwitz, ed., *The Moral Foundations of the American Republic*. Charlottesville: University of Virginia Press, 1979.

———. "The Undemocratic Party System." In Robert A. Goldwin, ed., *Political Parties in the Eighties*. Washington, D.C.: American Enterprise Institute, 1980.

———. *Strong Democracy: Participatory Politics for a New Age*. Berkeley: University of California Press, 1984.

———. *The Conquest of Politics: Liberal Philosophy in Democratic Times*. Princeton: Princeton University Press, 1988.

———. "Liberalism and the Costs of Consent." In Nancy Rosenblum, ed. *Liberalism and the Moral Life*. Cambridge, Mass.: Harvard University Press, 1989.

Barnard, F. M. "Patriotism and Citizenship in Rousseau: A Dual Theory of Public Willing?" *Review of Politics* 46 (1984).

Barnard, F. M., and Porter, Jene. "Will and Political Rationality in Rousseau." Paper presented at Canadian Political Science Association annual meeting, Vancouver, Canada, 1983.

Beck, Lewis W., ed. *Kant: On History*. Indianapolis: Bobbs-Merrill, 1974.

Bellah, Robert N., Madsen, Richard, Sullivan, William, Swidler, Ann, and Tipton, Steven M. *Habits of the Heart*. New York: Basic Books, 1984.

Berlin, Isaiah. "Two Concepts of Liberty." In *Four Essays on Liberty*. London and New York: Oxford University Press, 1969.

Berman, Marshall. *The Politics of Authenticity*. New York: Athenaeum, 1972.

Berns, Walter. "Does the Constitution Secure These Rights?" In Robert A. Goldwin and William Schambra, eds., *How Democratic Is the*

Constitution? Washington, D.C., and London: American Enterprise Institute Press, 1980.

Birnbaum, Pierre, Lively, Jack, and Parry, Geraint, eds., *Democracy, Consensus and Social Contract*. London and Beverly Hills, Calif.: Sage, 1978.

Bloom, Allan. "Jean-Jacques Rousseau." In Leo Strauss and Joseph Cropsey, eds., *History of Political Philosophy*. 2nd ed. Chicago: Rand McNally, 1972.

———. *The Closing of the American Mind*. New York: Simon and Schuster, 1987.

Bluhm, William T. *Force or Freedom? The Paradox in Modern Political Thought*. New Haven: Yale University Press, 1986.

———. "Liberalism and the Aggregation of Preferences: Problems of Coherence and Rationality in Social Choices." In Kenneth Deutsch and Walter Soffer, eds., *The Crisis of Liberal Democracy*. Albany: State University of New York Press, 1987.

Bobbio, Norberto. *The Future of Democracy*, trans. Roger Griffin. Minneapolis: University of Minnesota Press, 1987.

Braybrooke, David. "The Insoluble Problem of the Social Contract." *Dialogue* 15 (March 1976).

Burke, Edmund. *Reflections on the Revolution in France*, ed. Thomas H. D. Mahoney. Indianapolis: Bobbs-Merrill, 1955.

Canavan, Francis. "The Levels of Consensus." *Modern Age* 5 (1961).

Canovan, Margaret. "Arendt, Rousseau and Human Plurality in Politics." *The Journal of Politics* 45 (1983).

Cassirer, Ernst. *The Question of Jean-Jacques Rousseau,* trans. Peter Gay. Bloomington: Indiana University Press, 1954.

Charvet, John. *The Social Problem in the Philosophy of Rousseau*. Cambridge: Cambridge University Press, 1974.

Cobban, Alfred. *Rousseau and the Modern State*. London: Allen and Unwin, 1964.

Cohler, Anne. *Rousseau and Nationalism*. New York: Basic Books, 1970.

Connolly, William. *Appearance and Reality in Politics*. New York and London: Cambridge University Press, 1981.

———. *Political Theory and Modernity*. New York: Blackwell, 1988.

Constant, Benjamin. *Ouevres*. Paris: Pléiade, 1964.

Cranston, Maurice. *Social Contract*. Hammondsworth, U.K.: Penguin Books, 1968.

Cranston, Maurice, and Peters, R. S., eds., *Hobbes and Rousseau*. Garden City, N.Y.: Anchor Books, 1972.

Crocker, Lester. *Jean-Jacques Rousseau: A New Interpretive Analysis of His*

Life and Work. 2 vols. Cleveland: Case Western Reserve University Press, 1968.

———. *Roussau's "Social Contract": An Interpretive Essay.* Cleveland: Case Western Reserve University Press, 1968.

Dahl, Robert A. *Dilemmas of Pluralist Democracy.* New Haven: Yale University Press, 1982.

Derathé, Robert. *Jean-Jacques Rousseau et la science politique de son temps.* Paris: Presses Universitaires de France, 1950.

Diggins, John P. *The Lost Soul of American Politics.* New York: Basic Books, 1984.

Eden, Robert. "Tocqueville on Political Realignment and Constitutional Forms." *Review of Politics* 48 (Summer 1986).

Emberley, Peter. "Rousseau Versus the Savoyard Vicar." *Interpretation* 14 (1986).

Flathman, Richard. *The Practice of Political Authority.* Chicago and London: University of Chicago Press, 1980.

Foucault, Michel. "Governmentality." *Ideology and Consciousness* 6 (1979).

Galston, William. *Kant and the Problem of History.* Chicago and London: University of Chicago Press, 1975.

———. "Defending Liberalism." *American Political Science Review* 76 (September 1982).

Gardiner, Patrick. "Rousseau on Liberty." In J. N. Gray and Z. Pelcynski, eds., *Conceptions of Liberty in Political Theory.* London: Athlone Press, 1984.

Gauthier, David. "The Politics of Redemption." In James MacAdam, M. Neumann, and Guy LaFrance, eds., *Trent Rousseau Papers.* Ottawa: University of Ottawa Press, 1980.

Gildin, Hilail. *Rousseau's Social Contract.* Chicago and London: University of Chicago Press, 1983.

Glendon, Mary Ann. *Rights Talk: The Impoverishment of Political Discourse.* New York: Free Press, 1991.

Goldschmidt, Victor. *Anthropologie et politique: Les principes du système de Rousseau.* Paris: Vrin, 1974.

Gossman, Lionel. "Time and History in Rousseau." *Studies on Voltaire and the Eighteenth Century* 30 (1964).

Gould, Carol. *Rethinking Democracy: Freedom and Social Cooperation in Politics, Economy, and Society.* Cambridge: Cambridge University Press, 1988.

Graham, George J., Jr. "Rousseau's Concept of Consensus." *Political Science Quarterly* 85 (March 1970).

———. "Consensus." In Giovanni Sartori, ed., *Social Science Concepts.* Beverly Hills, Calif.: Sage, 1984.

Grant, George Parkin. *English Speaking Justice.* Toronto: Anansi, 1974.

Groethuysen, Bernard. *Jean-Jacques Rousseau.* Paris: Gallimard, 1949.

Habermas, Jurgen. *Legitimation Crisis,* trans. Thomas McCarthy. Boston: Beacon Press, 1975.

———. *Communication and the Evolution of Society,* trans. Thomas McCarthy. Boston: Beacon Press, 1979.

Hanson, Russell L. *The Democratic Imagination in America.* Princeton: Princeton University Press, 1985.

Heineman, Robert. *Authority and the Liberal Tradition.* Durham, N.C.: Carolina Academic Press, 1984.

Hobbes, Thomas. *Leviathan,* ed. C. B. Macpherson. London: Penguin Books, 1968.

Holmes, Stephen Taylor. *Benjamin Constant and the Making of Modern Liberalism.* New Haven and London: Yale University Press, 1984.

———. "The Permanent Structure of Antiliberal Thought." In Nancy Rosenblum, ed., *Liberalism and the Moral Life.* Cambridge, Mass.: Harvard University Press, 1989.

Horowitz, Asher. "Will, Community and Alienation in Rousseau's *Social Contract.*" *Canadian Journal of Social and Political Theory* 10, no. 3 (Fall 1986).

Huntington, Samuel. "The Democratic Distemper." *The Public Interest* 41 (Fall 1975).

———. *American Politics: The Promise of Disharmony.* Cambridge: Harvard University Press, 1983.

Ignatieff, Michael. *The Needs of Strangers.* Hammondsworth, U.K.: Penguin Books, 1984.

Jones, W. T. "Rousseau's General Will and the Problem of Consent." *Journal of the History of Philosophy* 25 (January 1987).

Jouvenel, Bertrand de. "Essai sur la politique de Rousseau." In *Du Contrat social.* Genève: Éditions Cheval-Ailé, 1947.

———. "A Discussion of Freedom." *Cambridge Journal* 6 (September 1953).

———. *Sovereignty.* Chicago: University of Chicago Press, 1957.

———. "Rousseau the Pessimistic Evolutionist." *Yale French Studies* 28 (1961–62).

———. "Rousseau's Theory of the Forms of Government." In Maurice Cranston and R. S. Peters, eds., *Hobbes and Rousseau.* Garden City, N.Y.: Anchor Books, 1972.

Kant, Immanuel. "Idea for a Universal History." In L. W. Beck, ed., *Kant: On History.* Indianapolis: Bobbs-Merrill, 1974.

Kelly, George A. *Idealism, Politics and History.* Cambridge: Cambridge University Press, 1969.

Kosselleck, Reinhard. *Critique and Crisis: Enlightenment and the Pathogenesis of Modern Society.* Cambridge, Mass.: MIT Press, 1988.

Kryger, Edna. *La Notion de liberté chez Rousseau et ses repercussions sur Kant.* Paris: Librarie A.G. Nizet, 1978.

Larmore, Charles. *Patterns of Moral Complexity.* Cambridge: Cambridge University Press, 1987.

Launay, Michel. "L'Art de l'écrivain dans le *Contrat social.*" In *Études sur le Contrat social de Jean-Jacques Rousseau.* Paris: Société Belles Lettres, 1964.

———. *Jean-Jacques Rousseau: Écrivain politique.* Grenoble: A.C.E.R., 1972.

Leduc-Fayette, Denise. "Le Materialsme du sage et l'art de jouir." *Revue philosophique* 3 (1978).

Lerner, Ralph. *The Thinking Revolutionary.* Chicago: University of Chicago Press, 1987.

Lincoln, Abraham. *Collected Works,* ed. Roy P. Basler. 9 vols. New Brunswick, N.J.: Rutgers University Press, 1953.

Lovejoy, Arthur. "The Supposed Primitivism of Rousseau's Discourse on Inequality." In *Essays in the History of Ideas.* New York: Capricorn Books, 1960.

MacIntyre, Alasdair. *After Virtue,* 2nd ed. Notre Dame, Ind.: Notre Dame University Press, 1984.

Macpherson, C. B. *The Real World of Democracy.* Toronto: CBC Publications, 1965.

Manent, Pierre. *Naissances de la politique moderne.* Paris: Payot, 1977.

Manin, Bernard. "On Legitimacy and Political Deliberation." *Political Theory* 15 (August 1987).

Mansfield, Harvey C., Jr. "Impartial Representation." In Robert A. Goldwin, ed., *Representation and Misrepresentation.* Chicago: Rand McNally, 1968.

———. *The Spirit of Liberalism.* Cambridge, Mass.: Harvard University Press, 1978.

———. "The Forms and Formalities of Liberty." *The Public Interest* 70 (Winter 1983).

———. "Constitutional Government: The Soul of Modern Democracy." *The Public Interest* 74 (Winter 1987).

Masters, Roger. *The Political Philosophy of Rousseau.* Princeton: Princeton University Press, 1986.

McWilliams, Wilson Carey. "Democracy and the Citizen: Community, Dignity and the Crisis of Contemporary Politics in America." In

Robert Goldwin and William Schambra, eds., *How Democratic Is the Constitution?* Washington and London: American Enterprise Institute Press, 1980.

———. "Parties as Civic Associations." In Gerald Pomper, ed., *Elections in America.* New York: Praeger, 1980.

Meier, Heinrich. 1989. "The *Discourse on the Origin and the Foundations of Inequality Among Men*: On the Intention of Rousseau's Most Philosophical Work." *Interpretation* 16 (Winter 1988–89).

Melzer, Arthur. "Rousseau and the Problem of Bourgeois Society." *American Political Science Review* 74, no. 4 (December 1980).

———. "Rousseau's Moral Realism." *American Political Science Review* 77 (September 1983).

———. *The Natural Goodness of Man: On the System of Rousseau's Thought.* Chicago: University of Chicago Press, 1990.

Mill, J. S. *On Liberty*, ed. Gertrude Himmelfarb. London: Penguin Books, 1974.

Miller, James. *Rousseau: Dreamer of Democracy.* New Haven: Yale University Press, 1984.

———. *Democracy Is in the Streets.* New York: Simon and Schuster, 1987.

Murray, Charles. *In Pursuit of Happiness and Good Government.* New York: Simon and Schuster, 1988.

Offe, Claus. *Contradictions of the Welfare State.* Cambridge: MIT Press, 1984.

Pangle, Thomas. *Montesquieu's Philosophy of Liberalism.* Chicago and London: University of Chicago Press, 1973.

———. "The Federalist Papers' Vision of Civic Health and the Tradition out of Which That Vision Emerges." *Western Political Quarterly* 39 (December 1986).

———. *The Spirit of Modern Republicanism.* Chicago: University of Chicago Press, 1988.

Pateman, Carole. *Participation and Democratic Theory.* Cambridge: Cambridge University Press, 1970.

———. *The Problem of Political Obligation.* New York: John Wiley and Sons, 1979.

Plamenatz, John. *Man and Society.* 2 vols. London: Longman, 1963.

———. "Ce qui ne signifie Autre Chose qu'on le forcera d'être libre." In Maurice Cranston and R. S. Peters, eds., *Rousseau and Hobbes: A Collection of Critical Essays.* Garden City, N.Y.: Anchor Books, 1972.

Plant, Raymond. "Community: Concept and Ideology." *Politics and Society* 8 (1978).

Plattner, Marc. *Rousseau's State of Nature*. Dekalb: Northern Illinois University Press, 1979.

Polin, Raymond. *La Politique de la solitude*. Paris: Éditions Sirey, 1971.

Ravier, André. *L'Éducation de l'homme nouveau*. 2 vols. Paris: Issoudon, 1941.

Rawls, John. *A Theory of Justice*. Cambridge, Mass.: Harvard University Press, 1971.

Riedel, Manfred. "Transcendental Politics? Political Legitimacy and the Concept of Civil Society in Kant." *Social Research* 48 (1981).

Riker, William H. *Liberalism Against Populism: A Confrontation Between the Theory of Democracy and the Theory of Social Choice*. San Francisco: W. H. Freeman, 1982.

Riley, Patrick. "A Possible Explanation of Rousseau's General Will." *American Political Science Review* 64 (March 1970).

———. *The General Will Before Rousseau: The Transformation of the Divine into the Civic*. Princeton: Princeton University Press, 1986.

Rosenblum, Nancy, ed. *Liberalism and the Moral Life*. Cambridge: Mass.: Harvard University Press, 1989.

Rousseau, Jean-Jacques. *The Political Writings of Jean-Jacques Rousseau*, ed. C. E. Vaughan. 2 vols. 1915. Reprint. New York: John Wiley and Sons, 1962.

———. *Politics and the Arts: Letter to D'Alembert on the Theatre*, ed. Allan Bloom. Ithaca, N.Y.: Cornell University Press, 1960.

———. *The First and Second Discourses*, ed. Roger Masters. New York: St. Martin's Press, 1964.

———. *Oeuvres complètes*. ed. Bernard Gagnebin and Marcel Raymond, 4 vols. Paris: Pléiade, 1964.

———. *On the Social Contract, with Geneva Manuscript and Political Economy*, ed. Roger Masters. New York: St. Martin's Press, 1978.

———. *Émile or On Education*, ed. Allan Bloom. New York: Basic Books, 1979.

———. *The Reveries of the Solitary Walker*, ed. Charles Butterworth. New York: Harper and Row, 1979.

———. *The First and Second Discourses and the Essay on the Origin of Languages*, ed. Victor Gourevitch. New York: Harper & Row, 1986.

Russell, Bertrand. *History of Western Philosophy*. New York: Simon and Schuster, 1945.

Salien, Jean-Marie. "Dialectique de la raison et des passions dans la pensée de Jean-Jacques Rousseau." *International Studies in Philosophy* 12 (1980).

Salkever, Stephen. "Virtue, Obligation and Politics." *American Political*

Science Review 68 (March 1974).

Sandel, Michael. *Liberalism and the Limits of Justice.* Cambridge: Cambridge University Press, 1982.

———."Morality and the Liberal Ideal." *The New Republic,* May 7, 1984.

———."The Procedural Republic and the Unencumbered Self." *Political Theory* 12 (1984).

Sartori, Giovanni. *The Theory of Democracy Revisited.* 2 vols. Chatham, N.J.: Chatham House, 1987.

Schaefer, David L. "The Good, the Beautiful and the Useful: Montaigne's Transvaluation of Values." *American Political Science Review* 73 (March 1979).

Shell, Susan Meld. *The Rights of Reason.* Toronto: University of Toronto Press, 1980.

Shklar, Judith. *Men and Citizens: A Study of Rousseau's Social Theory.* 2nd ed. Cambridge: Cambridge University Press, 1985.

Simon, Yves. *Freedom and Community.* New York: Fordham University Press, 1968.

Starobinski, Jean. *Jean-Jacques Rousseau: La transparence et l'obstacle.* Paris: Presses Universitaires de France, 1957.

———. "Rousseau and Modern Tyranny." *New York Review of Books* (November 29, 1973), 20–25.

———. "La Prosopopée de Fabricius." *Revue des sciences humaines* 161 (1976).

———. "Eloquence and Liberty." *Journal of the History of Ideas* 38 (1977).

———. "The Accuser and the Accused." *Daedalus* (Summer, 1978), 41–58.

Storing, Herbert, ed. *The Complete Anti-Federalist.* Chicago: University of Chicago Press, 1981.

Strauss, Leo. *Natural Right and History.* Chicago and London: University of Chicago Press, 1953.

———. *What Is Political Philosophy? and Other Essays.* Glencoe, Ill.: The Free Press, 1953.

Taylor, Charles. *Hegel.* Cambridge: Cambridge University Press, 1974.

———. "Atomism." In Alkis Kontos, ed., *Power, Possessions and Freedoms.* Toronto: University of Toronto Press, 1979.

———. *Philosophy and the Human Sciences.* 2 vols. Cambridge: Cambridge University Press, 1985.

———. "Cross-Purposes: The Liberal-Communitarian Debate." In Nancy Rosenblum, ed., *Liberalism and the Moral Life.* Cambridge, Mass.: Harvard University Press, 1989.

Tocqueville, Alexis de. *Democracy in America*, ed. Phillips Bradley. 2 vols. New York: Vintage Books, 1945.

Tussman, Joseph. *Obligation and the Body Politic*. New York: Oxford University Press, 1960.

Unger, Roberto Mangabeira. *Knowledge and Politics*. New York: The Free Press, 1975.

Vatarian, Aram. "Necessity or Freedom? The Politics of an Eighteenth Century Metaphysical Debate." *Studies in Eighteenth Century Culture* 7 (1978).

Walzer, Michael. *Obligations*. Cambridge, Mass.: Harvard University Press, 1970.

———. "Philosophy and Democracy." *Political Theory* 9 (August 1981).

———. *Spheres of Justice*. New York: Basic Books, 1983.

Weil, Eric. "Rousseau et sa politique." In Gérard Genette and Tzvetan Todorov, eds., *Pensée de Rousseau*. Paris: Éditions du Seuil, 1984.

Wokler, Robert. "Rousseau's Perfectibilian Libertarianism." In Alan Ryan, ed., *The Idea of Freedom*. Oxford: Oxford University Press, 1979.

———. "Rousseau's Two Concepts of Liberty. " In George Feaver and Frederick Rosen, eds., *Lives, Liberties and the Public Good: New Essays in Political Theory for Maurice Cranston*. New York: St. Martin's Press, 1989.

Wolin, Sheldon. *Politics and Vision*. Boston: Little Brown, 1960.

———. "The Idea of the State in America." In John P. Diggins and Mark Kann, eds., *The Problem of Authority in America*. Philadelphia: Temple University Press, 1981.

———. *The Presence of the Past: Essays on the State and the Constitution*. Baltimore: Johns Hopkins University Press, 1989.

Zetterbaum, Marvin. "Self and Political Order." *Interpretation* 1 (Winter 1970).

———. "Self and Subjectivity in Political Theory." *Review of Politics* 44 (January 1982).

Index

passivity of, 60, 134–36; political, 132; primacy of, 12; as *qualité d'homme,* 4, 16, 75; reconciled with citizenship, 161; recreating conditions of, 122; requirements of, 105; and solidarity, 117; as spontaneity, 124; and tranquility, 46. *See also* Civil freedom; Democratic freedom; Independence; Moral freedom; Natural freedom

Galston, William, 182n.30, 187n.89, 209n.95
Gardiner, Patrick, 188n.116
Gauthier, David, 152, 217n.165
Gildin, Hilail, 198n.92, 215–16n.153, 219–20n.193
Glendon, Mary Ann, 174n.42, 211n.117
Golden age, 52–55, 126
Goldschmidt, Victor, 39, 184n.42
Goodness, natural, 33, 63–64, 67–68, 163–65
Gossman, Lionel, 185n.47
Gould, Carol, 212–13n.136, 215n.150
Governability, 109–10, 116
Government, 110–11, 120; distinguished from sovereignty, 85, 118, 151; and formation of citizens, 102; role of, 152–53; and tutelage of will, 114
Graham, George, J., Jr., 218n.174
Grant, George, 141
Groethuysen, Bernard, 190n.150, 202n.164
Grofman, Bernard, 214n.146
Généralité. See Generality
Generality, *xi,* 10, 19, 21, 24–25, 27, 128, 151

General will, *xi,* 9, 24, 27–30, 79–85, 123; antipolitical nature of, 156; as attribute of citizen, 9, 77; and civic identity, *x*; as a constant will, 89–91, 95; and constitutional forms, 105; and criticism of Rousseau, 18; as defense mechanism, 83; and deliberation, 104; in Diderot, 74–75; encounters no obstacle, 159; expression of, 10; as fence to freedom, *ix;* and the festival, 135; limited scope of, 22; and majority decision, 149–54; modeled on condition of natural man, 6; multiplication of, 160; no substantive task for, 136; opposition to private will, 88, 92; of patriots, 137; perfection of, 99; and popular assemblies, 148–51; and popular will, 19; and social unity, 118; sovereignty of, 7, 19, 22; and voting, 153–54; distinguished from will of all, 92, 155

Habermas, Jurgen, 24, 210n.97
Happiness, 5, 32, 35, 40, 45, 59, 61–65, 89, 96, 131, 135
Hayden, Tom, 26
Heineman, Robert, 172n.21
Holmes, Stephen T., 170–71n.9, 211n.118
Horowitz, Asher, 176n.71
Hobbes, Thomas, *ix,* 5, 12–16, 33, 55, 72, 83–84, 116, 134, 152, 163–64, 175n.57
Huntington, Samuel, 146, 210n.97

Identity, 101, 109; civic, *x,* 23, 83, 119–20; creation of, 78, 110;

178nn.95, 98, 201n.150, 202n.158

Moeurs, 55, 104, 129–30, 136, 145; of the first men, 125; and general will, 150; and government, 111; patriotic, 126–27; permanent influence of, 28; power of, 127; and social unity, 118–24

Moi commun, ix, xi, 20–21, 23, 29, 77, 79, 87, 89, 99–100, 107, 135, 144, 153–54

Montaigne, Michel de, 37–38, 127

Montesquieu, Charles de Secondat, Baron de, 5, 20, 101, 127, 200n.136

Moral freedom, *ix,* 3, 6, 8, 159; distinguished from higher freedom, 60–61, 66–67; and civil education, 99, 101, 103; as obedience to law, 57; as a political requirement, 132–33, 159; political significance of, 86–94; related to general will, 82–83

Morality, 3, 5, 47, 61, 66–67, 69; as a political construct, 75, 88; great maxim of, 76. *See also* Moral relations

Moral relations, 25, 46, 57, 86, 131, 133, 163; and denaturing, 97; onset of, 69

Murray, Charles, 194n.24

Natural condition. *See* State of nature

Natural freedom, *ix,* 3–9, 14, 31–69, 115; contrasted with civilized oppression, 38; destruction of, 47; as equilibrium of desire and power, 56; and general will, 80; in last

stage of state of nature, 72; as negative, 34, 49; relevance to the social problem, 51; restoration of, 79; and solitude, 46; worth of depreciated, 58–59. *See also* Independence

Natural man, 7–8, 29, 53; contrasted with civil man, 81; contrasted with moral man, 59; as a critical concept, 41, 50; encounters no obstacle, 42, 60–61, 67; forced out of natural condition, 38; independence of, 28; in golden age, 52–55; goodness of, 43–44, 164–67; as *l'homme physique,* 39–40; limited needs of, 34–35; metaphysical side of, 49; model for civil independence, 87–88; moral side of, 43–47; outside dialectic of reason and passion, 56; and pity, 166; as solitary, 33–34

Nietzsche, Friedrich, 28

Offe, Claus, 210n.97

Pangle, Thomas, 201n.136

Passivity: of the citizen, 25, 30; of freedom, 32, 68, 134; of the people, 110, 153; of the soul, 136, 166

Participation, *ix,* 10, 23, 112, 153–56, 161

Participatory democracy, 25, 30, 113, 138. *See also* Strong democracy

Pateman, Carole, 209n.93

Patriotism, 27, 108, 113–15, 128, 130, 133, 137, 151

Perfectibility, 33, 37–39

Plamenatz, John, 5, 67–68